TO **SERVE** THE **LIVING**

TO **SERVE** THE **LIVING**

FUNERAL DIRECTORS

AND THE

AFRICAN AMERICAN WAY OF DEATH

Suzanne E. Smith

The Belknap Press of Harvard University Press
Cambridge, Massachusetts · London, England
2010

Library of Congress Cataloging-in-Publication Data

Smith, Suzanne E., 1964–
To serve the living : funeral directors and the African American
way of death / Suzanne E. Smith.
p.   cm.
Includes bibliographical references and index.
ISBN 978-0-674-03621-5 (alk. paper)
1. Funeral rites and ceremonies—United States.   2. African Americans—
Funeral customs and rites.   3. African Americans—Social life and
customs.   4. Undertakers and undertaking—United States.
5. United States—Social life and customs.   I. Title.
GT3203.S75 2010
363.7'508996073—dc22   2009035231

For Doug, Evan, and Jeremy,

with all my love

And in memory of

Lawrence W. Levine and Roy A. Rosenzweig

Contents

ABBREVIATIONS   VIII

PROLOGUE: An Undertaker Like Him   1

1. From Hush Harbors to Funeral Parlors   15

2. The Colored Embalmer   46

3. My Man's an Undertaker   79

4. A Funeral Hall Is as Good a Place as Any   112

5. The African American Way of Death   156

EPILOGUE: She Has Gone Home   194

NOTES   211
ACKNOWLEDGMENTS   245
INDEX   251

Illustrations follow page 78

Abbreviations

ACMHR	Alabama Christian Movement for Human Rights
CORE	Congress of Racial Equality
FTC	Federal Trade Commission
GABEO	Georgia Association of Black Elected Officials
GBI	Georgia Bureau of Investigation
INFDA	Independent National Funeral Directors Association
LIP	Lincoln Independent Party
MFSA	Metropolitan Funeral System Association
MIA	Montgomery Improvement Association
NAACP	National Association for the Advancement of Colored People
NFDA	National Funeral Directors Association
NFDMA	National Funeral Directors and Morticians Association
NNBL	National Negro Business League
NNFDA	National Negro Funeral Directors Association
NRA	National Recovery Administration
RCNL	Regional Council of Negro Leadership
SCLC	Southern Christian Leadership Conference
SNCC	Student Nonviolent Coordinating Committee
WCC	White Citizens Council

TO **SERVE** THE **LIVING**

Prologue

An Undertaker Like Him

Dan Young, the owner of Young's Funeral Home in Monroe, Georgia, was on a personal mission in early 1968. The sixty-three-year-old funeral director had spent most of his adult life as one of the most respected business leaders and civil rights organizers in Walton County. Down in the basement of his funeral establishment, Young had faithfully stored the last remnants of a long-forgotten tragedy that he now wanted to resurrect. He decided to reach out to two young civil rights activists, Tyrone Brooks and Robert "Bobby" Howard, in an effort to bring justice to a crime that had never been solved. Brooks, who was only twenty years old, had just started working as a field organizer in Georgia for the Southern Christian Leadership Conference (SCLC). Howard was a local activist in Walton County. In his conversations with the men, Young felt compelled to show them photographs he had kept for more than twenty years. The images were graphic portraits of the corpses of Roger Malcom, Dorothy Malcom, George Dorsey, and Mae Murray Dorsey, victims of the 1946 Moore's Ford lynching, also known as the "last mass lynching in America." Young, who had directed the victims' funerals, had a painfully intimate relationship to the murders and was haunted by the fact that the perpetrators of the crime had never been caught.[1]

By 1968, the photographs of the Moore's Ford lynching victims were among the few remaining pieces of physical evidence from the crime. Young had carefully stored them in the basement of his funeral home since 1946. Now he used them to warn Brooks and Howard about the dangers of being civil rights activists in Walton County, what he called "the lynching capital of Georgia." More urgently, however, he wanted the men to help him rekindle the long-dormant effort to identify suspects in the crime and seek their prosecution. Young hoped to work with Brooks to establish an SCLC chapter in Walton County and perhaps bring Martin Luther King, Jr., to Monroe for a visit to renew public interest in the largely forgotten murders. Young wanted Howard, who was a member of the local community, to conduct a private investigation into the crime, which had remained a cold case for more than two decades. To serve this end, Young gave Howard two lists that he had kept about the crime: one was a list of whites in the area who were alleged suspects, and the other was a list of blacks who might know something about what had happened that day.[2]

The Moore's Ford photographs would not have existed at all if it had not been for the foresight of Dan Young, whose role as Monroe's leading black funeral director put him in a pivotal position to both publicize the lynching to the black press and secretly assist its criminal investigation. Young's commitment to pursuing justice in the case began almost immediately after the crime took place. Roger Malcom, Dorothy Malcom, George Dorsey, and Mae Murray Dorsey were shot to death on July 25, 1946, near the Moore's Ford Bridge, which lay across the Apalachee River that divided Walton County from Oconee County. The precipitating event that led to the lynching happened on July 14, when Roger Malcom stabbed his white landlord, Barnette Hester. Malcom, who was twenty-four years old at the time, had heard rumors that Hester had made sexual advances toward his common-law wife, Dorothy. Although Malcom's stabbing of Hester was not fatal, the attack, which was apparently driven by an interracial love triangle, quickly inflamed local Ku Klux Klan members. When word of the stabbing spread through Walton County, a group of local whites, including Hester's older brother, Weldon, chased Malcom down in a cornfield, bound his ankles and wrists, and prepared to lynch him on the spot. Hester's mother stopped the mob and called in the Walton County deputy sheriffs to arrest Malcom and take him to the local jail in Monroe.[3]

The day after Malcom was arrested, Dorothy Malcom and Malcom's friends George Dorsey and Mae Murray Dorsey showed up at Young's Funeral Home to ask Dan Young if he would post Roger

Malcom's bond to get him released from jail. As one of the most respected and economically secure members of Monroe's black community, Young was often the first person local black sharecroppers turned to when they needed financial assistance—whether it was for a small loan or to post bond. Young's funeral business gave him not only financial stability but also a degree of political clout. The black community admired him for his ability to live and work independent of the peonage embedded in rural Georgia's agricultural economy; and local whites often saw him as a reliable mediator when racial tensions arose in Walton County. In one incident, Young had posted a $500 bond to help a black man from neighboring Winder, Georgia, get released from jail after he had been "picked up by a group of armed white men and charged with peeping into the room of a white woman." Trumped-up charges were a common tactic to extort labor from local blacks. Typically, the accused was fined for the alleged wrongdoing; a white farmer would then pay the fine in exchange for labor. Dan Young's intervention in the Winder case helped the man escape this fate.[4]

Somewhat uncharacteristically, then, Young refused to help Roger Malcom get out of jail. Dorothy Malcom's request for help with Roger's bond came at a particularly challenging time—just two days before the first primary election in Georgia in fifty years in which blacks were allowed to vote. Young, who was the president of the Walton County Civic League, had been leading a major voter-registration drive and wanted to distance himself from the controversial stabbing case. Young needed to focus all his energies on getting black voters to the polls. The stakes were high in the gubernatorial primary election, which pitted James Carmichael, a political moderate, against Eugene Talmadge, an ardent white supremacist who opposed "nigger voting." Just two days later, Young's fears were realized when Talmadge won, even though Carmichael had carried the popular vote. A combination of Georgia's county unit voting system, which was similar to electoral voting; intimidation of black voters; and voter purging handed the final victory to Talmadge, who secured his fourth nomination as governor of Georgia. The political repercussions of Talmadge's win were immediately evident when he addressed his supporters the night of the election and declared that "no Negro will vote in Georgia for the next five years." As one reporter wrote of Talmadge's win, "the season on 'niggers' was automatically opened, and every pinheaded Georgia cracker and bigoted Ku Kluxer figured he had a hunting license."[5]

Just one week later, on July 25, 1946, Roger Malcom was released from jail when Loy Harrison, a local white farmer, agreed to post his $600 bond in exchange for his labor. Harrison brought Dorothy Malcom, George Dorsey, and Mae Murray Dorsey with him to Monroe when he went to get Roger released. On the drive back to Harrison's farm, Harrison's car was ambushed by a mob of approximately twenty white people, who took the four black field hands out to a clearing near the Moore's Ford Bridge and shot them to death by firing squad. Although Harrison later portrayed himself to investigators as an innocent bystander to the crime, his decision to take the victims down a less-traveled and circuitous route back to his farm raised local suspicions that he was actually a key participant and perhaps an organizer of the lynch mob.

Later that evening, the local coroner telephoned E. L. Almand, Jr., the mayor of Monroe and owner of E. L. Almand's Undertaking Company, to come pick up the bodies. Almand's was a white-owned funeral home that accepted both white and black customers. Almand's one black employee, Isaac Brooks, cleaned and embalmed the bodies that night, but the next day, the victims' remains were transferred to Young's Funeral Home at the request of the victims' families, who preferred that the funerals be directed by Dan Young. Given the racially charged circumstances of the lynching, Young's Funeral Home, which was located in the heart of Monroe's black business district, was the safest haven for a public viewing of the victims' remains.[6]

As the embalmed bodies were moved to Young's Funeral Home on Friday morning, Walter White, executive director of the National Association for the Advancement of Colored People (NAACP), who spearheaded the NAACP's antilynching campaign, immediately sent a press release about the Moore's Ford attack to the major newspapers and radio networks in the country as well as to all major black newspapers. White, who had been tracking violent attacks against Negro veterans, was particularly interested in the fact that one of the victims, George Dorsey, had been "recently honorably discharged from the United States Army." For this reason he also sent telegrams to U.S. Attorney General Tom Clark and to President Truman to alert them of the mass lynching, which he described as an "outbreak of lawlessness which threatens not only minorities but democracy itself." White then contacted the director of the NAACP's Atlanta office, Eugene M. Martin, to request that he send investigators to Monroe immediately to gather as much evidence and information as possible and to ascertain whether the Ku Klux Klan was responsible for the crime. By Friday evening, NBC's national radio news bulletin included a report on the "most vicious lynchings to stain our national record in a long time." The story was soon headline news across the country.[7]

Back in Monroe, Dan Young prepared the victims' bodies for the public viewing scheduled for the following day. The task was extremely challenging because the shotgun blasts had destroyed much of their faces. As one of Young's associates later recalled, the grim task of attempting to restore the victims' faces was unsettling and had knocked Young "off his feet." By Saturday morning, a large crowd of black people had descended on Young's Funeral Home for the viewing. The line of onlookers snaked back over three blocks and included several hundred people by midday. Once admitted to the funeral home, the public was given a rare opportunity to bear direct witness to the atrocity of lynching. As the mourners and the curious entered Young's establishment, they were led into the funeral home's central viewing room, where the corpses of the four victims—draped in dark velvet shrouds—lay starkly on stretchers. There, in the somber stillness of the funeral parlor, Monroe's black community was left alone to pay its respects to the victims and to behold up close their mutilated remains—"mute evidence in human form" of local white supremacy.[8]

After the crowds dispersed that Saturday afternoon, Dan Young surreptitiously brought J. Richardson Jones, a photographer and reporter from the *Pittsburgh Courier* newspaper, into his funeral home to photograph the victims' remains. Monroe city officials had made it clear to Young that they did not want photographs taken of the victims, but Young ignored the edict in order to help publicize the crime in the black press. These images, published in the nationally circulated *Pittsburgh Courier*, brought the visual horror of the crime to black readers across the country. Young's foresight in allowing the photographer access to the bodies foreshadowed the media sensation that would occur nine years later in the 1955 Emmett Till case, when Mamie Till Bradley not only opened her son's casket but allowed *Jet* magazine and the *Chicago Defender* to publish graphic images of Till's disfigured corpse, "so the world could see what they did to my boy." In the weeks following the lynching, Young kept in close contact with his brother-in-law, C. A. Scott, who was editor of the nation's first black daily newspaper, the *Atlanta Daily World,* to keep the press updated on the latest news about the crime.[9]

Young assisted the investigation of the Moore's Ford lynchings from behind the scenes. Within days of the lynching, he made the first of several trips to Atlanta to meet privately with A. T. Walden, a civil rights activist and prominent black attorney, and Eugene Martin, director of the Atlanta NAACP, to share insider information about the murders. Young wanted to discuss the criminal investigation and "stated definitely that he did not think that the F.B.I. and the G.B.I. [Georgia Bureau of Investigation] were doing a good job." He was irritated that the agents were not being thorough in ascertaining even basic facts about the case. To illustrate his point, Young mentioned that Loy Harrison, a witness and possible suspect in the crime, "stated that the women who were lynched were drinking." According to Young, "his experience in embalming led him to know whether or not the person he was embalming had been drinking. He stated definitely that these women had not been drinking." He went on to tell Martin that if the FBI "really meant business . . . [they would] protect those that gave information [and then] . . . people who knew [about the lynching] would talk and the crime could be solved." Despite some of his frustrations, Young told Martin that "the lynching had not by any means intimidated the Negro population [of Monroe] . . . they felt outraged but their spirits were high. He said this was especially true of young Negroes who when a fiery cross was burned some few weeks ago by the Klan, stood nearby and watched and laughed and joked and wished they had a few of the hand grenades that they used when they were over in Europe."[10]

If Young's first meeting with Martin ended on a note of optimism, his subsequent visits had a more tense and despairing tone. In a letter dated August 8, 1946, Martin described a visit from "the colored undertaker from Monroe, Georgia," in which Young was trying to arrange for protection for a possible witness to the crime, a young black man named Johnnie Burdette. At this meeting, Young asked that his own name not be used in relation to the information he was sharing because it "might cause him to be killed." He also wanted "guaranteed protection and sufficient funds" to help Burdette leave the South after he testified, because "his life would not be worth a tinker's dam if the crackers even thought that he would tell his story." Young again reiterated his lack of confidence in the GBI and the FBI to solve the case. The only person Young trusted was Thomas Johnson, a white attorney who had been sent by the NAACP to investigate the crime. In one of his first reports to Walter White on the case, Johnson noted Young's exceptional position in Monroe as someone in whom both blacks and whites confided. In the days immediately after the lynching, both Roger Malcom's first wife and Loy Harrison, a rumored suspect, visited Young at his funeral home to share insider information about the racial tensions that had led up to the crime.[11]

On August 24, 1946, Martin noted that Young's involvement in the case had reached a point such that even though "he has made money in Monroe and is a property owner . . . [he is] beginning to wonder whether or not he should remain." Young's fears were heightened when Isaac Brooks, the black embalmer who worked for E. L. Almand Undertaking Company, suddenly went missing. Young told Martin that E. L. Almand, Sr., was rumored to be a member of the Ku Klux Klan and that Brooks had recently made off-the-record comments speculating "about one of the Almands being a member of the [lynch] mob." Young then offered the name of "one of the leading merchants in Monroe," who matched "the description of the leader of the lynch mob given by Loy Harrison," which supported the growing opinion "that the sheriff of the county, the jailer, and other prominent citizens were the leaders and planners of the [lynch] mob." Young also reported that "a Negro was beaten up on the outskirts of Monroe last week." Given the perilous circumstances, Young reiterated to Martin that "under no circumstances does he want his name mentioned in any shape, form, or fashion as he had been sought after and talked to so much that he is beginning to fear that he might in some way be considered a dangerous man by the guilty parties." Martin then added, "You see, an undertaker like him is an important character in the town."[12]

Dan Young was indeed "an important character" in Monroe, Georgia, and his position as an undertaker was the foundation of his role as a black leader in the small Southern town. His story, though exceptional in many ways, is representative of the unique role funeral directors have always played in African American life. As individuals charged with orchestrating the African American funeral—often described as a "homegoing celebration" in African American folklore, funeral directors have always been culturally valued for their ability to help their communities honor their dead with dignity and the requisite pageantry. As entrepreneurs in a largely segregated trade, funeral directors were usually among the few black individuals in any town or city who were economically independent and not beholden to the local white power structure. For these reasons, African American funeral directors like Dan Young often found themselves serving the living as much as they buried the dead.

Dan Young's career as a funeral director began when he opened Young's Funeral Home in 1938, during the Great Depression, when starting such a venture was risky at best. To get support and professional help, he joined the Georgia Colored Funeral Directors and Embalmers Association, the main trade organization for black funeral directors in his state. In May 1939, the group held its annual convention in Atlanta, which commenced awkwardly when then-former Governor Eugene Talmadge decided to make a public appearance to greet the conventioneers. Talmadge, a confirmed white supremacist, was an odd choice to open the convention, but his presence revealed the complexity of racial politics in Depression-era Georgia. As the black press reported, Talmadge, "a rabid avid Negro-baiter . . . aroused only lukewarm interest . . . as he spoke in welcome to delegates." Talmadge, "an avowed anti–New Dealer," argued against "governmental charity" and astonishingly claimed that "Negroes [had] weathered" the economic depression "better than some whites." He told the funeral directors that "true wealth lies in the soil" rather than in government relief, and so he advocated a "back-to-the-land movement." The former governor told the audience of undertakers that they "could set an example for others by going back to the farms and intensively cultivating the soil." As might be expected, Talmadge's recommendation fell on deaf ears. The funeral directors in attendance—including Dan Young—already knew that their financial self-sufficiency lay not in the peonage of the agricultural sharecropping economy that dominated rural Georgia but in pursuit of success in the growing funeral industry.[13]

Throughout the twentieth century, the modern funeral industry provided one of the most economically viable careers for the aspiring African American entrepreneur. Beginning at the turn of the century, Jim Crow segregation laws clearly divided the consumer marketplace by race. For the first half of the twentieth century, the insulated world of black business provided African American funeral directors and other economic leaders with a relatively secure base of African American consumers. The financial stability that resulted from the segregated economy ultimately laid the foundation for the modern civil rights movement that emerged at midcentury. Funeral directors like Dan Young and other black entrepreneurs used their financial independence to fight for civil rights and racial integration, a goal that would ironically threaten the relative economic security of a segregated marketplace. This tension between the desire to maintain control of the African American market and the drive to fight for racial equality resonated in the lives of black funeral directors.[14]

Dan Young's personal story is compelling because it exemplifies how complex, contradictory, and challenging the role of funeral director could be in any black community. In 1946, Young did not simply run his funeral home business. He worked tirelessly to register black voters and to get out the vote in the 1946 gubernatorial election in the hopes of keeping a white supremacist like Eugene Talmadge out of office. Just days after the political forces behind Talmadge's campaign maneuvered their victory, it was Dan Young who worked late into the night in the basement of his funeral home trying, albeit futilely, to reconstruct the faces of Roger Malcom, Dorothy Malcom, George Dorsey, and Mae Murray Dorsey, victims of the brazen racial hatred that Talmadge's election had stirred in Walton County. As one reporter who observed the scene wrote, "nothing in the undertaker's art could put back the faces of Roger Malcom or May Dorsey. Shotgun shells fired at point blank don't leave much of a face." Yet instead of hiding the disfigurement of the corpses, as Monroe's city leaders would have preferred, Young had the political instincts to secretly allow a black press photographer to document the atrocity in all its graphic horror.

Although Young's efforts to secure Talmadge's defeat in the 1946 election failed, his covert role in publicizing the mass lynching that was committed in its wake was not in vain. The public outcry over the Moore's Ford lynching was national in scope and, with the help of leaders like Walter White of the NAACP, successfully reached the White House. In the weeks that followed the mass lynching, President Truman not only "expressed his horror at the crime and his sympathy for the families of the victims" but also ordered Attorney General Tom Clark and the Department of Justice to "proceed with all of its resources to investigate" the crime. Most impressively, Ellis Arnall, the acting governor of Georgia—in an unprecedented move—offered a substantial reward for any information that might lead to the apprehension of the perpetrators of the crime.[15]

As the news and pictures of the Monroe lynching received national press coverage, black communities across the country from Dallas to Philadelphia held public memorial services and prayer vigils to honor the victims. In Washington, D.C., fifteen hundred people joined in a funeral march to the base of the Lincoln Memorial to hold a service for the Moore's Ford dead and to call upon Congress to pass a federal antilynching bill. In late August, when Dan Young went to Eugene Martin to share his worries about his own personal safety, three hundred of his colleagues in the National Negro Funeral Directors Association were meeting in Atlantic City for their annual convention. To show their collective support for the victims, the group passed resolutions to condemn the Monroe lynchings, to appeal to President Truman and Attorney General Tom Clark to prosecute the case, and to raise reward money.[16]

Yet the Moore's Ford lynching case could not be solved. By December 1946, the press reported that the federal grand jury investigating the crime "unanimously agreed that, from the evidence furnished by the FBI, they could not identify 'any person or persons participating in the murders or in any violation of the civil rights statutes of the United States.'" The jury, which included twenty-one whites and two blacks, had heard the testimony of more than one hundred witnesses and reviewed "reams of FBI reports," but "any evidence which would justify the return of indictments was missing."[17]

The federal grand jury's failure to return indictments in the case painfully illustrated how, in Talmadge's Georgia, vigilante violence could be used with impunity to suppress any progressive efforts to engage blacks in the democratic process. As one black activist in Georgia remarked in the wake of the election, "a spirit of hope . . . went gurgling down the drain when Gene Talmadge was elected." In an unexpected twist to an already controversial gubernatorial election, Eugene Talmadge died on December 21, 1946, just as the federal grand jury announced its inconclusive findings in the Moore's Ford investigation and weeks before he was officially to take the oath of office. Talmadge's son, Herman, was eventually elected to office by the state legislature to replace his father and keep his political agenda afloat. As a result, an era of white supremacy and racial repression began in Georgia that was almost unprecedented in the South. NAACP membership in Georgia, which had peaked at 11,000 in 1946, dropped to 3,168 by 1949; and the organization's branch offices in the state fell from a high of 55 in 1946 to fewer than 20 by the early 1950s.[18]

Dan Young's own political activism became more muted in the years immediately following the Moore's Ford lynching. It was not until 1954—after the U.S. Supreme Court's decision in *Brown v. Board of Education* declared racial segregation in public schools to be unconstitutional—that Young and other black activists in Georgia began to reorganize their political campaign to fight for voting rights. By August 1954, Young and other black leaders in Georgia had formed a new, nonpartisan committee with the goal of "getting out the largest possible Negro vote . . . and increasing voter registration in the future." By 1958, Young was a district vice president of the Georgia Voters League.[19]

It wasn't until early 1968, however, that Young decided to dust off his photographs of the Moore's Ford lynching victims and share them with Tyrone Brooks and Bobby Howard. Young clearly believed that the crime could still be prosecuted. He had lived long enough by 1968 to witness the many victories of the modern civil rights movement, which might not have dramatically changed race relations in Monroe, Georgia, but did open up the possibility that a new generation of civil rights activists might be able to revive the fight for justice in the Moore's Ford case. They did. Both Brooks and Howard never forgot Young's mission to solve the Moore's Ford lynching case. Howard, a lifelong civil rights activist in Georgia, continued his personal investigation into the crime for decades, and Brooks went on to become a representative in Georgia's state legislature as well as president of the Georgia Association of Black Elected Officials (GABEO).

In August 1997, nine years after Young himself had died, Howard and other local leaders in Monroe, Georgia, officially founded the Moore's Ford Memorial Committee, Inc., a biracial group that was "committed to telling the story [of the Moore's Ford lynching], honoring the dead, promoting healing and social justice, and creating a living memorial to the victims of this horrible crime." In May 1998, the group held its first annual memorial service for the victims of the crime and announced its first achievement, which involved locating and cleaning the gravesites of three of the victims. The group also erected—in conjunction with the Georgia Historical Society—a permanent historical marker about the event near the site of the crime. The Moore's Ford Memorial Committee focused its mission on community reconciliation and providing scholarships to deserving local high school students.

By July 2005, new interest in the Moore's Ford case arose when Tyrone Brooks and GABEO decided to stage a dramatic reenactment of the lynching in order to generate a new commitment to solving the crime. Brooks and others were inspired by the June 2005 conviction of Edgar Ray Killen, a former Ku Klux Klansman, who had been involved in the 1964 murders of Andrew Goodman, James Chaney, and Mickey Schwerner, three civil rights activists who were working to register voters in Mississippi's "Freedom Summer" project. Organizers hoped that the reenactment of the Moore's Ford lynching would reignite public interest in identifying and convicting any individuals still alive in Walton County who may have participated in the lynching. The Moore's Ford reenactment did garner national press coverage and raise public awareness about the crime, but it also created its own controversies. Some questioned the theatrics of a staged lynching as tactless, while others took issue with the veracity of the reenactment itself.[20]

On July 2, 2008, *USAToday* reported that FBI and Georgia Bureau of Investigation agents had "swarmed the backyard of a modest white house along a windy stretch in rural northeast Georgia . . . in search of clues that could be linked to living suspects involved in the 1946 unsolved lynchings of four people." Though some observers, including Bobby Howard, expressed cautious excitement about the investigation's latest development, others soberly acknowledged that since "most of the suspects and possible witnesses have died . . . it will be nearly impossible to try the case unless compelling new evidence is found."[21]

Although the Moore's Ford lynching case may never be solved, the fact that investigators were still actively pursuing evidence about the crime sixty-two years after it was committed was a testament to the perseverance and community leadership of Dan Young. Young's role as a funeral director in Monroe, Georgia, clearly went far beyond burying the dead, and the work he did to serve the living continued even after his own death. "An undertaker like him" was "an important character" in his town because his work managing death could never be separated from life in a time and place when someone could get killed simply for being black.

Young's career as a funeral director began in 1938, but his story is part of a larger history of African American funeral directing that can be traced back to the transatlantic slave trade and the earliest slave burials in the New World. There—in the "hush harbors" of the slave quarters—African Americans first began to use funerals to both bury their dead and plan a path to freedom. In African American culture, death was never simply the end of life and funerals were never simply occasions to mourn. This fact explains not only how someone like Dan Young came to be but also why serving the living is such an essential feature of the African American way of death.

1

From Hush Harbors to Funeral Parlors

A cold mist hovered in the air and rain started to fall as twenty-eight weary fugitive slaves gathered on the banks of the Ohio River to contemplate the next obstacle on their perilous journey on the Underground Railroad. The husbands, wives, children, and one young mother carrying a newborn all came from the same neighborhood in Kentucky and had worked odd jobs to accumulate a small amount of money to pay someone to guide them to freedom. All of their hopes rested with the skills of their conductor, John Fairfield, a curious and somewhat controversial character. A white Virginian by birth, Fairfield had spent most of his life in the South but hated slavery. His Southern background helped him pose among other whites as a proslavery advocate while he worked surreptitiously to locate slaves who needed help escaping to freedom. Among his cohorts in the Underground Railroad, Fairfield was known as "devoid of moral principle, but a true friend to the poor slave." On this damp evening as his charges collected themselves at the edge of the river near Lawrenceburg, Indiana, Fairfield quickly had to devise a plan to get all of them across the river and on their way to Cincinnati, which was another twenty miles north.[1]

Fairfield brought the group to this particular spot on the river, near the mouth of the Big Miami, because he knew he might find some skiffs tied to the bank. Within a few minutes, Fairfield found three small boats and broke them free of their moorings. When later asked if he had any qualms about this act of larceny, Fairfield simply replied, "No; slaves are stolen property, and it is no harm to steal boats or anything else that will help them gain their liberty." After he dragged the skiffs over to the fugitive slaves, they all crowded onto the three rather fragile vessels and began their voyage. The overloaded and rickety boats almost immediately began to take on water. When the skiff carrying Fairfield started to sink only a few yards from the Ohio shore, he jumped out onto a sandbar and found himself in water two to three feet deep. As he attempted to drag the boat to land, Fairfield began to sink in the mud and quicksand. The others jumped in to help him, and they all ended up wading to the shore. The muddy journey left everyone soaked to the skin, and some lost their shoes in the struggle.[2]

Finally on the Ohio riverbank, Fairfield tried to get his bearings, as he needed to hide the large—and now very conspicuously disheveled—group while he figured out how he might navigate them through the next passage of their journey. Although they were all exhausted and chilled from the rain, the fugitives followed Fairfield's instructions to hide in the ravines outside of Mill Creek while he went to get help. Fairfield, who had many contacts in the Underground Railroad, went to John Hatfield, "a worthy colored man, a deacon in the Zion Baptist Church . . . a great friend to the fugitives—one who had often sheltered them under his roof and aided them in every way he could." Once Hatfield understood the dire situation of the runaway slaves, he sent a messenger to Levi Coffin, the reputed "President of the Underground Railroad," to ask for assistance. Coffin quickly decided that the best way to move the fugitives through the area was to stage a mock funeral procession. In his own words, Coffin recounted the drama:

> Several plans were suggested, but none seemed practicable. At last I suggested that some one should go immediately to a certain German livery stable in the city and hire two coaches, and that several colored men should go out in buggies and take the women and children from their hiding-places, then that the coaches and buggies should form a procession as if going to a funeral, and march solemnly along the road leading to Cumminsville, on the west side of Mill Creek. In the western part of

Cumminsville was the Methodist Episcopal burying ground, where a certain lot of ground had been set apart for the use of the colored people. They should pass this and continue on the Colerain pike till they reached a right-hand road leading to College Hill. At the latter place they would find a few colored families, living in the outskirts of the village, and could take refuge among them . . . We knew we must act quickly and with discretion, for the fugitives were in a very unsafe position, and in great danger of being discovered and captured by the police, who were always on the alert for runaway slaves.

Coffin's plan worked quite well, and the escapees, with provisions from Hatfield's black neighborhood, were able to make it through to College Hill. One sad footnote haunted the story, however, as the smallest fugitive, the one infant, died during the mock funeral procession. The baby apparently had fallen ill during the cold, wet escape across the river. The child's mother had wrapped the infant tightly in blankets to muffle its cries. When they finally reached their destination, she was stunned to discover that her baby, whom she had thought was just sleeping, had passed away. The group quickly but respectfully buried the child in the Methodist Episcopal cemetery and moved on.[3]

This evocative story highlights the profound relationship that African Americans have always had to death and the funeral experience. During slavery, from its beginnings in the transatlantic slave trade through the antebellum period, death was often imagined as the ultimate "freedom" from a life of oppression. When African slaves first began arriving in the New World, many believed that death was a way for their spirits to return home to Africa. In this account from the Underground Railroad, the mock funeral procession acted as a protective façade that literally conveyed the enslaved African Americans to their freedom. Yet in the loss of the infant it also acknowledged that the specter of actual death was ever present. Throughout African American history, death and funerals have been inextricably intertwined with life and freedom.[4]

Historically, death in the African American cultural imagination was not feared but rather embraced as the ultimate "homegoing," a welcome journey to a spiritual existence that would transcend the suffering and injustices of the mortal world. As W. E. B. Du Bois wrote in *The Souls of Black Folk*, "Of death the Negro showed little fear, but talked of it familiarly and even fondly as simply crossing the waters, perhaps—who knows?—back to his ancient forests again." The vision of death as a homegoing was most powerfully captured in the lyrics of the famous slave spiritual "Oh, Freedom":

Oh Freedom, Oh Freedom, Oh Freedom over me!
And before I'll be a slave,
I'll be buried in my grave
And go home to my Lord
And be free.

Death, therefore, was not only mourned as a loss but also celebrated, since the afterlife signified complete emancipation from the oppression of enslavement. For these reasons, the funeral director was destined to have an unusually powerful role in African American culture as the person who oversaw death and burial, which were so heavily invested with spiritual meaning and the hope of ultimate liberation.[5]

The roots of African American burial and mourning customs can be traced back to West and Central Africa. These rituals traveled to the New World via the transatlantic slave trade and ultimately influenced the traditions of African American slave funerals from the early colonial period through the antebellum period. The Civil War, which ended slavery in the United States, also marked the beginning of what would become the modern funeral industry. Significantly, then, the funeral profession emerged directly parallel to the rise of Jim Crow segregation, which began during Reconstruction and intensified at the turn of the century. African Americans actively participated in the early development of modern funeral practices such as embalming and saw the funeral industry as a promising avenue for economic independence and social uplift in a racially divided world. Thus the combination of the cultural significance of funeral customs and the economic potential of the funeral industry secured the funeral direc-tor's place as a central and complex figure in African American life.

*   *   *

Hear more often things than beings,
The voice of the fire listening,
Hear the voice of the water.
Hear in the wind
The bushes sobbing,
It is the sigh of our forebears . . .

Those who are dead are never gone,
they are in the breast of the woman,
they are in the child who is wailing,
and in the firebrand that flames.
The dead are not under the earth:
they are in the fire that is dying,
they are in the grasses that weep,
they are in the whimpering rocks,
they are in the forest, they are in the house,
the dead are not dead.
                                   —Birago Diop

In African cosmologies about death, the dead and the living are never separated from one another but are, in fact, always intimately con-nected.[6] In contrast to Western ideas of death as an irrevocable loss for the living survivors, African religious beliefs imagine deceased ances-tors as dynamic spiritual forces that guide life for those still alive. The vast diversity of Africa makes it difficult to make specific claims about every aspect of death and burial practices. Nevertheless, it is possible to describe the basic contours of West and Central African burial ritu-als and religious beliefs about death to explain how they may have in-fluenced African American death and funeral rituals over time.

The profound cultural significance of the funeral in African society, and subsequently in African American life, arose from the basic but essential belief that one's deceased ancestors have direct relationship with and authority over the lives of their descendants. The dead are not "alive" in the most literal sense; rather, they exist as powerful spiritual beings who continue to influence the living world through the actions of their descendants. In his seminal text *The Myth of the Negro Past*, Melville Herskovits writes that in the African worldview, "the dead are everywhere regarded as close to the forces that govern the universe, and are believed to influence the well-being of their descendants who properly serve them." He notes that the worship of ancestors in West Africa created an "ancestral cult," which demanded strict observance:

> The ritual for the ancestors begins with the death of a person, who must have a funeral in keeping with his position in the community if he is to take his rightful place in the afterworld. As far as surviving relatives are concerned, two drives cause them to provide proper funeral rites. The positive urge derives from the prestige that accrues to a family that has provided a fine funeral for a dead member; negative considerations arise out of the belief that the resentment of a neglected dead person will rebound on the heads of surviving members of his family when neglect makes him a spirit of the kind more to be feared than any other— a discontented, restless, vengeful ghost.

The combination of the longing for the status accrued from a "fine funeral" and the fear of being haunted by the spirit of the "neglected dead person" clearly fueled the intense interest in proper burial in West African culture.[7]

The largest percentage of North American slaves came from West Africa and, specifically, from the West Coast of Central Africa or the Congo-Angola region. This area, therefore, offers critical insight into the way African burial customs influenced African American death rituals. The Bakongo people of the West African Kongo civilization embraced a cosmology that contained what has been described as two worlds or divided worlds, simply expressed as "this world" and "the other world." "This world" was the world of the living in which birth and death occurred along with all the tribulations and joys in between.

"The other world" was the world of the ancestors, ghosts, witches, and other types of spirits, who exerted their power in many often unforeseen ways. Unlike the world of the living, the other world of the deceased was free of difficulty, injustice, birth, and death. It exemplified pristine order and contrasted with the unpredictable and disordered world of the living.[8]

Central to the two-worlds concept was an acknowledgment that life had no end but was, rather, a cycle reflected in the natural world. The Bakongo imagined the two worlds in concrete physical terms:

> The N'Kongo thought of the earth as a mountain over a body of water, which is the land of the dead, called Mpemba. In Mpemba the sun rises and sets just as it does in the land of the living. Between these two parts, the lands of the dead and the living, the water is both a passage and a great barrier. The world, in Kongo thought, is like two mountains opposed at their bases and separated by the ocean . . . The setting of the sun signifies a man's death and its rising his rebirth, or the continuity of his life. Bakongo believe and hold it true that man's life has no end, that it constitutes a cycle. The sun, in its rising and setting, is a sign of that cycle, and death is merely a transition in the process of change . . .
> Death is a way of changing one's body and location; he will continue in the cycle on earth.[9]

Here the land of the dead, or the Mpemba, existed as a direct inversion of the lived world. Water was imagined as "both a passage and a great barrier" between the two worlds and, therefore, was considered a highly mystical and primal element. The Bakongo believed that when sunlight sparkled on the surface of lakes or streams, the spirits of their ancestors were near. The movement of the sun symbolized the continuity of the life cycle and the dynamic relationship between the worlds of the living and the dead. The importance of the sun to burial rituals is evident in the common practice among West Africans and African Americans of burying a corpse on the east-west axis, with the head laid to the west. Folklorists have cited this practice as a desire to lay the deceased in the direction of the rising sun rather than "crossways uv de world."[10]

In Kongo and other West African traditions, the moment of death marked the beginning of a series of sacred acts that sought to guide the spirit of the deceased safely into the next world. Several key rituals characterized most West African mortuary practices, including the offering of libations, the bathing of the corpse, the presentation of gifts to the deceased, public bewailment, interment, a special visit to the gravesite the morning after burial, and a celebratory memorial service weeks after the burial. Before any other preparations of the corpse, the mourners offered libations to appease the gods of the household and to placate the spirit of the deceased. Immediately following the offering of libations, most West African tribes had a select group—usually composed of older women—wash the corpse. No one else was allowed to touch the body until the ritual bathing was complete. In some tribes, for instance among the Ga, it was fairly common to embalm the corpse after the ritual bathing to preserve the remains until all living relatives could come to view the deceased. In these instances, embalming did not hold religious meaning but was viewed as a practical measure.[11]

After the corpse was bathed and embalmed, the deceased was dressed in his or her best apparel and laid out for what was called the public bewailment. This communal weeping was often the emotional climax of traditional mortuary practices. In many cases, the older women who oversaw the bathing began the weeping ceremony, and the congregation of family and other mourners then joined in with wailing and lamentations. Those who did not participate in the ritual weeping risked being viewed by other mourners with contempt and suspicion. During the period of weeping, mourners presented gifts to the deceased, usually in the form of money, fine clothes, or other objects that might serve the dead person in the spirit world.[12]

After the public bewailment, mourners placed the corpse and the gifts the deceased had received in a coffin in preparation for the interment—the culmination of the West African funeral ceremony. The location of the burial depended on the type of death that had occurred. A natural death was viewed positively and warranted burial in a communal cemetery. Accidental or sudden death was viewed with suspicion, often as a sign of evil spirits at work. Consequently, individuals who died suddenly or by accident were buried in seclusion in the hopes of keeping the malevolent spirits away from others. The procession to the burial often involved intricate drumming ceremonies and dancing around the grave in the form of a ring shout. On the morning after the burial, mourners usually gathered at the grave to pray that the spirit of the deceased was at peace.[13]

Anywhere from several weeks to one year after the burial, many West African tribes held an elaborate memorial celebration or "second burial" to honor the deceased one final time with singing, drumming, dancing, and feasting. These festive ceremonies marked the official end of the funeral ritual and offered a dramatic contrast to the mournful tone of the earlier phase of public bewailment. The second burial was in some sense spiritually more significant than that of the first burial. The special memorial service released the deceased from "the region of the dead in which all souls are confined . . . to usher him triumphantly . . . into the abode of his fathers in the world of the spirits."[14]

After the official funeral ceremonies were over, grave decoration—particularly among the Bakongo people—became the primary means to communicate with the spirit of the deceased. In Kongo cosmology, the cemetery grave was viewed not simply as a burial place for the deceased but as a mystical portal between the two worlds of the living and the dead. For this reason, the Bakongo decorated the gravesite with charms, which were called *minkisi,* to cultivate this metaphysical connection with the spirit world of the ancestors. Grave decoration allowed mourners to allay any lingering fears of improper burial through symbolic acts that sought to free the deceased's spirit from the earthly realm. Most commonly, survivors decorated gravesites with the last objects that the deceased had touched or with objects that the deceased had particularly cherished. Among the most prevalent items left on the burial site were plates, cups, or drinking glasses, as it was believed that the spirit of the dead person was still present in these objects. Given the symbolism associated with water as the barrier between the worlds of the dead and the living, many objects used in grave decoration were either receptacles for holding water, such as pitchers and cups; objects that simulated water, such as mirrors; or objects found in water, such as seashells. As an observer commented, "The shells stand for the sea. The sea brought us, the sea shall take us back. So the shells upon our graves stand for water, the means of glory and the land of demise." The Bakongo also planted trees on or near the gravesite so their descending roots could visually represent the journey of the soul to the other world.[15]

The position and condition of the items left on the gravesite were also significant. Grave decorations were often inverted, an emblematic gesture in the Kongo tradition signifying that the spirit world was upside-down or a mirror of the living world. As Robert Farris Thompson has described, "the verb 'to be upside down' in Ki-Kongo also means 'to die.' Moreover, inversion signifies perdurance, a visual pun on the superior strength of the ancestors, for the root of *bikinda*, 'to be upside down, to be in the realm of the ancestors, to die' is *kinda*, 'to be strong,' 'because those who are upside down are strongest.'" Another important burial ritual involved breaking or damaging the objects left on the grave. In an 1891 article entitled "Fetishism in the Congo," E. J. Glave observed that the "crockery, empty bottles, and old cooking pots" left on Kongo graves were "rendered useless by being cracked or perforated with holes." Unaware of the spiritual significance of the damaged objects, Glave speculated that mourners broke these items to prevent them from being stolen. Subsequent research revealed that—rather than a deterrent to theft—the damage was intended to free the deceased's spirit from the earthly objects and facilitate a transition to the spiritual realm.[16]

West African, and specifically Kongo, cosmologies about death espoused a vibrant dynamism that existed between the living and the spirits of the deceased ancestors. Death was not an end but only a transition to another state in the life cycle. For this reason, the preparation of the corpse and the burial involved an elaborate set of rituals and procedures to honor the spirit of the deceased and properly guide its soul to its new existence in the land of the dead. Although elaborate burial rites are evident in many world cultures, the transference of African funeral customs to the New World via the transatlantic slave trade was exceptional. Evidence of the endurance of these beliefs and rituals in African American culture can be seen most dramatically in the death practices of the slave community. The trauma of capture, the

Middle Passage, and enslavement in the New World only strengthened Africans' and African Americans' beliefs that death represented a freedom to return home to a spirit world superior to life on earth. In the New World, African Americans used these West African death rituals to their own ends.[17]

*   *   *

I know moon-rise, I know star-rise,
Lay dis body down.
I walk in de moonlight, I walk in de starlight,
To lay dis body down.
I'll walk in de graveyard, I'll walk through de graveyard,
To lay dis body down,
I'll lie in de grave and stretch out my arms;
Lay dis body down.
I go to de judgment in de evenin' of de day,
When I lay dis body down,
And my soul and your soul will meet in de day,
When I lay dis body down.
—TRADITIONAL SLAVE SPIRITUAL

The African American slave funeral from the colonial era through the antebellum period was one of the most central ways the slave community was able to assert its essential humanity.[18] In colonial times, the funeral ceremony allowed many recently enslaved Africans to honor their heritage and practice religious rituals that gave them a sense of connection with their homeland. In the early Republic, the slave funeral took on new meaning as most enslaved African Americans were more fully acculturated to North American life but had not yet converted to Christianity in significant numbers. Throughout the eighteenth century, the funeral stood as one of the few religious ceremonies in which slaves experienced some degree of autonomy from their masters' control. The slave funeral traditionally took place late at night in the "hush harbors," the secluded, usually wooded, places near the slave quarters where the enslaved could congregate for religious services and social gatherings. By the early nineteenth century, fear arose among masters that slaves were using the late-night funeral services to plan insurrections. Consequently, the antebellum slaves' desire to assert their spiritual life through their own funeral ceremonies directly conflicted with the masters' need to monitor all such observances. Throughout all these time periods, the funeral was a powerful communal refuge where slaves found shelter from the horrors of enslavement and where they reasserted the bonds of family and community at a time of loss. Most significantly, the slave funeral served as the foundation of several key elements of African American life, including the early origins of an independent black church, the organization of mutual aid and burial societies, and ultimately—through the establishment of the funeral industry—a very successful form of black entrepreneurship. [19]

If slave funerals laid the groundwork for African American communal life, they also revealed the power dynamics of the slave-master relationship. Some scholars have argued that slave funerals were one of the most consistent acts of benevolence on the part of slaveowners toward their chattel. They emphasize the frequency with which slave funerals were allowed to take place; the testimony on the part of some masters about their own grief upon the death of a particularly beloved slave; and the willingness of slaveowners to either be present at or preach the sermon at a slave funeral. The counterargument to this view of paternalistic benevolence highlights evidence that the majority of slaves were rarely given time off to honor and bury their dead, and that many slaves were denied proper burial. As one former slave recalled, "When we die, dey bury us the next day and you is just like any of the other cattle dying on de place. Dat's all 'tis to it and all 'tis of you. You just dead, dat's all." Even worse, runaway slaves, slaves who challenged their masters, or slaves who were caught planning a revolt were sometimes killed and their corpses mutilated or left to decay as a means of intimidating other slaves. These forms of terrorism began on the transatlantic slave ship but were documented well into the nineteenth century. In 1811, when whites in Louisiana discovered plans for a slave insurrection, they not only killed the suspected rebels but also publicly displayed their dismembered corpses.[20]

Most slave funerals existed somewhere between the two extremes of familial benevolence and violent mutilation of the corpse. Slaveowners usually allowed their chattel to bury their dead with some small measure of dignity, even if it simply meant providing them with materials to build a coffin and time after dark to gather for a burial or funeral service. Nevertheless, knowing that funerals allowed slaves to gather in private and assert their spiritual beliefs with some degree of independence, masters tended to resist the idea of lengthy slave funerals and sought some measure of control over even the most basic burial rituals. Historical records from as early as 1680 reveal that colonial lawmakers in Virginia perceived that when large numbers of "Negro slaves [met] under the pretense of . . . burials," the situation was "dangerous." To lessen the risk they legislated a stringent pass-and-patrol system to monitor the gatherings. By 1772, a New York City law mandated that slave funerals could only be held during the day, and that attendance at slave wakes could not exceed ten people. The policing of funerals reflected anxiety on the part of slaveowners that the ceremony provided too much of an opportunity for the enslaved to congregate away from the watchful eyes of their masters. Ironically, the owners' own unwillingness to give their slaves time off to honor their dead resulted in most slave funerals being held at night or on Sundays in the hush harbors. This restriction actually reaffirmed the common West African belief that the dead should be buried after sunset.[21]

In 1800, slaveowners' fears that slave funerals were subversive were realized when white authorities discovered the plot of what became known as Gabriel's Rebellion in Richmond, Virginia. Gabriel, a slave owned by Thomas Prosser, held one of the key organizational meetings for his planned insurrection at a slave infant's funeral on August 10—only days before the attack was to occur. Gabriel and his co-conspirators were "appropriately dour during the service, but with the end of the funeral 'Gabriel gave an invitation to some of the Negroes to drink grog at the Spring.' There he announced—significantly—that he had a plan to fight not just for black freedom but also 'for his Country.'" In the aftermath of Gabriel's Rebellion, whites demanded more vigilant surveillance of slave funerals, which now required the presence of white owners or clergy. Later, in 1831, Nat Turner would lead his violent slave revolt in Virginia, which resulted in the deaths of fifty-seven white men, women, and children. Although there was no evidence that Turner organized his uprising at a funeral, the Commonwealth of Virginia responded to the attack with legislation that completely forbade black preaching at unsupervised slave funerals.[22]

In the face of these heightened restrictions, slaves persisted in their efforts to maintain their own cultural traditions for proper burial. These traditions reflected both African and African American religious rituals as well as general trends in funeral customs in nineteenth-century America. The antebellum slave funeral evoked many West African burial rituals, including bathing and wrapping of the corpse, laying out of the body on a cooling board, the "settin' up" wake, procession to the grave for burial, postburial feasting, and finally a much more elaborate "second funeral," weeks, months, or even up to a year after burial. At the moment of death, which was often signaled by a loud, mournful wail or piercing scream from the family members of the deceased, the women in the slave household were most often called upon to prepare the deceased for burial. These preparations included washing the corpse, wrapping it in a white shroud or "winding sheet," and laying it out on a wooden plank called a "cooling board." As one former slave recalled, "Dere warn't no undertakers dem days. De homefolks jus' laid de corpse out on de coolin' board 'til de coffin was made . . . A coolin' board was made out of a long straight plank raised a little at de head, and had legs fixed to make it set straight. Dey wropt 'oman corpses in windin' sheets." While the corpse was prepared, word of the slave's death was sent through an informal slave messenger network or, less frequently, through the African tradition of beating the "drum of death" to summon mourners.[23]

Mourners then gathered to conduct the settin' up vigil or wake throughout the night in the slave quarters. Here slaves shared their grief through communal acts of praying, chanting, dancing, singing, and sometimes touching the corpse as an intimate way to bid farewell to the deceased. As one former slave recalled, "At de wake we clapped our han's an' kep' time wid our feet—*Walking Egypt,* dey calls hit—an' we chant an' hum all night 'til de nigger was *funeralized.*" Another common ritual at the settin' up involved passing an infant over the corpse to protect the living from the spirits of the dead.[24]

The lively communal nature of slave burial rituals continued during the procession to the slave graveyard, which could involve up to several hundred mourners marching solemnly by torch light and often included drumming and dancing an African-inspired ring shout in a counterclockwise circle around the grave. Mourners sang spirituals such as "Hark from de Tomb, a Doleful Sound," "Lay Dis Body Down," and "Deep River," which includes the lyrics "Deep River, my home is over Jordan,/Deep river, Lord; I want to cross over into camp ground." Spirituals like "Deep River," which foreground the African American religious and folklore belief that when a person died his or her soul crossed over the River Jordan, also evoked the West African belief that water or bodies of water connected the living to the dead. The final act of burial, which was usually the shortest part of the ceremony, involved mourners dropping handfuls of dirt on the coffin or working together to shovel the dirt over the grave. The procession back to the slave quarters from the graveyard was markedly more festive, with the mourners sometimes singing and dancing in celebration of the memory of the deceased. Often these festivities continued throughout the night.[25]

One of the most striking similarities between the West African death practices and African American slave funerals was the importance of the "second funeral," which happened weeks to months—and sometimes as long as a year—after the actual burial. This second funeral, usually celebratory in tone, was considered essential because it allowed all family members to gather to honor the deceased. The length of the delay between the actual burial and the second funeral ceremony was largely determined by the availability of a black preacher to perform the funeral sermon. One of the most renowned black funeral preachers in the antebellum period was John Jasper from Richmond, Virginia. A passage from a 1908 biography of Jasper vividly captures the importance of the second funeral in slave communities:

> There was one thing which the Negro greatly insisted upon, and which not even the most hard-hearted masters were ever quite willing to deny them. They could never bear that their dead could be put away without

a funeral. Not that they expected, at the time of burial, to have the funeral service. Indeed, they did not desire it, and it was never according to their notions. A funeral to them was a pageant. It was a thing to be arranged for a long time ahead. It was to be marked by the gathering of kindred and friends from far and near. It was not satisfactory unless there was a vast and excitable crowd. It usually meant an all-day meeting, and often a meeting in a grove, and it drew white and black alike, sometimes in almost equal numbers. Another demand in this case—for the slaves knew how to make their demands—was that the Negro preacher "should preach the funeral" as they called it. In things like this, the wishes of the slaves usually prevailed. "The funeral" loomed up weeks in advance, and although marked by sable garments, mournful manners and sorrowful outcries it had about it hints of an elaborate social function with festive accompaniments.

The slave funeral was thus one of the most important venues for the plantation or itinerant black preacher, who might travel great distances to perform funeral sermons. Until a black preacher preached the official funeral sermon, the family did not have peace of mind that the deceased's spirit was free. In this way, the slave funeral was an important training ground for what evolved into the independent black church.[26]

Long after the last funeral sermon was preached, African American slaves, like their West African forebears, used grave decoration as another tangible way to honor the spirits of the dead. One former slave recalled, "Dis wuz a common ting wen I wuz young. Dey use tuh put duh tings a pusson use las on duh grabe. Dis wuz suppose tuh satisfy duh spirit an keep it frum followin yuh back tuh duh house." Ernest Ingersoll wrote of visiting South Carolina burial sites in 1881 and observing grave decoration:

> When a negro dies, some article or utensil, or more than one, is thrown
> upon his grave; moreover it is broken . . . Nearly every grave has bor-
> dering or thrown upon it a few bleached sea shells . . . Mingled with
> these is a most curious collection of broken crockery and glassware. On
> the large graves are laid broken pitchers, soap-dishes, lamp chimneys,
> tureens, coffee-cups, sirup jars, all sorts of ornamental vases, cigar

boxes, gun-locks, tomato cans, teapots, flower-pots, bits of stucco, plaster images, pieces of carved stone-work from one of the public buildings destroyed during the war, glass lamps and tumblers in great number, and forty other kitchen articles. Chief of these, however, are large water pitchers; very few graves lack them.

Ingersoll's level of detail confirms the astonishing array of items left on African American gravesites in the mid- to late nineteenth century. They were strikingly similar to the objects that were commonly left on Kongo graves, including seashells, water pitchers, and other everyday containers. These African American decorative rituals offered a dramatic contrast to the more austere tombstones that marked most Anglo-American graves at the time and revealed how significant it was for slaves to honor the spirit of the dead in very tangible, symbolic ways.[27]

The funeral was a fundamental act of kinship in the slave community. The rituals involved in the preparation of the corpse, the settin' up, the burial, and the second funerals gave enslaved African Americans a concrete and meaningful way to share grief, assert family ties, and build an independent spiritual and religious life. The outbreak of the Civil War, which stirred new hopes of emancipation among slaves, profoundly changed all Americans' relationship to death. When the war ended and the slaves celebrated their newfound freedom, they no longer needed to gather in the secret hush harbors of the slave quarters to bury their dead. Nevertheless, the most meaningful traditions of the slave funeral did not disappear with the end of slavery. On the contrary, the newly freed African Americans continued to view the funeral as one of the most sacred communal acts they could perform. For these reasons, the emergence of funeral directing as a profession in the late nineteenth century was particularly significant in the African American community, which placed such a high value on a proper and dignified burial.

Over the course of the nineteenth century, America witnessed a remarkable transformation in funeral and mourning practices. In the antebellum period, simple, private family funerals in rural settings were the norm. By the end of the century, as increasing numbers of Americans moved to cities in search of industrial work, funerals reflected a more urban and urbane sensibility. Although most people still died at home in the late nineteenth century, the preparation of corpses was no longer overseen by family members but was instead given over to the local undertaker or funeral director, who would come directly to the house and embalm the deceased for viewing. The undertaker would manage all other funeral arrangements, which now involved ordering a range of products from factory-made caskets to burial robes. Burial no longer took place at a private graveyard but at a lawn cemetery with landscapes that evoked the restfulness of a park rather than the sober setting of the early nineteenth-century graveyard. A funeral ultimately became a commodity that was purchased in the free market and, therefore, was used to determine one's status in American society.[28]

The marked shift in American funerals from intimate family affairs to more commercialized and public rituals began at the time of the Civil War, a national trauma that permanently altered Americans' relationship to death and mourning. The staggering carnage wrought by the war, including the more than 600,000 deaths that resulted from the conflict, created a cultural crisis that demanded new ways of managing death and burial. The massive casualties left many Americans struggling to reconcile their most cherished beliefs about what constituted a dignified burial with the grim realities of sudden death on the battlefield. For logistical reasons, soldiers who died in battle were buried as soon as possible, often in makeshift graves near the site of combat. As death tolls rose over the course of the war, many families—especially those of Union soldiers—demanded that the bodies of their dead be returned home for what was deemed a proper burial. Transporting these deceased soldiers home was not a simple task, however, especially in the heat of the summer months, when decomposition occurred more rapidly.[29]

In response to these dire wartime conditions, embalming gained sudden and widespread popularity as an effective means to preserve the corpse for shipment home. Before the war, embalming was used only to maintain cadavers for dissection in medical schools. The Civil War created a new and practical use for the technique as a means to facilitate the grieving process. During the war, the early embalming industry was centered in the nation's capital and was led by Thomas Holmes, who has been called the "Father of American Embalming." Holmes, who trained as a physician in New York City in the 1840s, became interested in embalming while dissecting cadavers in medical school. Critical of the poisonous compounds—such as arsenic and mercury—used in early embalming, Holmes worked to develop a less toxic fluid that would be safe for broad use. He also invented an effective injection pump for arterial embalming.

Early in the war, Holmes relocated to Washington, D.C., and began a calculated campaign to popularize embalming as a means to preserve the war dead properly. Holmes's efforts included distributing circulars that extolled the benefits of embalming and staging public exhibitions of embalmed bodies at local undertaking establishments. Some of his promotional endeavors met with resistance, as when he was arrested for creating a public nuisance at one exhibition. Nevertheless, throughout the war embalming became increasingly popular. Some ambitious early embalmers brazenly went directly to the front lines of battle to advertise their ability to preserve the "honored dead."[30]

One particularly successful embalmer at this time was W. R. Cornelius, whose undertaking career illustrates the evolution of the trade in the nineteenth century. Earlier in the century, undertaking had been an informal commercial venture, most commonly an offshoot of the furniture business. Cornelius began his career as an undertaker in 1844, when he apprenticed to a cabinetmaker in Pennsylvania. After his apprenticeship, he relocated to Nashville, Tennessee, to become the foreman of undertaking at the cabinet firm of McComb and Carson. At this time, undertaking involved not only providing the coffin but also transporting it from the home to the graveyard in a horse-drawn carriage or wagon. Cornelius's reputation grew when, in 1849, he had the honor of conducting the funeral of President James K. Polk. The 1850s proved less than prosperous for Cornelius when the McComb and Carson firm, of which he had become a partner, suffered financial troubles and, in 1856, lost its cabinet factory to fire. The Civil War, however, proved a boon to Cornelius's undertaking career when he secured contracts for burying both the Confederate and the Union dead. As he later recalled, "I took a contract to bury the confederate dead and I continued to bury them (about 1800 in all) until the arrival of the Union Army, when I took a contract from Capt. Gilliam . . . basing my prices on what I had received from the Confederate government." As a result of these war contracts, Cornelius was able to establish branch offices of his undertaking business in Tennessee, Alabama, and Georgia. By the end of the war, he claimed to have "buried and shipped to their homes something over 33,000 soldiers, employees, etc. of which I kept record."[31]

Throughout his career as an undertaker, Cornelius employed an assistant by the name of Prince Greer, who was an ex-slave and one of the first African American embalmers mentioned in historical records. Cornelius first began to embalm the war dead in 1862, when Dr. E. C. Lewis, a representative of Thomas Holmes and his embalming fluid company, offered to train him in the skill. As Cornelius recalled, "I undertook embalming myself with a colored assistant named Prince Greer, who appeared to enjoy embalming so much that he became himself an expert, kept on at work embalming through the balance of the war, and was very successful." Greer arrived at Cornelius's establishment from Texas, where he had been the servant of Colonel Greer of the Texas Confederate Regiments. When Colonel Greer was killed during the storming of Fort Donelson, Prince Greer accompanied his body to Cornelius's funeral establishment. After the colonel's body was shipped back to Texas for burial, Prince Greer stayed on to work for Cornelius. In his assessment of his assistant's skill at embalming, Cornelius remarked that Greer could "raise an artery as quickly as anyone, and was always careful." He needed Cornelius's guidance only when there was "a critical case," indicating that Cornelius viewed Greer not simply as an assistant but as a skilled technician in his own right.[32]

While the popularity of embalming grew during the war, it became firmly established as an essential part of the mourning experience after the assassination and funeral of Abraham Lincoln. Lincoln's corpse, which traveled across the country on an extended funeral procession, dramatically advertised the marvel of embalming. Starting in Washington, D.C., Lincoln's funeral journey lasted a full twenty days before coming to an end in Springfield, Illinois. The cross-country cortege allowed American citizens of all races to view the president's embalmed body as a way to pay their respects to their fallen leader. When the cortege finally arrived in Springfield, the embalmer who had been escorting the corpse across the country struggled to maintain its integrity. Nevertheless, the nation's ability to witness Lincoln's remains for such an extended period of time showed the American public that embalming could allow them one last look at the deceased. In the decades following the war, the appeal of embalming increased, as undertakers promoted not only its ability to preserve the corpse for viewing but also its importance as a sanitary measure that might prevent the spread of disease.[33]

America's adoption of embalming as a regular feature in the preparation of the dead in the late nineteenth century was instrumental in the formation of the modern funeral industry. Embalming gave undertakers the ability to claim a specialized scientific skill, which was a critical step in their effort to redefine funeral directing as a distinct profession. Professionalism became highly prized in the mid-nineteenth century as many Americans sought to establish a middle-class identity and distinguish themselves from the industrial working class. The rise of industrialization, which resulted in the mass production of commodities such as coffins, allowed undertakers to distance themselves from trades such as furniture- or cabinetmaking. Freed from the task of individually constructing coffins, undertakers could emphasize instead their ability to offer specialized services to assist the bereaved. In the 1880s, funeral directors used embalming to associate themselves with the prestige of the medical profession by adopting titles such as "embalming surgeon" and "mortician," which evoked the title "physician." Equally important, funeral directors argued that their role as grief counselors put them on par with the clergy in terms of professional status.[34]

By the early 1880s, two concurrent developments illustrated the shift toward a more professional public image for undertakers: the founding of embalming schools and the establishment of a national association of funeral directors. At embalming schools, leading practitioners worked strategically to institutionalize the skill as a requirement for any legitimate undertaker. Dr. Auguste Renouard, sometimes referred to as the dean of early embalming education, published *The Undertakers' Manual,* the first textbook on embalming and undertaking, in 1878. A few years later, in 1883, Renouard opened the Rochester School of Embalming in New York. In 1882, another preeminent embalmer, Joseph Henry Clarke, had established the Cincinnati School of Embalming. Before these schools were created, training in embalming occurred only in medical schools or very informally as embalming chemical salesmen demonstrated their wares on the road. Embalming schools allowed funeral directors to receive formal training and credentials, although formal licensing did not begin until the mid-1890s. By the 1890s, Dr. Auguste Renouard relocated to New York City and founded the U.S. College of Embalming, which—in 1900—merged with the Renouard Training School for Embalmers, a school founded by Renouard's son, Charles. Significantly, many of these schools admitted African American students and were responsible for training many of the earliest African American funeral directors. These efforts to formalize embalming education promoted the idea that embalming was a specialized professional skill that required advanced training in anatomy and chemistry.[35]

The establishment of formal embalming schools occurred contemporaneously with the movement among undertakers to organize themselves into professional trade associations. In 1864, the first formal organization of undertakers was founded in Philadelphia under the name the Undertakers' Mutual Protection Association of Philadelphia. Other major cities including Chicago and New York established similar groups from 1865 through 1880. In 1880, Michigan was the first state to found an undertakers' association; the following year the name was changed to Michigan Funeral Directors Association. Other states quickly followed suit, and in 1882, these separate state associations met in Rochester, New York, to establish the National Funeral Directors Association (NFDA). The delegates at this first convention sought to protect themselves from unfair competition, to cultivate a professional public image for undertakers, and to provide educational instruction for members. The main educational feature of the first NFDA convention, not surprisingly, was Dr. Auguste Renouard's embalming demonstrations. One of the most important debates to be resolved at this first meeting of the NFDA was the decision to replace the term "undertaker" with "funeral director" as the official appellation of this new "profession." The campaign to confer professional status on funeral directors would prove challenging, however, and was never completely successful because the burgeoning funeral industry lacked the standards, regulation, and prestige of medicine or law. Ultimately, funeral directing gained a more positive public image by the end of the nineteenth century but never earned full legitimacy and remained a quasi-profession.[36]

In part, the funeral directors' struggle to gain professional prestige resulted from their active role in promoting and profiting from the commercialization of the funeral experience. They were never able to separate their primary identity as trades people involved principally in the sale of death-related commodities from their role as professionals offering a specialized service, whether it be embalming corpses or counseling the bereaved. By definition, professionalism is supposed to operate as a counterbalance to commercialism. The professional was perceived as driven by a moral code of ethics and a desire to serve the public good rather than by a profit motive alone. Given this ideal, it was difficult for funeral directors, who were foremost entrepreneurs, to make a convincing claim to a professional identity. The challenge was accentuated by the fact that their efforts occurred simultaneously with the exponential growth of the commercial funeral industry in the Gilded Age.

The movement to professionalize funeral directing and the commercialization of the funeral industry were inextricably intertwined. Most prominent embalmers either worked for or established their own embalming chemical companies and built their reputations on their ability to find new and innovative ways to sell embalming fluid. Thomas Holmes invented what he called "Inominata" embalming fluid, which he sold for $3.00 a gallon. The Egyptian Chemical Company completely underwrote Dr. Auguste Renouard's Rochester

School of Embalming in 1883. When Renouard established his embalming school in New York City, he began marketing his own "Renouard Special Embalming Fluid" and "Renouard Face Tint" products. The institutionalization of embalming education, which clearly raised the occupational status of the undertaker, was never separate from the direct commerce of the funeral industry.[37]

Perhaps the most striking example of the interrelationship of marketing and the professionalization of funeral directing was the Stein Manufacturing Company of Rochester, New York. Samuel Stein, who founded the company in 1870, invented the cloth-covered "showcase" casket, which featured velvet-covered wood panels, solid silver handles, and an interior lined with Venetian lace, silk tassels, and satin. An expert marketer, Stein showcased his high-end caskets in a special exhibit hall at the Philadelphia Centennial Exposition in 1876 and set a new standard for advertising caskets in public. At the same time, the Stein Company began publishing the trade journal the *Casket,* which kept funeral directors abreast of the latest merchandising and business trends in the funeral industry. The James Cunningham Company, a hearse and carriage manufacturer, also subsidized the publication of the *Casket* to advertise its line of increasingly ornate hearses. As a result of the success of the journal, funeral directors began selling consumers a wider array of ancillary products, including burial robes, elaborate floral arrangements, and "mourning cards," which were given as mementos to grieving relatives and friends. The proliferation of these funeral products demonstrated the degree to which the death experience in America had changed by the end of the nineteenth century into a very profitable enterprise offering a new form of conspicuous consumption to the American public. When the NFDA hosted its first annual convention in 1882, the new organization not surprisingly decided to meet in Rochester, New York, home of the Stein Manufacturing Company, the *Casket,* and the renowned embalmer Auguste Renouard. The site of the convention reflected the merger of the marketing of the funeral industry with its aspirations to professional status.[38]

The evolution of funeral directing from a modest trade before the Civil War into a quasi-profession and highly lucrative business by the turn of the century was a remarkable example of the way industrialization, urbanization, and the rise of a professional middle class completely redefined the death experience in nineteenth-century America. The career potential that the emergent funeral industry represented from the 1880s through the turn of the century was not lost on African Americans. On the contrary, from the triumph of Emancipation through the hopes and failures of Reconstruction, African Americans were actively seeking ways to become economically independent and respected by white society through self-help and a spirit of racial uplift. By the 1880s, the burgeoning field of "funeral directing" presented what appeared to be a perfect opportunity. It offered not only the promise of economic security and social respectability but also the ability to honor and cultivate African Americans' longstanding and most cherished homegoing traditions.

African Americans' relationship to the nascent funeral industry illustrated both the possibilities and the limitations of black capitalism in the late nineteenth century. In many ways, the history of the early funeral industry, which paralleled the rise of Jim Crow segregation after the Civil War, offers a unique case study of the relationship between race and capitalism in American life. It is almost impossible to imagine the many challenges most newly freed African Americans faced in their search for any form of economic security in the immediate aftermath of the Civil War. As W. E. B. Du Bois wrote in 1899 in *The Negro in Business,* "Physical emancipation came in 1863, but economic emancipation is still far off. The great majority of Negroes are still serfs bound to the soil or house servants. The nation which robbed them of the fruits of their labor for two and a half centuries, finally set them adrift penniless." Consequently, the business opportunity that the formation of the funeral industry represented to many black Americans in the decades after the war offers a particularly vivid example of the way death and funerals continued to represent a symbol of hope and freedom within black communities.[39]

As the funeral industry first became officially established in the 1880s, African Americans were particularly well positioned to capitalize on its business potential through the exponential growth of their own mutual aid societies, secret societies, and burial leagues. These organizations, which provided members with sickness and death insurance, were critical to the development not only of the African American funeral industry but also of its banking and insurance industries. African American mutual aid began in the late eighteenth century when free blacks founded the first black benevolent societies, including the African Union Society in Newport, Rhode Island, in 1780 and the Free African Society, which Richard Allen established in Philadelphia in 1787. Also in 1787, Prince Hall, a black minister and leader in Boston's free black community, founded the first black Masonic fraternal order, known as the Prince Hall Masons, which eventually inspired other blacks to found their own branches of fraternal groups such as the Knights of Pythias, the Odd Fellows, and the Grand United Order of True Reformers.[40]

The early benevolent societies, which were inspired by African secret societies, and the fraternal orders, which followed the European tradition of fraternal organizations, were founded primarily to assist fellow blacks through economic cooperation and to offer social support in times of need. The most significant aspect of most black benevolent societies, however, was aid given for burial. In addition to burial insurance, these early organizations promised to provide dignified funeral rites and a cemetery plot. Securing land for black burials was not always easy and often involved acquiring significant capital. In both the North and the South, elite free blacks constituted the core membership of these organizations, and enslaved blacks were usually unable to benefit from their efforts. Nevertheless, early black benevolent societies in the South such as the Brown Fellowship Society, founded in Charleston, South Carolina, in 1790, used their membership dues to purchase a burial plot in 1794 that would "serve Charleston's entire black population, slave or free, mulatto or not."[41]

Throughout the antebellum period, these benevolent societies and fraternal lodges enjoyed great popularity among free blacks, but quickly gained widespread appeal among freed slaves after the Civil War, when African Americans realized that white society was not going to assist them in times of financial crisis, sickness, or death. In the earliest stages of Reconstruction, the Freedman's Bureau offered critical assistance to newly emancipated slaves, but this aid was limited in scope and in duration. As Carter G. Woodson wrote, "The Negroes in the final analysis had to learn to look out for themselves. The deep-seated idea of solving a social and economic problem through benevolent societies, then, seemed more practical than ever." Moreover, the ceremonial and social aspects of fraternal organizations and secret societies also appealed to freed blacks, who took pride in the regalia and celebratory parades that the groups regularly held for holidays such as Emancipation Day. Offering important social and economic benefits, the secret society or fraternal organization soon rivaled the black church in terms of its importance to the black community throughout the Gilded Age.[42]

From the 1880s through the 1890s, African American mutual aid societies, secret societies, and burial leagues reached the peak of their popularity. Members of secret societies and burial leagues usually contributed about fifty cents a month to a central fund that would act as insurance to help pay or defray the costs of sickness or, in the case of death, embalming and other funeral services. During this period, African Americans faced more direct discrimination from white insurance companies, which began to publish studies claiming that blacks were a much higher insurance risk than whites. African Americans had yet to form their own insurance companies to compete with the white insurance industry. The first major African American insurance company, the North Carolina Mutual Life Insurance Company, was not founded until 1898. Consequently, African American secret societies and burial leagues offered their members the best option for securing burial insurance and death benefits for family members.[43]

These organizations promised their members a dignified home-going that would include all the new accoutrements of the late nineteenth-century funeral. The guarantee of a proper burial held particular appeal for poor African Americans, who sought to avoid a pauper's grave. For this reason, purchasing burial insurance and maintaining these policies became an unusually high priority even in the poorest black communities. As the anthropologist Hortense Powdermaker observed, "Burial insurance is usually the first to be taken out and the last to be relinquished when times grow hard. It is considered more important by the very poor than sickness or accident insurance . . . No Negro . . . can live content unless he is assured a fine funeral when he dies." Consequently, the early African American funeral industry profited directly from the success of these secret societies and burial leagues, which generated both the demand and the capital needed to support any aspiring black funeral director.[44]

It was not long, however, before prominent Negro leaders began to debate the value of secret societies and burial leagues as a community activity and a business practice. Critics of these groups believed that elaborate funerals were a misplaced and, therefore, ineffective financial investment. W. E. B. Du Bois commented in 1898 that "secret societies represent much extravagance and waste in expenditure . . . and to some extent they divert the savings of Negroes from more useful channels." James Weldon Johnson later wrote, "They [secret societies or lodges] . . . care for the sick and bury the dead. In many of them, however, burying the dead has called for a financial outlay so far out of proportion to that used in caring for the living as to make the 'high cost of dying' a live question." Booker T. Washington was more blunt in a speech at the Tuskegee Institute in the 1890s: "The trouble with us is that we are always preparing to die. You meet a white man early Monday morning and ask him what he is preparing to do, and he will tell you that he is preparing to start a business. You ask a colored man at the same time, and he will tell you that he is preparing to die."[45]

Washington, as well as others, had a clear change of heart about the value of secret societies and burial leagues once their overall value to the development of black capitalism became more obvious in the first decade of the twentieth century. In 1909, in his book *The Story of the Negro*, Washington argued that secret benevolent societies encouraged black Americans to save money and develop sound investments. In his chapter on secret societies, Washington stated:

I think that it may be safely said that these organizations have collected from the masses of coloured people large amounts of money that would not otherwise have been saved. In doing this they have created a considerable capital, which has been at the disposal of Negro business men. It has enabled Negroes to erect buildings, invest in lands, and greatly increase property in the hands of members of the race. Indirectly, these organizations have stimulated thrift and industry among the masses of people.

Washington went on to note that the business people who most obviously benefited from the growth of secret societies and burial leagues were undertakers:

> Another business in which the Negro early found an opportunity to be of service to his people is that of undertaking. As far as they are able, the Negro people have always tried to surround the great mystery of death with appropriate and impressive ceremonies. One of the principal features of the Negro secret organizations has been the care for the sick and the burial of the dead. The demand that these organizations sought to meet has created a business opportunity, and Negro business men have largely taken advantage of it.[46]

Washington first articulated his appreciation of undertaking as a growth industry for African Americans two years earlier in his 1907 book *The Negro in Business,* which featured a chapter titled "The Negro Undertaker," as well as profiles of several successful undertakers across the country. As one example, Washington singled out Elijah Cook, who was born a slave in Alabama and was taught the carpenter's trade through an apprenticeship. Soon after the Civil War ended, Cook realized that there were no black undertakers in his hometown of Montgomery and "that the corpses of colored people were being hauled to the cemetery in rough wagons." In response, Cook "bought a hearse, and went into business for himself." Twenty years later, he had accumulated a small fortune and had become "one of the most respected citizens of Montgomery, and is foremost in every plan for the betterment of the race."

Washington also presented the story of James C. Thomas, "the richest man of African descent in New York." Born in Texas in 1864, Thomas worked on steamboats in his youth and, through his nautical travels, eventually relocated to New York City in 1881. He opened his undertaking establishment in 1897, when there were only two other "colored undertakers" in business in the city. At this time, "the larger part of the [undertaking] business which should have come naturally to colored undertakers was in the hands of white men." Through his "conscientious dealings with colored patrons, and by his ability to meet their peculiar needs," Thomas was able to compete with white undertakers and secure "colored business largely for colored business men." Through the example of Thomas's career, Washington illustrated a major trend in black capitalism that had specific implications for the developing field of funeral directing: the growth of a segregated marketplace.[47]

Throughout the early and mid-nineteenth century, black entrepreneurs, who worked as barbers, tailors, blacksmiths, and other artisans, had largely succeeded through their ability to attract white patronage. By the 1880s, as Jim Crow segregation increased throughout the country, black business leaders began to realize that the key to future success lay in securing the African American market for themselves. W. E. B. Du Bois described this trend as the development of a "group economy," which he defined as "a cooperative arrangement of industry and service in a group which tends to make a closed economic circle, largely independent of surrounding whites." For many aspiring black entrepreneurs of the late nineteenth century, the realities of racial segregation were impossible to ignore. Booker T. Washington directly addressed racial separatism in his famous 1895 Atlanta Exposition Address when he remarked, "In all things that are purely social we can be as separate as fingers, yet one as the hand in all things essential to mutual progress." Racial segregation in public facilities only intensified one year later in 1896, when the U.S. Supreme Court legally upheld the "separate but equal" doctrine of public accommodations in its *Plessy v. Ferguson* decision.[48]

Given these circumstances, it is not surprising that Du Bois, Washington, and other prominent black leaders began, at the turn of the century, not only to champion the idea of group economy as a key platform for racial uplift but also to see funeral directing as unique in its potential to thrive in a racially segregated marketplace. Undertaking, as Washington had argued, was a particularly promising enterprise for the aspiring black entrepreneur who hoped to secure "colored business." As the twentieth century dawned, many more African American entrepreneurs would follow James C. Thomas's lead and pursue their economic dreams through funeral directing. The hopes of these funeral directors were complicated, of course, by the reality that their business success was bound in part to Jim Crow segregation, which would always limit the degree of their achievements. As they worked together to fulfill the ideals of black economic cooperation, these funeral directors would quickly face the challenges of navigating a funeral industry that was both growing exponentially and working actively to make sure that the largest opportunities in the field were reserved for "whites only."

2

The Colored Embalmer

On November 16, 1918, a small news story ran in the black press under the provocative headline, "Race Chauffeurs Block a Funeral Procession." The story came out of Jacksonville, Florida, but received national coverage when it was picked up by the black wire service, which sent it to black newspapers across the country. The report was brief but engaging as it described a rather unusual protest. Apparently, a group of "Colored chauffeurs who owned and operated their own cars" decided to form a blockade with their vehicles to thwart a funeral procession that was trying to advance down a Jacksonville street one mid-November day. To disrupt the sacred act of burying the dead must have involved a serious offense. For the "race chauffeurs," the wrong committed was egregious indeed and involved the fact that a "prominent Colored family uncompromisingly employed a white undertaker, overlooking the race men in the same business." The chauffeurs sarcastically declared at the blockade that given the circumstances, "it would be better for all whites to handle the affair, even to the minister." Their request for a white minister, clearly an affront to time-honored African American funeral traditions, revealed the level of contempt the protestors felt toward the mourning family. Back at the church, the "crowd of mourners waited while the white undertaker was compelled to hold the remains" until the chauffeurs' demands were met.[1]

Meanwhile, an entirely different type of conflict involving race and the funeral business arose in Hattiesburg, Mississippi. In 1916, E. W. Hall and Malachi C. Collins decided to open Hall and Collins Funeral Home, the first black-owned funeral establishment in Hattiesburg.

A white funeral director in town, threatened by the potential competition, initially tried to sabotage their plan by circulating handbills among local blacks that read, "Don't patronize those niggers, we can give you better service." An organized campaign of intimidation continued for two years and escalated from handbill propaganda to violent threats. The local Ku Klux Klan made a practice of racing cars in front of the Hall and Collins Funeral Home late at night. Tensions became so high that Hall and Collins armed themselves with shotguns after hours and took turns guarding their new business from possible attack.[2]

The Jacksonville blockade and the hostilities in Hattiesburg offer two very different snapshots of the racial politics of the early funeral industry. Yet both resonate with the central paradox that faced African American funeral directors at the beginning of the twentieth century: how to negotiate both the costs *and* the benefits of the strict Jim Crow segregation that divided most of America into clearly marked worlds of "white" and "colored." On the one hand, the racism that fueled the pervasive segregation led to all types of discrimination that limited African Americans' ability to succeed socially, politically, and economically. For African American funeral directors, racial discrimination within the funeral industry began in 1912, when the most recognized professional trade organization in their field, the National Funeral Directors Association, officially banned them from membership. Moreover, as the Hattiesburg case attests, racist whites often actively fought African Americans' efforts to establish their funeral businesses through any number of legal and illegal means.

On the other hand, the strict boundaries of the racially divided world of early twentieth-century America meant that African American funeral directors and other black entrepreneurs had a clearly defined consumer market that was, supposedly, all theirs. In the strange calculus that evolves from a Jim Crow world, racial segregation was— for all practical purposes—in the best interests of the black business people, since it theoretically guaranteed them a captive and steady base of consumers. In reality, the loyalty of the African American consumer was not a given for the black entrepreneur, but something that had to be secured through an active campaign advocating that true racial uplift could be achieved only through the economic cooperation of all people of color. Given these circumstances, we can appreciate the motives of the race chauffeurs in Jacksonville in obstructing a solemn funeral procession when the "Colored" family involved made the decision to employ a white undertaker.[3]

The ways African American funeral directors navigated Jim Crow racial segregation in the first decades of the twentieth century provide an important case study of the paradox of early black capitalism. Black entrepreneurs tried to use their businesses as a form of self-help and racial uplift and—at the same time—as a strategy for fighting racial prejudice and discrimination. These two goals, however, were sometimes directly at odds with each other, which ultimately led to internal dissension among black leaders about the best way for black business to serve the race. At the turn of the century, both Booker T. Washington and W. E. B. Du Bois agreed that black economic independence was central to the overall campaign for racial equality. Soon after Du Bois refined his theories of the benefits of a group economy for the advancement of the race in 1899, Booker T. Washington founded the National Negro Business League (NNBL), an organization that would exemplify the spirit of economic cooperation among black entrepreneurs. The league's central philosophy was defined, however, by a distinct dualism which "asserted that the economic laws of laissez faire were blind to color differences and that economic usefulness and success were the best way to eliminate prejudice, but [the league] also vigorously propagandized for Negro support of Negro business." In other words, the campaign for black economic cooperation at the turn of the century was based both on the belief in a color-blind free market as a means to end racial prejudice and on the importance of maintaining a color-bound segregated group economy.[4]

African American funeral directors struggled with this dualism most acutely in the first decades of the twentieth century as the funeral industry became more established, modern, and profitable. Given African Americans' reverence for proper burial, black funeral directors were especially well positioned to promote the idea that blacks should support their businesses for cultural as well as for economic reasons.

As one funeral director in the NNBL argued at the annual convention in 1917, "we realize . . . that it is important that the remains of members of our race, both men and women, be looked after by funeral directors who respect them, who revere them, and who will treat them justly and fairly in all respects." Moreover, in the face of discrimination from within the funeral industry and by the NFDA, African American funeral directors were forced to unite and form their own professional associations and trade journals in order to succeed.[5]

Yet even as they were advocating the insularity of a group economy, African American funeral directors at the turn of the century led some of the most important early battles against racial segregation in the Jim Crow era. These entrepreneurs had both the financial resources and the prestige as leaders of their respective communities to stand at the forefront of the formative campaigns for civil rights, including the 1896 Supreme Court case *Plessy v. Ferguson*. In the end, many African American funeral directors found themselves actively advocating black patronage for black business while, at the same time, fighting for the larger cause of racial equality and desegregation in their local communities.

Booker T. Washington's National Negro Business League, founded at the dawn of the new century in 1900, provided the first formal organization through which African American funeral directors could band together to gain a foothold in the funeral industry. The early history of the league not only revealed how the philosophy of black economic cooperation had come to the forefront of the national campaign for racial equality but also set the stage for the ongoing debate between the militant and the accommodationist strategies for fighting this campaign in the twentieth century. Somewhat surprisingly, W. E. B. Du Bois, who would soon lead the militant front with the founding of the Niagara Movement and the NAACP, was the first black leader and intellectual to articulate a clear vision of black economic independence as a central platform in the fight against racial inequality. Du Bois hosted the Fourth Conference for the Study of Negro Problems at Atlanta University in May 1899, which focused on the topic "The Negro in Business." One of the final resolutions of the conference read: "The mass of the Negroes must learn to patronize business enterprises conducted by their own race, even at some slight disadvantage. We *must* cooperate or we are lost. Ten million people who join in intelligent self-help can never be ignored or mistreated." Moreover, the final resolution of the conference included a call for the "organization in every town and hamlet where colored people dwell, of Negro Business Men's Leagues, and the gradual federation from these of state and national organizations."[6]

Almost exactly a year after Du Bois's Atlanta University conference, Booker T. Washington issued a call for black businessmen to gather in Boston, Massachusetts, in August 1900 "to organize what will be known as the National Negro Business League." Although Washington had consulted with Du Bois when he began to compile a list of active black businessmen around the country, he chose not to acknowledge Du Bois's inspiration for such an organization. This lack of attribution was one of the first steps in the growing rift that would divide the two leaders and their respective philosophies.[7]

For African American funeral directors, the NNBL provided a forum through which they could promote their achievements in undertaking to a larger supportive group. At the first convention in Boston, George C. Jones, a funeral director from Little Rock, Arkansas, was one of the 115 businessowners in attendance who was given the floor to make public remarks. True to the spirit of the occasion, Jones emphasized the inroads that he had made not only in his undertaking establishment but also in supporting other blacks in business. He noted that at "every funeral [I handle] that turns out in Little Rock, everything needed in the line, from a buggy up, is owned by the Negro that drives it or by the undertaker that conducts it." Five years later, at the fifth annual meeting of the NNBL, James C. Thomas, the leading black funeral director in New York City, gave a similar speech in which he noted that undertaking had become an especially promising business profession for *any* aspiring black entrepreneur. Thomas observed not only that funeral directing now required formal training and a state license for embalming, but that the field was open to the "lady embalmer . . . whose duty is to prepare for burial the bodies of the women and children." Most notably, Thomas continued that his own success in funeral directing, which included conducting more than 400 funerals in the last year, enabled him "to enter into another field of investment which has for its purpose no other than to meet the needs of my race." Thomas's new business venture was the Afro-American Realty Company, which was founded in response to "the difficulty encountered by our people in securing comfortable homes in any respectable neighborhood in any part of New York." Clearly, through the example of Thomas and others, funeral directing was a business that held tremendous potential to fulfill the larger mission of the NNBL.[8]

By 1907, the funeral directors in the NNBL had established their own auxiliary organization, the National Negro Funeral Directors Association, which was the first of its kind in the country. In 1911, J. N. Shelton, a representative of the association, gave a report on the organization at the annual NNBL convention in Little Rock, Arkansas. Shelton noted that "twenty-five years ago the Negro funeral director was almost an unknown quantity," and yet now he was "one of the most substantial business factors making for the success of our race, as well as one of the most valuable assets of the National Negro Business League." When Shelton opened the floor for questions, a delegate promptly asked him how much Negro patronage funeral directors received, a query which revealed that race patronage was not guaranteed for any black entrepreneur. Shelton garnered much applause when he responded confidently, "They receive ninety-five per cent of the patronage of the colored people in the communities in which they live."[9]

Just two years later, in 1913, the report of the National Negro Funeral Directors Association to the NNBL convention again addressed the issue of race patronage. In this instance, however, it became clear that the topic was more politically charged than it had been in the past. Speaking once again to the floor, J. N. Shelton declared, "I say the time has come when we ought to make it impossible for any white man to bury a Negro in any community in which you live." Another funeral director, Basil F. Hutchins of Boston, Massachusetts, then reported that when he began his undertaking career sixteen years earlier, "ninety per cent of the work [of black funerals] was then being done by white undertakers . . . to-day, I am glad to know, ninety-five per cent of the work is done by colored undertakers." Hutchins then continued, however, "I have a good percentage of white trade . . . [and] recently conducted the funeral of one of the richest white citizens of Boston." Hutchins admonished other NNBL members not to depend only on race patronage but to "prepare yourselves and be able to successfully meet any kind of competition. Let us rely solely upon our merit as business men and not depend upon our color alone as the drawing card . . . I am succeeding alongside of white funeral directors, and make apology to no man of my color."

In the wake of Hutchins's impassioned speech, Booker T. Washington felt compelled to make his own comments to the floor on the highly charged issue:

> All things being equal, of course it is our duty to support Negro enterprises, but don't let us have the short-sightedness to say that we *must* patronize black people and absolutely ignore the white people . . . *for you know the white man can come back at us in a hundred ways, where we can't get back at him in one way.* We have too much at stake to be narrow either in our thought or our action. If other people want to be narrow, let us be broad. Let our business men count on support and patronage, as Mr. Hutchins said, not simply because we are colored, but rather because we manufacture the best goods and render the highest service.[10]

Here, the internal contradictions of a race-patronage philosophy bubbled quickly to the surface of the convention's proceedings. Was a "successful" black funeral director someone who kept whites from burying blacks or someone who earned the trust of black and white customers alike and allowed white funeral directors to do the same? Clearly, the public rhetoric of black economic cooperation could easily get entangled in its own inconsistencies, when the idealism of free-market economic theory ran into the reality of the racism so entrenched in American society at the height of Jim Crow segregation. For evidence of racial discrimination, the members of the NNBL did not need to look any further than the national funeral industry itself, which was, by 1913, actively excluding black funeral directors from key aspects of professional and business development. Most obvious, of course, was the decision of the National Funeral Directors Association to bar black funeral directors from membership just one year earlier in 1912.

When the NFDA was founded in 1882 in an attempt to legitimize funeral directing as a profession, its membership was officially open to all undertakers regardless of race. Membership in the association had many benefits, including protection from unfair competition and fraud; continuing education; and access to trade publications that disseminated trends in the industry. Then, beginning in 1912, membership was restricted to whites only. Specifically, the NFDA constitution adopted at the organization's national convention on October 4, 1912, included the following language in its membership clause: "But no delegate or ex-officio member shall be admissible to membership in this association, however he or she may be accredited by a state or territorial association, who is not of the white race and actively engaged in the profession of funeral directing and caring for the dead." The language of this clause, which makes particular mention of "state or territorial" associations, responded to an earlier practice in which nonwhite funeral directors—particularly in the Northeast—had been given membership in the NFDA through their membership in local or state associations that did not discriminate by race.[11]

A few members of the NFDA questioned the decision to add overtly discriminatory language to the organization's constitution, although no one staged a formal protest. The minutes of the proceedings of the 1912 convention reveal that some members voiced concerns about the legality of the new clause. Fred Hulberg, a funeral director from New York, took the floor to express his reservations: "I rise to inquire why the White Race has been inserted into this article. We must not forget the 14th amendment to the Constitution of the United States, and I call your attention to this objection to that article. I have no motion to make, but I simply want the attention of the Convention called to it."

NFDA President Cookerly promptly responded: "The Chair will say this in answer to that, that all the funeral directors of this Association, I believe, do not want to sit in the hall with a negro." To which Hulberg replied, "I am thoroughly in accord with the President's announcement, but can we afford to put this into our constitution?" President Cookerly's final comment ended all discussion on the matter: "If there is no further objection, the section will stand adopted as read."[12]

The NFDA's discriminatory membership policy was revisited and expanded yet again in 1926, after the organization's legal incorporation two years earlier prompted revision of the constitution. In the middle of this transition, the association had inadvertently dropped specific references to the "white race" as qualifications for membership in the group. In 1926, the NFDA sought to remedy this oversight in the membership clause to ensure that active members of the organization included "any person of the white race engaged in the profession of funeral directing or caring for the dead."[13]

Once again, the revised membership clause did not get approved without dissenting comments from a few NFDA members from the Northeast. Jeffrey Sullivan, a funeral director from Fall River, Massachusetts, remarked that some state associations, including his own, had colored members. Other NFDA delegates then "pointed out to him that the state associations could do as they pleased with colored funeral directors, but it was desired to make the National association for whites alone." When it was also noted that "the colored member of Massachusetts can thus save himself five dollars a year—the National per capita [membership dues]," Sullivan replied, "Will you return to us the per capita tax we have been paying for years on this member?" Another voice of dissent came from Elwood Heacock of Philadelphia, who expressed serious concern about the association's racially exclusionary membership practices:

We should recognize here every man entitled to membership, and I feel any man is acceptable as a business man, regardless of his color or religion, should be acceptable to us. If this association slips backward for such a reason and becomes unjust, unfair, and un-American, I shall feel that I must withdraw from it.

Here, Heacock articulated one of the essential beliefs of the National Negro Business League: that laissez-faire capitalism should be, in theory, color-blind. The practice of racism, however, overruled any pure economic ideal. The final word in this debate came from the past NFDA president C. C. Reel, who noted, "Our constitution already bans the colored fellow, and you [the By-laws Committee] are not proposing anything new." At that point, "Mr. Heacock insisted that his vote in the negative be recorded in the minutes." In the end, the committee voted to include the "white race" language in the 1926 constitution.[14]

Given the history of the NFDA's discriminatory practices, the efforts of the NNBL and the National Negro Funeral Directors Association to promote black business can be understood more fully. In many ways, black funeral directors embodied the NNBL's highest hopes for the growth of black business and black economic cooperation. At the 1915 NNBL convention, George W. Franklin, president of the National Negro Funeral Directors Association, proudly proclaimed, "Fifteen years ago there were less than 500 Negro funeral directors in the United States; today there are over 1100 men and women actively engaged in the business." Just two years later at the NNBL's national meeting in Chattanooga, Tennessee, A. L. Garrett, founder of the Fayetteville Coffin and Casket Company of North Carolina, gave a talk titled "Financing and Developing a Co-operative Business Enterprise." Garrett decided to invest in his business, which was "the only colored casket factory in the United States of America," after researching the growth of the black funeral industry. At the Chattanooga session, Garrett reported that

the number of deaths yearly among our people in the South [is] estimated at two hundred and twenty-five thousand. The average yearly amount heretofore paid by colored undertakers in the United States to white manufacturing concerns for caskets and other funeral supplies required in burying our people is more than three million, five hundred thousand dollars ($3,500,000). The amount heretofore paid colored factories of this kind, none. Those figures and facts alone speak eloquently of the need of a Negro co-operative enterprise of the kind that I have mentioned, and it should be liberally patronized by Negro funeral directors all over the United States.

In addition to the casket factory, Garrett was establishing an embalming school in the hopes of training more young black men and women in the field; in fact, nineteen of the twenty-one applicants to Garrett's new embalming school were women. In a stirring conclusion, Garrett expressed the hope that "if the Fayetteville Coffin and Casket Company in North Carolina can obtain the support and patronage of a large number of the 1700 Negro undertakers in this country . . . a large part of the more than three million dollars now being spent among white casket factories will flow into the pockets of colored people . . . [and] the success of this co-operative enterprise in North Carolina will prove a practical inspiration to Negroes everywhere."[15]

Although most of the reports about the black funeral industry at the NNBL conventions were optimistic and motivational, some black funeral directors did not hesitate to take the floor to lament the racism they had witnessed in their chosen line of work. In 1918 at the Atlantic City NNBL convention, Mr. Lightner of Raleigh, North Carolina, reported on the "small white undertakers" who were doing business in the country around Raleigh and were "maltreating our people." In one incident, a white undertaker who had come to the house of a black family "just pushed the coffin of the colored person on the porch." He refused to help the family of the deceased move the corpse into the coffin and brusquely remarked, "We don't do anything about putting bodies in the coffin." On the day of the funeral, the same undertaker reserved his best horses for a white funeral and left the black family his mules to transport the casket to the burial. A few years later, at the 1921 NNBL convention in Atlanta, Georgia, another undertaker, Thomas H. Hayes, commented about discrimination in the funeral industry. Hayes noted that "very few white [casket] companies would employ our men and a certain company which did employ them would only promote them to the position of a shipping clerk; while the white employee would be advanced to higher positions and larger pay." Hayes also remarked that the white undertakers who accepted black customers never consulted "the colored undertaker about the wants of the colored people, because the white undertaker does not know the wants of our people and really does not care."[16]

Racial discrimination in the funeral industry, including the NFDA's membership policies, reflected the general racial tensions of early twentieth-century America. In the 1910s and 1920s, the country witnessed the continuing proliferation of Jim Crow legislation; the ongoing terror of lynching, particularly in the South; and, in the North, race riots in cities such as Chicago during the infamous "Red Summer of 1919," which reflected the strain between blacks and whites competing for jobs and housing in crowded urban centers. These trends created an environment in which it became increasingly common for most aspects of the black funeral business to be segregated from the white funeral industry. The establishment of black-owned casket companies, such as the Fayetteville Casket and Coffin Company, was only one example of this phenomenon. Another was a movement to ban the burial of blacks in white cemeteries. In response, many African American funeral directors were working to establish black-owned-and-operated cemeteries to secure a dignified burial ground for their respective communities. These efforts by African American funeral directors to alleviate some of the humiliations of Jim Crow were not new; rather, they can be traced back to the initial campaign to stop Jim Crow segregation from becoming legalized.

The role of the African American funeral director in the fight against legal racial segregation began with the landmark *Plessy v. Ferguson* Supreme Court case of 1896, which established the concept of "separate but equal" segregation of public facilities. The history of de facto racial segregation, however, dated back to the colonial era. While strict segregation was counterproductive to the management of slavery, free blacks in the North and South from the colonial period to the Civil War were regularly segregated from whites in schools, churches, and other public areas. In the immediate aftermath of the Civil War, newly freed blacks throughout the South were subjected to what became known as Black Codes, a series of laws that sought to keep them in a state of perpetual servitude. Black Codes restricted the ability of free blacks to rent or purchase property, subjected those accused of vagrancy to forced labor, and denied them political and legal rights. These laws—as well as many forms of de facto racial segregation—were commonplace throughout the Reconstruction era.[17]

De jure segregation of public facilities did not begin in earnest, however, until after the end of Reconstruction in 1877, when many Southern states began passing statutes to segregate railroad cars by race. Public transportation became the front line in the battle to maintain racial hierarchies because it was a public space that most immediately challenged racial boundaries. Tennessee passed the first railroad segregation law in 1881, which stated that "all railroad companies located and operated in this State shall furnish separate cars . . . in which all colored passengers who pay first class passenger rates of fare, may have the privilege to enter and occupy." The Tennessee law and others like it were designed to provide separate public facilities for black citizens, which some people viewed as better than the alternative of total exclusion. In 1890, the city of New Orleans passed the Separate Car Act, which ruled that "passenger trains shall have the power . . . to assign each passenger to the coach . . . used for the race to which such passenger belongs." Highly educated and politically active members of New Orleans's black Creole society, who were well accustomed to a life without such restrictions, took particular offense at the legislation and quickly began to organize a strategic campaign to challenge the new law.[18]

On September 1, 1891, a group of eighteen elite black Creole leaders founded the "Comité des Citoyens," or the Citizens Committee for the Annulment of the Separate Car Act. Among the leaders of this organization were two prominent funeral directors, Alcée Labat and Myrthil J. Piron. Although Piron died soon after the formation of the Citizens Committee, Labat worked diligently to fight New Orleans's segregationist laws. The Comité des Citoyens considered the Separate Car Act, which they described as a "malicious measure" that would "encourage open persecution" of black citizens, an unambiguous violation of the equal protection clause of the Fourteenth Amendment. The group decided to challenge the Separate Car Act through a legal test case in which Homer Plessy, a light-skinned octoroon, would purposefully violate the act and then challenge its constitutionality by bringing the entire idea of racial classification into question.[19]

One of Alcée Labat's most important contributions to the committee's cause was his role as a board member of the *Crusader,* the black newspaper of New Orleans, which was one of the most essential organizing tools for the Comité des Citoyens. Labat paid a price, however, for his willingness to be a leader in the fight against racial segregation in New Orleans. In the middle of the *Plessy* case, his funeral home was burned to the ground in an act of retaliation against his work as a civil rights activist.[20]

When the Supreme Court ultimately ruled in favor of "separate but equal" facilities in the *Plessy* decision, the defeat stunned Labat and all the members of the Comité des Citoyens. The disheartened activists could only look to Justice John Harlan's eloquent dissent as evidence that their arguments had resonated with one member of the high court. Harlan wrote: "The destinies of the two races, in this country, are indissolubly linked together, and the interests of both require that the common government of all shall not permit the seeds of race hate to be planted under the sanction of law." After the *Plessy* decision was handed down, the Comité des Citoyens made a defiant public statement: "We, as freemen, still believe that we were right and our cause is sacred . . . In defending the cause of liberty, we met with defeat, but not with ignominy." The activism of funeral directors such as Alcée Labat in the *Plessy* case was not an isolated occurrence, but instead marked the beginning of a growing trend in which black undertakers, who were often among the most admired leaders in their respective communities, stood at the forefront in local battles against the humiliations of Jim Crow legislation throughout the South.[21]

Perhaps no one person better exemplifies the way black funeral directors used their business capital and prestige as local community leaders to fight the indignities of racial segregation at the turn of the century than the Reverend Preston Taylor of Nashville, Tennessee. Born into slavery in Shreveport, Louisiana, in 1849, Taylor spent his childhood years in Lexington, Kentucky. Near the end of the Civil War, he enlisted in the Union Army as a drummer and was an eyewitness to the final defeat of the Confederate forces during the siege of Richmond and the surrender of Robert E. Lee at Appomattox in April 1865. After the war, Taylor learned the trade of stonecutting and became particularly skilled in monument work. He met with discrimination, however, when whites refused to hire him at the top marble yards in Louisville, Kentucky. After working a few years as a train porter, Taylor decided to follow his calling to become the pastor of the Christian (Disciples of Christ) Church in Mt. Sterling, Kentucky. Over the course of fifteen years, Taylor became one of his denomination's leading ministers as he built up the largest congregation of his church in Kentucky. By the mid-1880s, Preston Taylor had relocated to Nashville, Tennessee, to continue his career in the ministry as the pastor of the Gay Street Church and eventually the Lee Avenue Christian Church.[22]

In 1888 Taylor branched out from his career in the ministry and opened his own undertaking establishment, Taylor and Company Undertakers, on North Cherry Street. Taylor's dual career as a church pastor and an undertaker illustrated the close relationship that existed between the black church and the black funeral industry. Taylor decided to open his business when Thomas Winston, the only black undertaker in Nashville, passed away. At the same time, Taylor also purchased thirty-seven acres of land to establish Greenwood Cemetery, to provide Nashville's black citizens with a dignified burial ground. By the early 1890s, two more black funeral establishments were founded in Nashville, but Taylor was considered the city's premier black undertaker. He secured this honor in 1892, when he oversaw one of the city's most regal funerals. On January 2, 1892, three black firefighters were killed while battling a "great conflagration" in the city. To stage the funeral, Taylor built a special carriage hearse that held all three caskets side by side. Thousands of onlookers witnessed the funeral procession that included the wide hearse drawn by six horses, as well as sixty carriages, which held city officials, members of the police and fire departments, and other community leaders.[23]

Throughout black Nashville, Taylor was admired not only for orchestrating such pageantry but also for running his business with style and a commitment to the economic well-being of his community. In one Nashville news report, local blacks marveled at Taylor's fine undertaking establishment, described as

[a] building [that] is 42 x 180 feet . . . reception hall, office, chapel, show rooms, supply rooms, trimming rooms, dry rooms, carpenter shops, paint shops, and a morgue. In the rear stands a large stable occupied by eighteen head of horses, seven carriages, hearses and all kinds of vehicles used in the undertaker's business. The entire building is lighted with electric lights and fitted up with electric bells.

In the story, Taylor was also praised for being the only black undertaker in the city who "manufactures his own goods" and who employs "sixteen men" and "often is compelled to call in extra help." Taylor's funeral directing business made him one of the most esteemed black business leaders in Nashville and gave him the financial resources to address some of the most pressing issues facing the city's black community.[24]

In the first decade of the new century, the most urgent problem facing Nashville's black community was the proliferation of Jim Crow legislation throughout the South that sought to divide the public sphere by race. In March 1905, the Tennessee state legislature passed a bill to establish Jim Crow segregation on all streetcars in the state. When the law officially went into effect in July 1905, Nashville's black community responded swiftly by calling for a boycott of the city's streetcars. The Nashville boycott was one of more than twenty-five boycotts throughout the South against Jim Crow streetcar laws between 1900 and 1906. The streetcar boycott movement was remarkable for its scope, which included protests organized in all the states of the former Confederacy, and for the conservative strategy it employed, which sought to preserve the status quo and avoid "direct confrontation with the laws, such as would have occurred if Negroes had insisted on sitting in the white section [of a streetcar]."[25]

The conservative nature of the protests reflected the general tenor of race relations at the turn of the century, when the accommodationist philosophy of Booker T. Washington had reached the height of its popularity. In most of the cities involved, including Nashville, the streetcar boycotts were led by black elites—several of whom were undertakers like Preston Taylor. These businessmen were contemporaries of Washington, members of the National Negro Business League, and supporters of his nonconfrontational views. Although the boycotts employed tactics that avoided direct conflict with whites, they nevertheless were genuine forms of protest against laws that were, as the black press reported, "yielding to the wave of prejudice and vindictiveness that has swept the South . . . [and were] designed especially to humiliate colored people."[26]

Of all the Southern protests against streetcar segregation, Nashville's boycott was perhaps the most fully realized. Organizers not only asked black citizens to refuse to ride the white-owned streetcar lines but also founded the Union Transportation Company, a black-owned streetcar line headed by Preston Taylor, who acted as president. The establishment of the independent black transportation company gave Nashville blacks a proactive way to protest the streetcar legislation. By providing black riders with alternative transportation, the Union Transportation Company supported the boycott, shielded black riders from the humiliations of riding on the white-owned Jim Crow streetcars, and also fulfilled the goals of black economic cooperation.

Taylor and other black business leaders in Nashville, who were motivated to put the ideals of the NNBL into action, moved quickly to found the company in late August 1905 as a logical progression of the citywide boycott that had begun in July. In the first few weeks, the company used horse-drawn wagons to transport riders to their destinations, but by mid-September they had sold $7,000 worth of stock, had another $18,000 worth of stock subscribed, and were able to purchase five motor buses. By December 1905, the black press optimistically reported that the efforts of the boycotters and the Union Transportation Company had cost the Nashville Street Car Company $7,500 a month and that this was an example of how the "race means hereafter to make the white man pay for his prejudices."[27]

Within the first few months of operation, however, a series of mishaps and a lack of consistent financial backing hampered the Union Transportation Company's ability to serve Nashville's black riders in the long term. Early on, the company's first fleet of steam-powered buses was unable to manage Nashville's hilly terrain. All the original buses had to be sold, and another nine electric motor buses were purchased for the company. The Union Transportation Company was then plagued by the technical and financial challenges of maintaining the electric buses. Initially, the company was forced to purchase electric power from the Nashville Railway and Light Company, the white-owned business that was the target of the boycott. In addition to the difficult concession of giving money to its white competitor, the Union Transportation Company faced sabotage when the Nashville Railway and Light Company overcharged their batteries and damaged the bus equipment. In response, the company attempted to set up its own dynamo and generator in the basement of the National Baptist Publishing House, which was owned by Richard H. Boyd, one of the company's officers. The independent electrical system was never able to function consistently, however. As a result, the Union Transportation streetcar lines were notoriously unreliable and had difficulty maintaining the patronage of many working-class blacks whose job security depended on consistent transportation to work. Another financial setback occurred when Nashville's city government decided in April 1906 to levy a $42.00 privilege tax on electric cars, which added additional expenses to the struggling company.[28]

By the summer of 1906, main service on the Union Transportation Company's streetcar lines was discontinued. The following spring, Preston Taylor presided over a stockholders' meeting in which he reported on the financial difficulties of the company, which involved paying off the remaining debt from the $20,000 original investment that was made to purchase vehicles for the line. When many stockholders reneged on their promises to pay for the company's stock, Taylor was left to manage the company's debt from the sale of the electric buses and his own profits from his funeral directing business.[29]

Despite the Union Transportation Company's very limited success, the Nashville Streetcar Boycott remained a pivotal moment in one of the earliest organized fronts against Jim Crow segregation in the twentieth century. In the end, the company's ultimate failure to provide consistent service revealed how difficult it was to create from scratch a black-owned business that would have to compete with already established and fully funded white-owned transportation companies. The demise of the Union Transportation Company was not, however, a sign that all such efforts were futile. On the contrary, the overall objective of the Nashville Streetcar Boycott and other, similar boycotts across the South in the first decade of the new century illustrated quite dramatically that African Americans would not let themselves be subjected to the indignities of Jim Crow segregation without a fight. Most important, they would adopt economic strategies, whether this meant boycotting white-owned businesses or establishing competing black-owned businesses to serve black citizens. Given that black businesses were so central to these actions, African American funeral directors like Alcée Labat and Preston Taylor would continue to play leading roles in many local movements to fight racial discrimination.

Of all the indignities endured as the result of racial prejudice, discrimination during the death and burial of a loved one was perhaps the one that most readily prompted African American funeral directors to act on behalf of their local communities. When Preston Taylor founded Greenwood Cemetery in Nashville in 1888, he sought to secure proper burial grounds for the city's black citizens. Beginning in colonial times, blacks were buried in segregated areas of white cemeteries, which were usually located on the least desirable margins of the larger cemetery. By the late nineteenth century, these practices became much more prevalent as Jim Crowism began to pervade all aspects of daily life *and* death. As a response, many black communities worked to establish their own cemeteries to ensure that their deceased family members could truly rest in peace. This development of independent black cemeteries involved the urban North as well as the South.[30]

The founding of one black cemetery, the Detroit Memorial Park, exemplified the way African American funeral directors fought racial discrimination in death as a means to support black economic cooperation in life. Charles C. Diggs, Sr., a leading black funeral director in Detroit, originally proposed the idea of establishing a black-owned cemetery to a small group of the city's black funeral directors in early 1925. Diggs began his business, the House of Diggs, in 1921, and it quickly became the largest black funeral home in Detroit and financially one of the most profitable black undertaking businesses in the country. For Diggs, founding the Detroit Memorial Park was a direct way to respond to the many different forms of racism that black customers experienced at established white cemeteries in the city, including restrictions on when they could bury their dead (usually on specific days or during unpopular hours); insistence that black funeral processions use side or back entrances to the cemetery; and paying higher prices than white patrons. When the funeral directors first met to discuss the project, they imagined a cemetery that charged reasonable rates to anyone, regardless of race, who wanted to bury their deceased with dignity.[31]

Diggs had a very well conceived plan for launching the new cemetery, which would become the first African American corporation in Michigan. In June 1925, he asked twenty subscribers—including some of his fellow funeral directors—each to invest in five shares of stock to start the new company. Each share was worth $250.00, and the $25,000 raised was then used to purchase sixty acres of land located in Warren Township, an all-white suburb north of Detroit. When Diggs and his colleagues purchased the land, they did not face any initial resistance to the project. Yet when local whites discovered that the cemetery's black superintendent and family would reside in a farmhouse on the property, a local protest arose to stop the project. In a move to secure the property for its designated use, Diggs and one of his fellow funeral directors quickly buried the body of a stillborn infant to ensure that the land could not be reclaimed for other purposes. The cemetery conducted its first adult burial in November 1926.[32]

In its early years, the Detroit Memorial Park faced several challenges, including maintenance of the grounds, which were plagued by water-drainage problems. In 1928, the corporation faced another major setback when the Michigan Mutual Savings Bank, which had lent the cemetery its mortgage money, failed and was taken over by the state. Nevertheless, even in the difficult early years of the Great Depression, the company, largely through the generosity of its board of directors, was able to honor all its financial commitments to its stockholders. By the 1940s, the Detroit Memorial Park had not only achieved financial stability but also offered home loans to black Detroiters who were denied financial aid from white-owned banks. By using the funds from the Detroit Memorial Park to finance mortgages, the funeral directors who founded the cemetery created a viable means to private homeownership for African American Detroiters who were regularly discriminated against in the city's real estate market.[33] From the work of the New Orleans Comité des Citoyens on the *Plessy* case in the 1890s to the Nashville Streetcar Boycott of 1905 and the establishment of the Detroit Memorial Park in the 1920s, African American funeral directors regularly participated in civil rights organizing and business cooperatives that sought either to fight Jim Crow segregation directly or to ameliorate the effects of persistent discrimination against blacks. Within the funeral industry itself, African American undertakers continued to organize themselves as a means to navigate the discrimination and segregation they experienced from the NFDA and the white funeral industry in general. In 1925, a group of black funeral directors were ready to establish their own trade association separate from the auspices of Booker T. Washington's National Negro Business League. The group, the Independent National Funeral Directors Association (INFDA), felt that its autonomy from the NNBL would allow it to more directly address and assert the needs of black funeral directors in the white-dominated funeral industry. The founding of the INFDA would mark a new era in the history of African American funeral directing that would define the field and, in many ways, attempt to uphold the ideals of black capitalism for the rest of the twentieth century.

The early efforts to found the INFDA marked a decline in the power of the NNBL, which achieved the height of its influence when Booker T. Washington presided over the group from 1900 to 1915. After Washington's death in November 1915, the league struggled to maintain its focus and keep local chapters engaged with the larger mission of the group. From 1915 to the mid-1920s, the NNBL faced internal power struggles in its leadership, financial mismanagement, and increased public criticism from black radicals such as A. Philip Randolph, who saw the organization's promotion of laissez-faire capitalism as a misguided and unrealistic strategy for the Negro masses. In the end, the league's rhetoric about the promise of Negro business to uplift the race and defeat racial prejudice was always more of a motivational tactic than a realizable goal. Without the commanding presence of Washington to lead the group, the NNBL struggled in the years after his death to create an effective strategy to pursue its goal of black economic cooperation. For many African American funeral directors, the league and its auxiliary group, the National Negro Funeral Directors Association, had begun to outlive their usefulness.[34]

As the NNBL's influence weakened in the 1920s, the funeral industry grew exponentially and entered its modern era. From the 1880s through the 1920s, the number of funeral directors in the United States had expanded approximately as fast as the living population. In 1900, the NFDA had a membership of 3,920 members; by 1910, this membership had grown to 9,281. By 1927, the NFDA reported at its annual convention that the overall number of funeral directors had grown from 9,891 in 1890 to 24,469 in 1920. In 1915, the National Negro Funeral Directors Association estimated that the number of African American funeral directors more than doubled in number from less than 500 in 1900 to more than 1,100 in 1915. By the end of the 1920s, the estimated number of African American funeral directors jumped again to 3,000. In conjunction with the remarkable growth in the number of practicing funeral directors, the overall death rate in America dropped from 19.6 per 1,000 in 1890 to 12.1 per 1,000 in 1920, according to NFDA statistics. These two related trends heightened competition for customers throughout the funeral industry.[35]

In addition to the statistical increase in the number of funeral directors, the structure of the funeral business changed dramatically at this time. At the turn of the century, funeral directors tended to work out of small offices and travel to the home of the deceased to embalm the body. This practice reflected the general preference by most Victorian-era families to keep the deceased at home with visitation in the parlor before the funeral ceremony and burial. By the 1910s and 1920s, however, the funeral home began to take over as the location for all the funeral arrangements. The shift from the private parlor into the public funeral home reflected a number of larger cultural forces including urbanization and the rise of the modern hospital, which transformed death into a clinical rather than a familial experience. As death in hospital settings became more commonplace, funeral directors began to take more control over the management of the corpse. Increasingly, the embalming, viewing of the casket, and often the funeral ceremony itself were performed at the funeral director's business establishment. This allowed grieving relatives to segregate the often ominous presence of the deceased from the home and placed clear parameters around the mourning process. In the architectural world, a movement arose to remove any associations with death from the home. Edward Bok, the editor of *Ladies Home Journal*, "stipulated that home designs for the journal never show a 'parlor.' Instead, he preferred that the room be called the 'living room.'" Given these larger cultural shifts toward death and mourning, funeral directors gained credibility, greater control over the funeral service, and an ability to increase their range of services and prices.[36]

As the funeral business was becoming more established and more lucrative, the INFDA held its first meeting on September 4, 1924, in Chicago, Illinois, just two weeks after the NNBL and its National Negro Funeral Directors Association had met there for its annual convention. The participants at the meeting agreed that NNBL's broad-based and often vague agenda had started to limit the effectiveness of the National Negro Funeral Directors Association. They decided they needed an organization independent of the league.[37]

Somewhat surprisingly, the lead organizer of the new association, Robert R. Reed, was not a practicing funeral director but a journalist and a salesperson for the Champion Chemical Company, a white-owned embalming fluid business. Reed, who graduated in 1901 from Wilberforce University with a bachelor of science degree, worked for several years in the newspaper business before receiving his training in funeral directing in 1911 and becoming one of the first African Americans to earn an embalming license in West Virginia. After a number of years, he sold his funeral business, went back to journalism, and eventually was hired as the first and only "colored reporter" for the *Casket and Sunnyside*, the leading trade journal of the NFDA. Over time, Reed became increasingly frustrated with the editors' unwillingness to let him report on stories relevant to black funeral directors. Nevertheless, through his work reporting on black funeral directing and as the "first Negro salesman" for the Champion Chemical Company, Reed developed a unique perspective on the funeral industry and the position of the black undertaker within it. With an energetic, if somewhat egotistical, personality, Reed quickly became the guiding force behind the INFDA. Reed argued, for instance, that the association's name should emphasize that it was "independent" rather than "colored" or "negro." For Reed, this nomenclature best symbolized the group's break from Washington's NNBL and also the fact that "we are independent in personnel from the white National because they bar memberships of our race."[38]

From September 1924 to April 1925, the INFDA existed essentially as an idea on paper as Reed traveled around the country to support the formation of state associations and to raise funds to establish the organization more formally. Then, on April 30, 1925, thirty-one funeral directors gathered again in Chicago for their first executive committee meeting to design the overall structure of the new association. The group decided to model the organization after the NFDA, which used a system of regional districts to coordinate state chapters. At the April meeting, J. B. Cooper of Louisville, Kentucky, was elected the INFDA's first president, and the group officially named Reed its executive secretary and publicity agent. St. Julian Renfro, a funeral director from Cincinnati, Ohio, chaired the finance committee; and Wayman Wilkerson, a prominent funeral director from Memphis, Tennessee, who was the secretary of the National Negro Funeral Directors Association, volunteered to assist in the drafting of the organization's constitution and by-laws. In the group's first public bulletin, the INFDA announced its goals, which included a "closer affiliation of members of the profession for professional and racial uplift" and "the upholding of the ethics of the profession." Just one year later, in June 1926, the INFDA held its first national convention in Indianapolis with twelve states represented.[39]

Soon after the INFDA's first convention, Robert Reed, who had been writing the organization's monthly bulletin, began to publish the *Colored Embalmer,* the first black trade journal of any kind. The *Colored Embalmer* promised to be "A Medium of Education-Expression-Publicity-Co-Operation" for the INFDA as it kept members abreast of industry trends, announced important meetings and conventions, offered advertising space to vendors and members, and actively discussed debates about the future of the profession from a "Negro" perspective. The front page of the inaugural issue featured a portrait of George W. Saffell, Jr., a funeral director from Shelbyville, Kentucky, who was elected the second president of the organization at the Indianapolis meeting. The editorial page included a manifesto of the organization's broad goals, which included establishing and maintaining the credit of Negro funeral directors, promoting ethical business practices, stressing the importance of education to the elevation of the profession, and finally, appealing "to the white practitioner to allow Negro Funeral Directors in each center to bury their dead without contending with them for such rights." This final goal was revised over time and worded a bit more forcefully to read, "To use every instrument, argument within our realm to induce White Funeral Directors to refuse to bury Negroes who seek their services, when Negro Funeral Directors are equipped to bury their own dead."[40]

The INFDA's goal was, in essence, to encourage white funeral directors to discriminate against Negro customers. This took black businessowners' longstanding campaign for race patronage to a new extreme. The spirit of the INFDA's more aggressive stance on the issue revealed that African American funeral directors did not take for granted the loyalty of black customers but instead saw it as something that had to be won and sometimes perhaps even coerced with the cooperation of white funeral directors. Most significantly, the INFDA's policy on race patronage complicated the common assumption that racial segregation in the capitalist marketplace of the early twentieth century existed *only* as the result of racist practices on the part of white businessowners. On the contrary, African American funeral directors actively and publicly promoted segregationist business practices in order to maintain their foothold in a funeral industry that was becoming increasingly profitable and highly competitive.

From 1926 through 1929, Reed and the INFDA used the *Colored Embalmer* and its annual state and national meetings to build the organization into one of the most active black trade organizations in the country. One clear acknowledgment of its success was the decision by the leaders of the National Negro Funeral Directors Association, led by George W. Franklin of Chattanooga, Tennessee, to merge with the INFDA at their annual meeting in Birmingham, Alabama, in 1928. In early 1929, in a report on Negro business, the U.S. Department of Commerce commended the INFDA, noting that "the Undertakers are the most completely organized set of business men and women in the race group. This trade, or profession, has Local, State, and Tri-State Associations closely related to the National Organization."[41]

Reed, as well as other leaders of the INFDA, wanted the organization to be much more assertive in its advocacy of black funeral directing than the National Negro Funeral Directors Association had been. Specifically, Reed looked for ways to secure black corpses for black funeral directors. In 1927, he began a successful campaign to obtain for a black funeral establishment the burial contract for "departed Negro Service Men" at Government Hospital Number Ninety One in Tuskegee, Alabama, a segregated black veterans hospital. One year later, Reed reported that General Frank T. Hines of the U.S. Veterans Bureau had again awarded the contract to another black undertaking firm, even though "a white Funeral Director has underbid our colored firms." Then, in 1929, Reed wrote directly to James W. Good, the secretary of war, to express his dismay that white funeral directors had been handling the burials of "Colored Soldiers who die at Camp Bennings" in Georgia. Reed proceeded to make the case that "Negro Funeral Directors should be allowed to bury Negro dead" by openly acknowledging that racial segregation had created a situation of unfair competition between white and black funeral directors. In a letter to Good, Reed noted that "the race traditions of our country prohibit the general burying of any but those of our race by our group. On the other hand, the white Funeral Director can, and, in many instances, do seek to bury Negroes."[42]

In the end, black funeral directors faced two main obstacles to success in the modern funeral industry during the height of Jim Crow segregation. They regularly confronted the fact that many blacks continued to patronize white funeral establishments on the premise that white funeral homes offered better service or were simply more prestigious. As Reed himself editorialized, "It is an old tradition of race people believing in the service of white people to bury them being superior to their own." They also faced an ever-expanding, often saturated funeral industry that left many white undertakers in the position of seeking any and all customers regardless of race. Many white funeral directors, who originally resisted the idea of working with black clients, eventually sought out the race business in order to survive. Other white funeral directors, particularly in the rural South, actively tried to prevent black undertakers from establishing their own businesses in an effort to maintain a monopoly on the funeral industry in small towns. Some white funeral directors used deception to gain black business, hiring a black funeral director to manage a funeral home to give the appearance that the business was black-owned when it was, in fact, a white operation. In 1929, R. E. Hartley, president of the Georgia State Colored Funeral Directors and Embalmers Association, described the situation as follows: "In recent years the white man has refused service to our dead, but he has found competition so great in his own race and, the desire to make money [is] so strong that he is slowly but surely coming back. In some communities he is already there, maybe not as the whiteman seeking Negro business, but as the wolf in sheep's clothing."[43]

Given these difficulties, the INFDA struggled at times to motivate its members to succeed in a business that seemed full of opportunity yet also fraught with financial risks and dominated by white-owned interests. By 1928, African American funeral directors needed only to look to the career of Wayman Wilkerson of Memphis, Tennessee, to contemplate the bleak underside of the dream of black business success. Wilkerson, who was born in Illinois in 1873, moved to Memphis, Tennessee, in 1903 to pursue a career in business; like many others, he saw funeral directing as his best option. He and his business partner and brother, J. Jay Scott, purchased an established black funeral home from A. N. Johnson. The Scott and Wilkerson Funeral Home, which was incorporated in 1908, quickly became one of the most profitable black funeral homes in Memphis. Wilkerson, known for his aggressive business practices, moved quickly to parlay his earnings in undertaking into other business ventures. Most notably, he served as vice president of the black-owned Fraternal Savings Bank and Trust Company and president of the Tri-State Casket Company, one of the few black-owned casket companies in the country. Wilkerson's ambitions led him to the top of the black business elite in Memphis and into national leadership positions in the NNBL, the National Negro Funeral Directors Association, and the newly formed INFDA. He was also politically active in the Memphis "Lincoln League," a black Republican organization, while his wife, Hattie Foote Wilkerson, was head of the Memphis NAACP. By the time the INFDA held its first executive meeting in April 1925, few in attendance could do anything but admire Wilkerson's entrepreneurial talent and political influence.[44]

Yet by 1928 Wilkerson's reputation had taken a dramatic downturn. In early 1928, Wilkerson became caught up in a corruption scandal at the Fraternal and Solvent Savings Bank, of which he was chairman of the board. The bank, which represented a merger of the two major black banks of Memphis, was facing complete collapse from a practice of overdrawing its funds to support business ventures such as the Tri-State Casket Company. Executives including Wilkerson were accused of embezzlement as well as corruption and misuse of funds. Faced with disgrace, Wilkerson's wife promptly resigned from her position as head of the Memphis NAACP. Wilkerson, deeply ashamed by the public humiliation, shot himself in the mill of his Tri-State Casket Company after pinning a suicide note and a news clipping to his lapel. The note read: "I am now 56 years old, spirit crushed—nerves shattered—ambition gone—health failing—the attached clipping tells the tale":

> If satisfaction in life hinges on one thing more than another, it is on the idea that today is better than yesterday and that tomorrow will be better than today.
>
> When that idea falls out of the picture—when people are on the downgrade and know it—when they have to live on memories and reminiscences—without any hope that they can do as well—much less better than they have—life loses its thrill.[45]

For Robert Reed and other members of the INFDA, Wilkerson's suicide was a troubling loss. On the one hand, Wilkerson had been a prominent supporter of the organization. On the other hand, his loyalty to INFDA had recently been the subject of much debate in a lengthy editorial that Reed had written for the *Colored Embalmer*. In the editorial, published in April 1928, Reed accused Wilkerson of collusion resulting from his Tri-State Casket Company's partnership with the Charles Company, a purported black-owned embalming fluid company that was actually operating as a front for the white-owned Champion Chemical Company. For Reed, Wilkerson's covert involvement with the Charles Company was the ultimate act of treason against black economic cooperation. In his column, Reed scathingly wrote, "If there is anything . . . which deserves the disapproval of the whole profession, it is that act on the part of a few Negroes . . . who are such unjust members of our group and to our group, as to allow themselves to be the 'tool' of members of the other group [whites] to operate business for them . . . [and] against the bona fide members of our group actually operating business." Reed also recounted how, as early as 1926, Wilkerson and Charles Johnson, who was the owner of the alleged Charles Company, attempted to take control of the INFDA for their own commercial benefit. In the end, Wayman Wilkerson's rise and fall was not just an example of business corruption and personal failings, but a cautionary tale about the precarious state of many black business ventures that often relied on unsound financial investments and hidden alliances with white companies to survive. The Wilkerson scandal also revealed that behind INFDA's concerted efforts to present a united front of black economic cooperation in the funeral industry stood a more complicated reality involving intraracial competition, conflict, and betrayal.[46]

For the INFDA and other black business groups such as the NNBL, the ideal of black economic cooperation, which had seemed so full of promise at the turn of the century, became even more difficult to uphold with the onset of the Great Depression in late 1929. The country's financial collapse had long-reaching effects on all small business-owners and especially on black funeral directors, who were already struggling to survive. During the leanest years of the Depression, John T. Miles, a black funeral director in Atchison, Kansas, had to pawn his valuables, ask for small loans from friends, and fight the repossession of his hearse in order to save his business. As he lamented in an entry in his private diary, "Spent nothing [today], but 10 cent call, 5 cent tobacco. This is one of the most trying time[s] of my career as a funeral director. God alone can help me, and I trust Him."[47]

The financial hardships faced by Miles and thousands of other black businessowners prompted some leading black intellectuals to become much more forthright in their critique of what they perceived as the myth that black capitalism was a viable means for racial uplift. In an essay critiquing the NNBL, Ralph J. Bunche commented that the "hope for the salvation of the Negro masses by the erection of black business within the walls of white capitalism is clearly futile." In his influential 1936 book *The Negro as Capitalist,* economist Abram L. Harris argued that "Negro life has never afforded the economic basis for the development of a real black middle class. The future of this class is becoming more and more precarious because the future of Negro business and finance is increasingly uncertain in the face of unslackening growth in the size and power of white financial and industrial institutions." Harris then noted that white capital had begun to infiltrate "service and amusement enterprises where the Negro business man once enjoyed a monopoly . . . and of late, white capital has begun to push the Negro undertaker to the wall in southern cities!"[48]

For the INFDA, the best strategy to navigate the economic crisis of the Great Depression and to compete with white capital was to continue its ongoing campaign to ensure that black funeral directors were given first priority in burying the black deceased. When President Franklin D. Roosevelt signed the National Industrial Recovery Act on June 16, 1933, as part of his New Deal policies, the INFDA was encouraged that the emergency legislation might benefit black funeral directors. The act, which established the National Recovery Administration (NRA), sought to stabilize and revive the nation's faltering economy by setting standards for production, prices, and wages for all sectors of the economy. Although the act had multiple objectives, one of the most important goals was to eliminate unfair competitive practices in business through the formulation of industry-specific codes of fair competition.[49]

By mid-July 1933, Robert Reed and members of the INFDA met with representatives from the NFDA at a conference at the Palmer House Hotel in Chicago to discuss how to draft the code for the funeral industry. At the meeting, Reed spoke before an assembly of white funeral directors from the NFDA and made the case that it was much more efficient for their respective organizations to unite their efforts rather than to draft separate code proposals. Reed went further and argued that one of the key provisions for fair competition in the funeral industry code acknowledged that "it is unfair competition for White Funeral Directors to advertise for, or solicit business from our Race in communities where there are qualified Funeral Directors of our Group, in view of the fact that the Funeral Directors of our Group do not solicit business from the White Race." When the conference attendees adopted the provision unanimously, the practice of racial segregation in the funeral business was formally endorsed and recommended to the federal government as a key element of the proposed funeral industry code.[50]

In many ways, Robert Reed's work helping to establish the Funeral Service Industry Code for the NRA marked the high point of his tenure as executive secretary of the INFDA. After the Chicago meeting, Reed was invited by members of the NFDA to be on the committee that completed the final draft of the code and then traveled to Washington, D.C., to present, defend, and ultimately sign the code before the Federal authorities. As the black press noted, Reed's "defense of the Code and the rights of his Group before the Administration in Washington . . . brought forth highest praise from NRA officials and editors of white funeral directors' journals." In June 1934, Reed also lobbied for the election of T. M. Fletcher, acting president of the INFDA, as a member of the NRA Code Authority for the funeral industry. When Fletcher was elected and became the first black representative on any Code Authority in the NRA, Reed's political influence in the funeral industry and as an advocate for black business seemed unmatched.[51]

Ultimately, however, Reed's tenure at the INFDA paralleled the trajectory of the NRA itself, which President Roosevelt terminated in January 1936 after the Supreme Court's ruling in *Schechter v. United States* declared the code system unconstitutional because it gave the executive branch power that should only be granted to the legislative branch of government. As the NRA closed down in 1936, Reed traveled to the annual INFDA convention in Cincinnati besieged by criticism of his management of the organization. Some INFDA members resented Reed's large ego and the control he wielded over the organization, particularly given that he was not a practicing funeral director. Others accused him of mismanagement of funds and of using his power as editor of the *Colored Embalmer* to influence the election of INFDA officers. Despite a concerted effort to oust Reed from his position as executive secretary at the Cincinnati convention, he was reelected by a significant margin. Nevertheless, the INFDA's 1936 leadership crisis portended the larger conflicts to come, beginning with the demise of the *Colored Embalmer* in 1937 and culminating in a final showdown at the 1938 INFDA convention in Philadelphia. Here, as criticism mounted against Reed and his loyalists, another group of funeral directors, led by William J. Morsell of Chicago, broke away from the INFDA and founded their own group, the Progressive National Funeral Directors Association. The infighting between these two groups did not end until August 1940, when they agreed to merge again under the banner of the National Negro Funeral Directors Association, a name that ironically evoked the first funeral trade organization founded by the National Negro Business League, from which Robert Reed and the INFDA had originally sought independence. Reed, however, would never again hold a prominent leadership position in this new organization.[52]

When the country entered World War II in 1941, African American funeral directing began focusing less on organizational endeavors and more on supporting the war effort. Many black funeral directors and embalmers were drafted into the armed services, and those who remained on the home front had to manage their businesses during a time of scarcity, which included a moratorium on the purchase of new automobiles and hearses. Also, in an effort to conserve gasoline and rubber, the federal government's Office of Defense Transportation asked most professional and trade organizations to cancel their annual meetings. As a result, a number of state associations of African American funeral directors never met during the war years. In this interim period, the National Negro Funeral Directors Association developed a partnership with the Atlanta College of Mortuary Service, the first accredited black embalming school, which was founded in 1938.

The school's publication, the *Acomsinc Bulletin,* became the organization's official journal, replacing the *Colored Embalmer.* Also, in 1944, Thomas and Frieda Whibby founded Epsilon Nu Delta (E.N.D.), the first "Negro Mortuary Fraternity," at the well-established Worsham College of Embalming in Chicago.[53]

By midcentury, then, African American funeral directing had matured as a business and as a profession with its own independent training institutions and fraternal groups. Nevertheless, the central paradox of black funeral directing, as of all black capitalism, that one needed to both fight racial discrimination *and* cultivate race patronage to survive economically would continue to create its own challenges and contradictions for years to come. When the war finally ended in 1945 and the economy began to boom, black funeral directors continued to serve their communities as business leaders and activists, but the larger debates about the role of black capitalism in uplifting the race, which began in 1900 with the founding of Booker T. Washington's National Negro Business League, were far from resolved. In many ways, the economic devastation of the Great Depression and the rationing of the war years had only served to highlight the severe limitations of the dream of black capitalism as a viable tool for ending racial inequality. Yet African American funeral directors, who continued to be the most prominent and influential business leaders in their respective communities, kept the dream alive with their important role supporting African American life through their management of death.

Mourners gather in Young's Funeral Home in Monroe, Georgia, in July 1946 to view the victims of the Moore's Ford lynching, which became known as the "last mass lynching in America." Dan Young, owner of the funeral home, allowed a photographer from the black newspaper the *Pittsburgh Courier* to take images of the deceased, against the wishes of local authorities. The published images sparked a nationwide public outcry about the crime, but no one was ever prosecuted for the deaths of Roger Malcom, Dorothy Malcom, George Dorsey, and Mae Murray Dorsey. *(Copyright © Corbis)*

The gravesite of a Congo chieftain decorated with water pitchers, a broken pot, and dishes. In African burial traditions, these objects were believed to free the spirit of the deceased from the earthly realm. *(E. J. Glave, "Fetishism in the Congo," 1891)*

In 1936, Walker Evans photographed this gravesite of an African American child in Hale County, Alabama. Note the similarity between the items decorating this grave and those adorning the grave of the Congo chieftain (above). *(Farm Security Administration, Office of War Information Photograph Collection, Library of Congress Prints and Photographs Division)*

Slaves hold a midnight funeral in a hush harbor, a secluded, often wooded area, removed from the watchful eye of their master. These late-night services gave slaves an opportunity to honor mourning rituals that originated in Africa. Ultimately, however, such gatherings raised anxiety among slave owners, who saw them as opportunities to plan organized rebellions against the slave system. *(General Research and Reference Division, Schomberg Center for Research in Black Culture, The New York Public Library, Astor, Lenox, and Tilden Foundations)*

A 1907 promotional image of Preston Taylor's Nashville funeral home. Taylor, one of the most respected business leaders in Nashville, was a civil rights organizer who actively fought racial segregation through a number of business ventures, including an independent streetcar company, Greenwood Cemetery, and Greenwood Park, the first privately owned black recreational park in the city. This photograph highlights the importance of elegant funeral carriages to the reputation of a prominent funeral director. *(General Research and Reference Division, Schomberg Center for Research in Black Culture, The New York Public Library, Astor, Lenox, and Tilden Foundations)*

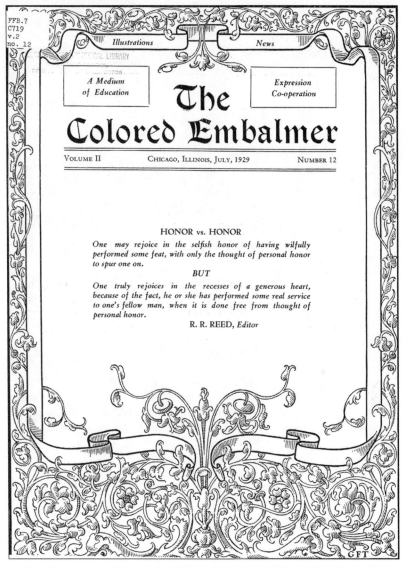

Illustrations   News

A Medium
of Education

The
Colored Embalmer

Expression
Co-operation

VOLUME II   CHICAGO, ILLINOIS, JULY, 1929   NUMBER 12

HONOR vs. HONOR

One may rejoice in the selfish honor of having wilfully performed some feat, with only the thought of personal honor to spur one on.

BUT

One truly rejoices in the recesses of a generous heart, because of the fact, he or she has performed some real service to one's fellow man, when it is done free from thought of personal honor.

R. R. REED, *Editor*

The front cover of the July 1929 issue of *The Colored Embalmer*. *The Colored Embalmer* was the first African American trade journal of any kind. The publication sought to be "a Medium of Education, Expression, and Co-operation" for the Negro undertaker. *(Abraham Lincoln Presidential Library and Museum)*

A 1929 portrait of members of the Independent National Funeral Directors Association, Western Division, which was based in Chicago, Illinois. Robert R. Reed, who founded the national organization in 1924, is pictured in the first row on the far left. *(Courtesy Barbara Miller Holmes)*

Portrait titled "Brotherly Love," from James Van Der Zee's classic work *Harlem Book of the Dead*. This vivid image depicts the lavish style of an African American funeral, which usually included elaborate floral arrangements, satin-lined caskets, and elegant hearses. This portrait, which features a banner from an Elks Lodge, also highlights the importance of fraternal organizations and secret societies to the staging and funding of a proper burial. *(James Van Der Zee, "Brotherly Love, 1929," copyright © Donna Mussenden Van Der Zee)*

The A. D. Price Jr. Funeral Home
208 East Leigh Street, Richmond, Virginia

THE A.D. PRICE Jr. FUNERAL HOME

Postcard advertising A. D. Price Funeral Home in Richmond, Virginia. When A. D. Price built this establishment at the turn of the century, he used the first floor for his funeral business and reserved the upper two floors as rental space. The well-furnished meeting rooms were used regularly by fraternal organizations, which enhanced Price's reputation as a community leader. (*Special Collections and Archives, Virginia Commonwealth University Libraries*)

This funeral fan from the 1940s depicts a warm scene of motherly love. With the rise of mass advertising in the mid-twentieth century, funeral fans offered an important venue to showcase respectable images of the black family—a direct counterpoint to many of the degrading images of African Americans that were commonplace in mass culture. *(Author's collection)*

Funeral fans featuring images of Martin Luther King, Jr., became very popular after the civil rights leader's assassination in 1968. Throughout the modern civil rights era, African American funeral directors often used their promotional fans to support the civil rights cause. In the Deep South in the late 1950s, some funeral fans included specific instructions on how to register to vote. *(Author's collection)*

Mamie Till Bradley weeps over her son's open casket at his funeral in September 1955. When Emmett Till's mutilated remains were discovered in Mississippi's Tallahatchie River one week after his disappearance in August 1955, local officials tried to bury his body as quickly as possible to suppress media attention to the case. Till's relatives in Mississippi stopped the burial and shipped the body back to Chicago. The horrifying death of Emmett Till and his mother's decision to open the casket so that "the world could see what they did to my boy" were a major catalyst of the modern civil rights movement. (*Courtesy of* Chicago Sun-Times)

Hundreds of mourners gather in front of the Frazier and Collins Funeral Home in Jackson, Mississippi, immediately after the funeral services for Medgar Evers in June 1963. Moments later a near-riot broke out as a group of young activists, unable to contain their anger over Evers's assassination, descended on the city's white business district. Although local and federal officials quelled the disturbance, the uprising revealed how quickly the funeral of a civil rights leader could become a politically charged event. *(Amistad Research Center, Tulane University)*

A. G. Gaston stands in front of his fire-bombed mansion in Birmingham, Alabama, in September 1963. The attack against Gaston reflected the still-heightened racial tensions in the city after the resolution of the Southern Christian Leadership Conference's Birmingham campaign. Throughout the campaign, Gaston had acted as a key mediator between the city's black activists and its white business community. While some activists thought he was too willing to appease the city's white power structure, others admired his courage as well as his financial and logistical support for the activists. *(New York World-Telegram and the Sun Newspaper Photograph Collection, Library of Congress Prints and Photographs Division)*

New York City police sharpshooters stand guard on the roof of Unity Funeral Home in Harlem during the viewing of Malcolm X's remains in February 1965. Unity Funeral Home received a number of bomb threats in the days surrounding Malcolm X's funeral services, illustrating how black funeral homes often found themselves literally caught in the crossfire of an intraracial conflict. *(New York World-Telegram and the Sun Newspaper Photograph Collection, Library of Congress Prints and Photographs Division)*

Jimmie Lee Jackson's funeral at Brown's Chapel in Selma, Alabama, in February 1965. Jackson, who was the first casualty of the Selma Voting Rights campaign, was shot in an altercation with an Alabama state trooper after an organizing rally in Marion, Alabama, and later died of his wounds. Jackson's fellow activists hung a banner proclaiming "Racism Killed Our Brother" on the church's edifice to make clear that Jackson did not die in vain and that their political fight would continue. *(AP/Wide World Photos)*

Memorial honoring Martin Luther King, Jr., and those who lost their lives during the 1965 Selma Voting Rights campaign: Jimmie Lee Jackson, James Reeb, and Viola Liuzzo. In August 1979, the National Funeral Directors and Morticians Association dedicated the memorial, which was one of the first in the country to honor victims of the modern civil rights struggle. The monument stands before Brown's Chapel in Selma, a regular meeting place for campaign organizers. *(QT Luong/terragalleria.com)*

Rosa Parks's body lies in state at the U.S. Capitol Rotunda in October 2005. Parks was the first woman and only the second African American in the nation's history to receive this honor. Her decision on December 1, 1955, not to relinquish her seat on a city bus to a white person sparked the Montgomery Bus Boycott and marked a turning point in the civil rights movement. *(Associated Press/Susan Walsh)*

3

My Man's an Undertaker

In 1953, Dinah Washington recorded a delightfully funny blues song titled "My Man's an Undertaker." The song capitalizes on the sassy vocal style that made Washington famous and earned her the moniker "Queen of the Blues." In the song, a jilted woman informs her ex-boyfriend that she has moved on to a new love: the local undertaker. The song's charm relies on a sly appreciation of the cultural importance that undertakers had achieved in black communities across the country by midcentury. In the song, Washington warns her ex-lover that he "better stop knocking on my door late at night," because "my man's an undertaker and he's got a coffin just your size." Perhaps most telling are the song's references to the undertaker's wealth: "You promised me a car but all you did was scheme/The only time I rode was in my dreams/And now my man's an undertaker and he's got a fleet of limousines." Here the playful jab at the ex-boyfriend works well only because the stable financial status of the black undertaker was tacitly understood. The song ends with a joke about the ultimate threat in any love triangle: "My man will come and get you in his big black hearse/Take you out of the house with your feet going first." In the end, the song's humor offers one glimpse of the role funeral directors played in the cultural imagination of the black community.[1]

Dinah Washington recorded the song "My Man's an Undertaker" for Mercury Records in late summer 1953, just a few months after *Ebony* magazine ran a lengthy feature story on the role of funeral directors in African American life titled "Death Is Big Business." Like the song, the *Ebony* article focused on the wealth and prestige that black undertakers had achieved in their respective communities. The article emphasized that "Negro undertakers gross more than $120 million for 150,000 race funerals each year," and that "death has become Negro America's third biggest business—only behind insurance and cosmetics." The story described undertakers who spent more money on elegant cars like Cadillacs to escort their customers to the cemetery than on the caskets in which to bury them. The article also noted that "undertakers are often among the wealthiest and most influential men in Negro society," and that the Smith and Gaston Funeral Home in Birmingham, Alabama, "which serves eight branch funeral parlors throughout the state of Alabama with more than 100 Cadillacs, most of them new models," was the most successful black funeral establishment in the nation. Although the article clearly highlighted the lucrative aspects of the funeral business, it did not hesitate to note that Negro undertakers were often accused of being unprincipled. The coverage included a quote from an undertaker criticizing his own profession with the biting comment, "I have never charged my colleagues with being unscrupulous. I just charged them with sucking all the dough they could get out of widows and orphan children unnecessarily."[2]

Both the song and the *Ebony* article bespeak the degree to which funeral directors had become significant figures in African American life at midcentury. The humor of the song and the depth of the article captured the conflicting stereotypes that surrounded the black undertaker, who could be seen simultaneously as both a model of financial success and a swindler. In many ways, these competing images worked together to create the legendary, and sometimes notorious, status that funeral directors held in African American culture.

On the positive side, the black public perceived local undertakers as heroes because they not only helped families at a time of loss but also often supported local politics, culture, and education through philanthropy. Moreover, African American funeral directors used their businesses and community standing to improve the public image of black Americans. Most notably, they maintained a high level of decorum at their funeral homes in an effort to cultivate respectability for the race.

Their advertising and subsidiary business ventures projected dignified images of black life that clearly sought to counter the degrading racist images of African Americans that pervaded American culture.

Despite these positive contributions, many blacks saw the local undertaker as a racketeer who cheated customers out of their hard-earned money in the name of needlessly extravagant funerals. This criticism was commonly leveled at all funeral directors regardless of race, but it was a particularly scathing condemnation in the black community, where so many customers had limited financial resources to pay for even a simple funeral, let alone the highly sought after and very elaborate homegoing. In some communities, especially in urban centers like Chicago and Detroit, black undertakers actively participated in informal, underworld economies and used their businesses as fronts for gambling and other illegal activities. Some of them used the profits from these illicit activities to help the black community in need—an act that ultimately transformed the concept of respectability itself. Whether they participated in the underground economy or simply provided dignified homegoings, funeral directors kept alive the ideal of black capitalism as a strategy of racial empowerment even as racism and discrimination continued to keep black entrepreneurs on the margins of America's capitalist economy.

The campaign to create a positive public image for African American funeral directing began with the formation of the modern funeral industry at the turn of the twentieth century. As the funeral business became more consolidated, commercialized, and lucrative in the first decades of the century, it attracted both sincere individuals looking for a professional and economic opportunity and other, more deceitful types searching for a quick road to financial gain. Given that training in embalming was still uneven and licensing practices inconsistent from state to state, it was relatively easy for individuals without proper training to advertise themselves as undertakers or embalmers in the hopes of making a quick profit from unsuspecting customers. In a 1925 article for the *Casket and Sunnyside* titled "The Negro Undertaker," Robert Reed described this problem:

The entrance of such unqualified men into the funeral directing field not only reflects discreditably on the profession as a whole, but casts a stigma upon the honest, efficient, self-respecting Negro undertaker. Where business rivalry is so keen we find that many of the unqualified "practitioners" are forced to resort to all sorts of unethical practices, to body-snatching, to sick-bed watching, to ruinous cutting of prices, to wire-pulling, and to formation of burial leagues . . . The cheating methods to which they have resorted while still in business have left a bad impression on those of the public who were so unfortunate as to fall in their clutches, and the just and the unjust alike are put into the same category—all undertakers are labeled as untrustworthy.[3]

Discussion about how to police the fraudulent practices of dishonest funeral directors appeared regularly in the pages of the *Colored Embalmer*. In March 1929, the journal published the annual address of Kelsey L. Pharr, president of the Florida Negro Embalmers Association. In the address, Pharr described the corrupt tactics that some fraudulent funeral directors used to get more customers. These schemes included paying "a grafting policeman" to ensure that the funeral director got "called in case of violent deaths," and offering a percentage of one's profits to "jack-leg preachers," who would then "use [their] influences with [church] members" to recommend the services of the bribe-paying funeral director. To remedy the situation, Pharr proposed "an Association Black List . . . to be peopled by members of our Association who run afoul [of] the code of ethics which I hope the Legislative committee will draw up." Pharr also echoed Reed's sentiments about unqualified practitioners, whom he described as "decided misfits," and recommended establishing safeguards to keep them out of the field.[4]

Debates about how best to promote ethical business practices in African American funeral directing reflected the larger public relations challenges faced by the funeral industry as a whole. When the profession modernized and became increasingly sales-oriented in the early twentieth century, funeral directors regularly faced public criticism that they were marketing unnecessarily costly funerals and thus ruthlessly profiting from the grief of others. Two early studies of the funeral industry opened the debate about the value of the modern profession to the American public: Quincy L. Dowd's book *Funeral Management and Costs: A World Survey of Burial and Cremation* (1921), and John C. Gebhart's study *Funeral Costs: What They Average; Are They Too High? Can They Be Reduced?* (1928), which was commissioned by the Metropolitan Life Insurance Company. Both Dowd and Gebhart documented the industry's creation of an array of goods and services—from embalming to grave vaults, floral arrangements, and ornate caskets—meant to entice consumers to spend more money on funerals. Most significantly, Dowd and Gebhart both expressed concern about the way some unethical funeral directors were taking advantage of the poor and working class, who were particularly susceptible to overspending in the name of an ostentatious funeral. Gebhart noted other corrupt practices by undertakers, including offering bribes or commissions to "doctors, nurses, and hospital employees" as well as "frequent collusion between undertakers and coroners, morgue superintendents and other officials" to obtain possession of corpses. Both authors called for reform in funeral practices that would include some type of government regulation of the industry and more societal emphasis on simplicity in burial customs. The funeral industry responded to these early critiques by emphasizing that funeral directors, rather than capitalizing on the vulnerabilities of grief-stricken mourners, sought to provide meaningful services to guide the bereaved through their loss.[5]

For black funeral directors, public critiques of profligate funerals did not take into account the longstanding imperative within African American culture for a triumphant homegoing ceremony, which had its origins in the slave funeral. As the modern funeral developed in the 1920s and 1930s, African Americans continued to honor venerable slave burial traditions, to which they added their own distinctive rituals. The twentieth-century African American funeral involved several characteristic features, including viewing at a wake or "settin' up"—usually held the night before the funeral; a highly emotive and unusually lengthy funeral service punctuated by spirited gospel music and numerous eulogies; the presence of uniformed female attendants to aid mourners overcome by grief; and a plentiful meal or "funeral banquet" after the service to honor the memory of the deceased.[6]

The first stage of the modern African American funeral was the wake, or settin' up, an expression dating to slavery, when mourners would "set up" all night praying and singing over the remains of the deceased. During the 1910s and 1920s, the settin' up evolved into a more traditional wake that was held in the home of the deceased, where friends and relatives would gather to offer emotional support and home-cooked food to the grieving family as well as to share cherished memories of the deceased. As one observer from South Carolina vividly recalled,

> Callers did not try to make the bereaved family cheer up. They talked about faith in God and quietly pressed a "piece of money" into the hand of the head of the house. There was something about the embers of the fireplace, the rocking chair, the solitude of friends that was comforting indeed. The small gathering, usually of women, seemed to be warding off the death of the next victim. Some of the men would have a drink on the back porch. In the days that followed, neighbors and church members would continue to visit, to reminisce, rocking on front porches even after the acute stages of mourning.

By midcentury, the wake was usually held at the local black funeral home. This was especially true in urban areas, since, as one observer noted, "the multitude of relatives and friends cannot be accommodated in the cramped confines of kitchenette apartments." Although the tradition of a wake was not unique to African American culture, it was particularly valued in black communities, not only as a means to celebrate communal bonds in a racially segregated world, but also as an opportunity to process grief in a tangible way by viewing the deceased's embalmed remains in an open casket.[7]

The funeral service that followed the wake was the centerpiece of the African American homegoing ceremony. Here, the community gathered in the sanctuary of the black church not just to mourn the dead but to exult in the triumph of the deceased's spirit's entrance into the next world. For these reasons, the somewhat open structure of the homegoing service, which included call-and-response gospel singing, testifying, and scripture readings, facilitated the free expression of emotions from grief to songs of praise. The famous New Orleans jazz funeral, which concludes with the joyous "second line" of upbeat jazz music and dancing, offers another example of the way African American funeral traditions fuse grief with the joy of remembrance. Historian Robin D. G. Kelley captured the celebratory essence of the modern African American funeral in a description of the funeral service of his grandfather, the Reverend Rafe D. Kelley, a prominent Baptist minister who died in April 1996:

Many congregants wore white and no one seemed sad or sullen, except for the little hungry and tired kids whose squirming behinds had to endure long hours on hard wooden church pews. And there really were no "eulogies" in the classical sense of the word. Music enveloped us. We rocked to the junior choir, the senior choir, the men's choir, and the women's choir, singing songs praising God and wishing my grandfather a safe passage "home." The congregation shouted, stomped their feet, clapped, and some got the Holy Ghost and had to be comforted by ushers in nurse's uniforms. Such deep emotional expression was encouraged by the congregation and by whoever occupied the pulpit at the moment. The most moving testimony came from the congregation itself. Men and women who knew my grandfather would get up, come to the microphone at the front of the church, and testify. Testifyin' frequently transmuted into lyrics or melodic moans, punctuated suddenly by a well-placed chord or a riff from the organist. Seconds later, a song would be in full bloom; half the congregation would be singing along and the organist was in full swing, always finding the right key.[8]

Expressive emotionalism was the most distinctive feature of the African American funeral, and black funeral directors organized their businesses to accommodate it. Most notably, the black funeral industry created the job of female funeral attendant—most commonly called "first lady" or mortician's nurse—to assist in the management of grief during the funeral service. The traditionally lengthy service offered multiple opportunities for mourners to publicly release their sorrow through clapping, shouting, sobbing, or fainting. The mortician's nurse, known as the "backbone of black funeral service," stood on hand to aid the bereaved and to maintain a certain level of decorum through the funeral service. Originally, the first lady assisted in the bathing and preparation of the corpse for burial; after embalming became popular, however, she became more of a grief counselor for the bereaved family. Often the wife of a funeral director, the mortician's nurse was expected to be emotionally sensitive and skilled in first aid in order to respond to the physical distress of grief. During services, mortician's nurses might fan mourners or offer beverages to the bereaved.[9]

While the first ladies attended to the emotions of mourners, the funeral director orchestrated the ceremony and supplied the necessary goods and services to fulfill the communal ideals of the proper homegoing. The pageantry of these funerals involved a variety of elements, including enormous floral arrangements, elegant caskets, and funeral processions led by only the most stylish hearses and limousines. Visual evidence of the regal quality of African American funerals in the early twentieth century can be seen in the acclaimed memorial photographs of African American dead taken by Harlem's renowned photographer James Van Der Zee. Van Der Zee's collection of funeral portraits, eventually published in the book *Harlem's Book of the Dead*, features numerous examples of ornate funerals. His stately portraits foreground the deceased dressed in finery, laid out in sumptuous caskets built of high-quality woods or metals with quilted satin linings, and surrounded by lavish floral arrangements. (See photo gallery.)[10]

The funeral director also staged the magisterial procession to and from the funeral service, which showcased the funeral home's fleet of hearses and limousines. At the turn of the century, African American undertakers regularly advertised the regal quality of their horse-drawn hearses and carriages. A. N. Johnson's Funeral Home, which opened in Nashville in 1907, appeared frequently in the city's black newspaper, the *Nashville Globe*, both in articles about the business and in press releases. Most of the coverage mentioned Johnson's stable of white Arabian horses and matching funeral cars, which were described in vivid detail:

> There is the large white funeral car with the milk white Arabian horses of full size, with which is used interchangeable drapery of white, grey, or purple. Then the two sizes of Ebony Funeral Cars, classic in design and of architectural beauty, colossal and massive. To these and to his carriages are magnificent steeds, appropriate in size, style and color, driven by men in uniform so that . . . [a] Johnson cortege has all the signs of superiority and excellence which have given him a reputation of which he is greatly proud.[11]

With the advent of the automobile, funeral directors often competed with one another when it came to the size or style of their "rolling stock" of motorized hearses and limousines. R. C. Scott of Richmond, Virginia, was bent on using his funeral cars to gain an edge on his competitors. Initially, Scott tried to combine the majesty of horse-drawn hearses with motorized limousines. As he recalled in an oral history, the plan literally backfired because the horses would get spooked and bolt from a solemn funeral procession when they heard "an explosion from a balking automobile . . . being made to run roughly one half as fast as the slowest speed it was designed for." As a result, Scott made the expensive but shrewd business decision to be the first funeral director in Richmond to "motorize one hundred per cent. That is, hearses, limousines and service cars." Scott's motorized fleet was exceptional not only among his fellow African American funeral directors but among most white funeral directors as well. By midcentury, as the *Ebony* article "Death Is Big Business" and Dinah Washington's song "My Man Is an Undertaker" attested, the reputation of the most successful black funeral homes in the country was directly associated with the style, make (usually Cadillac), and color of their limousines and hearses.[12]

For many African Americans, especially the working class and poor, securing funds to pay for all these accoutrements of the modern funeral meant purchasing burial insurance through a fraternal lodge, secret society, or black-owned burial insurance company. The existence of many of these burial leagues was a source of frustration for most African American funeral directors in the early twentieth century. Many of the burial leagues sponsored by fraternities and secret societies were notorious for not paying undertakers in a timely fashion. As Robert Reed reported in the *Casket and Sunnyside* in 1925, "The Negro funeral director who serves a number of secret societies is faced with a serious problem for the secret orders, as a rule, are unnecessarily slow in paying their funeral claims. In some cases the funeral director is forced to wait six months for his money." Not surprisingly, one of the first goals of the INFDA, as listed in the first issue of the *Colored Embalmer*, was to work collectively to secure "the payment of Burial Claims by secret societies in thirty days."[13]

A more pressing ethical concern for Reed and other leading black funeral directors was the growing trend in the 1920s of black funeral directors' establishing their own burial leagues in an effort to generate business for themselves. In a report on the controversial practice for the *Casket and Sunnyside,* Robert Reed pinpointed one of the main problems with these burial associations: "Most, if not all, of the contracts . . . become void if any undertaker other than the one operating the league is employed—and this notwithstanding that the member whose contract is voided may have paid in weekly contributions totaling many times the stipulated price of the funeral specified by the contract." Even in situations in which a contract was honored rather than voided, Reed argued that the undertaker involved would often "attempt to sell the family a far more expensive funeral than was stipulated by the contract of the league, thus seeking to gobble up the family's few remaining assets after having systematically 'milked' them of weekly contributions for an indefinite time." For all these reasons, Reed and the INFDA sought to put an end to burial leagues owned by funeral directors. While the campaign to end this questionable business arrangement was never completely successful, the public debate about the problem revealed the degree to which the African American funeral industry was aware of its own dubious business practices. In response, many funeral directors worked actively to gain the trust and admiration of their local communities through outreach and other business ventures that uplifted the race and cultivated respectability.

For most of these entrepreneurs, their most effective public relations tool was the funeral home itself.[14]

Of all the developments in the modern funeral industry in the 1920s, the emergence of the funeral home was perhaps the most significant. From a business perspective, the establishment of the funeral home was a masterly stroke of efficiency because it transformed what had been a largely decentralized and multistage funeral process into one uniform experience held under a single roof. More significantly, however, the funeral home—with its stately architecture, serene "slumber rooms," sanitary morgues, and sacred "chapels"—became one of the key tools in the funeral directors' public relations campaign to gain the trust and respect of a wary public. The funeral home, in other words, was the positive face of funeral directing, which could be used to ward off any skepticism about the extravagance of the modern funeral or any worries about the shady business practices of unscrupulous funeral directors.[15]

The industry's awareness of the importance of the funeral home to its public image was evident in both the white and the black trade journals. In March 1925, the *Casket and Sunnyside* published an article, "Popularizing the Funeral Home," which advised funeral directors on how to advertise. The piece highlighted the efforts of LaVerne Newkirk of Auburn, New York, who "frequently takes opportunity to invite friends and acquaintances to call upon him at his place of business just to see how beautifully it is equipped." Most important, Newkirk's invitations were "sincere as if inviting them to call at his own home." For many funeral directors, of course, the funeral home was located in their personal residence. The article also noted that Newkirk's newspaper advertisements featured a simple picture of the funeral home, which "impresses upon the public consciousness the up-to-dateness of this establishment." In April 1928, the *Colored Embalmer* published a list of tips on how to cultivate a respectable public image for the black funeral home. These pointers included making sure that casket boxes were stored away from public view rather than piled on the street; and ensuring that the funeral parlor did not become "a gathering place for tobacco-chewing, expectorating and story telling men." The home should, in contrast, be known for "neat, competent office girls . . . [and] cleanliness."[16]

In the first half of the twentieth century, African American funeral homes served an important purpose beyond promoting a positive image of the funeral business. In black communities, local funeral homes provided a safe place to meet in cities and towns where Jim Crow restrictions sharply circumscribed blacks' ability to gather or to be treated with respect in public places. Local black churches offered public meeting space to community groups, but these places of worship usually forbade social gatherings that might involve dancing, gambling, or drinking. Consequently, as an effort at community outreach and as a sound business strategy, black funeral directors regularly rented out rooms in their funeral homes to secret societies and fraternal orders for meetings and social events.[17]

In Richmond, Virginia, two prominent funeral directors, A. D. Price and R. C. Scott, specifically designed their funeral homes to accommodate secret societies and fraternal groups. When A. D. Price built his three-story funeral home at the turn of the century, he used the first floor exclusively for his funeral business and reserved the upper two floors for rental space, which included fourteen well-furnished meeting rooms. When R. C. Scott renovated his funeral establishment in the early 1920s, he included four "lodge rooms" on the second floor to accommodate fraternal meetings. With these facilities, Scott sought to tie his "profession to the community," and his foresight paid off. As he later recalled, "During this time there was a meeting of some one or more of the organizations each night in the week including weekends . . . This brought quite a number of people into my place constantly [through] a central door to the funeral home." For Scott and others, renting these rooms not only brought in revenue but also built up the undertaker's reputation as a community leader and broadened his base of clients.[18]

In some African American funeral homes, the history of the building could also have larger symbolic meaning in the racial politics of specific communities. When A. N. Johnson first opened his funeral business in Nashville in 1907, it was located at Carroll Street and Second Avenue. Two years later, in 1909, he relocated to Cedar Street when he was able to purchase the Porter Mansion, a downtown Nashville landmark that was previously owned by whites. The historic significance of Johnson's ownership was emphasized in the press release about the reopening of the funeral home:

> Those who have noted this ancient landmark of Nashville, one of the most valuable pieces of property, never dreamed that at any time it would become the possession of a Negro, whose magic touch would restore it to its ancient splendor for the service of the race . . . In other days fortunate and favored were the Negroes who were allowed to gaze on the splendors of festal occasions in that mansion and it was never contemplated that their walls would echo their tread except in an attitude of servility; but today the spacious parlor on the first floor has been converted into a Ladies Parlor and Resting Room as beautifully decorated as in ante-bellum days.

Significantly, Johnson designed the "Ladies Parlor and Resting Room" to be a daily refuge for black women, who often were treated curtly in white-owned shops and businesses. As the company noted, the parlor was where "the tired shopper can come and rest and be free from offense as at those places where our women are not wanted longer than they have made settlement for their purchases." For A. N. Johnson, his Porter Mansion funeral home gave the city's black community access to a piece of revered Nashville architecture in which mourners could stage a reputable funeral and everyday citizens could find sanctuary from the indignities of Jim Crow racial discrimination. Unlike white funeral homes, Johnson's Porter Mansion gave dignity to the dead *and* respectability to the living.[19]

In addition to opening their funeral homes to the black public for meetings and social gatherings, many black funeral directors used the profits from their funeral business to fund entertainment and leisure venues meant to counter the humiliations of Jim Crow segregation. A. N. Johnson eventually used revenue from his funeral establishment to open the Majestic Theater in Nashville's black business district. In acquiring the theater, Johnson followed the lead of one of his fellow black undertakers in Nashville, Preston Taylor. In 1905, the same year that Taylor founded the Union Transportation Company streetcar line in Nashville, this highly respected funeral director also established Greenwood Park, the first privately owned black recreational park in the city.[20]

Greenwood Park was adjacent to Taylor's Greenwood Cemetery and included a clubhouse, amusement hall, skating rink, and palatial grounds with "a bountiful spring" and more than six hundred trees. Taylor, who invested over $20,000 in renovating the site, advertised the park as "Owned by Colored People, Operated by Colored People, for Colored People" and actively worked to ensure that whites did not intrude on the leisure activities of his patrons in any way. In 1907, visitors to the park's Fourth of July celebration complained to Taylor after they witnessed three white men running some of the concessions at the event. In a public statement to the press, Taylor explained that the men had come on the park grounds through their association with some other "colored men" and without his knowledge. He emphatically reiterated the park's commitment to being owned and operated by colored people and reassured his clientele that there "will be no repetition of white men being on the ground[s]." In 1908, the park hosted the first annual Tennessee Colored State Fair. For Taylor, the goal of the park was to provide black patrons with a safe haven to enjoy recreation and the outdoors without fear of encountering racist whites.[21]

By contrast, Nashville's white community viewed the success of Greenwood Park's racial insularity as a threat. In April 1907, a group of white legislators from Davidson County attempted to pass a bill through the state legislature designed to close down Greenwood Park by focusing on Taylor's involvement in the funeral business. The legislation provided "that no park or amusement place . . . shall be maintained, used, or operated within two miles of a cemetery." Greenwood Park was the only park in the city in close proximity to a cemetery and, therefore, was the obvious target of the bill. Taylor and Nashville's other black leaders did not waste any time responding to the unjust legislation. The city's black newspaper, the *Nashville Globe*, editorialized:

The law says for its [white] authors: "We don't want you Negroes to be good citizens, therefore, we take from you one of the agencies which would tend to make you such. If you take any amusement you must take it on the curbing under police surveillance in the tender-loin districts or sweat it out within the compass of your homes. You shall not have a park inside corporate limits nor shall you have one outside of it, and you better not think of peeping through the fence at ours."

The effort to take away the only private black-owned park in the city was an affront to the entire black community, which knew that it was not welcome in any public or private white park in Nashville. As the black press noted, "If they [Nashville's black citizens] went to the re-sorts run by the street railway, they were confronted by a sign, 'Dogs and Niggers Not Allowed.' . . . [And] they did not feel like going to the city parks where they would be ordered around by a little 'tin horn' watchman." In the end, Tennessee Governor Malcolm Patterson vetoed the "Park Bill," as it came to be known, and saved Greenwood Park from closure. Nevertheless, the controversy revealed that even when elite blacks like Preston Taylor tried to navigate Jim Crow segregation by creating facilities for blacks that were separate and equal, they encountered active resistance from the white community. Despite this resistance, Greenwood Park endured and gave black Nashville a recreational facility that exemplified middle-class respectability.[22]

In the end, one of the most important contributions of black funeral directors to African American culture was the way they used their role as community leaders to promote the respectability of the race. The modern funeral industry emerged in the 1920s alongside other cultural phenomena of modern America, including radio, film, and mass advertising. Much of the newly emergent mass culture such as radio's "Amos 'n' Andy" show, D. W. Griffith's film *The Birth of a Nation,* and advertisements featured demeaning racist caricatures of black life. Many of the most popular advertisements and cartoons of the early twentieth century routinely depicted blacks as apelike buf-foons or as the overly cheerful mammies or servants known as Aunt Jemima and Uncle Ben. The public image of the black funeral director, who exuded affluence and impeccable decorum, stood in dramatic contrast to these ubiquitous images.[23]

Aware of the importance of a professional public image, Robert Reed advised funeral directors in a 1928 column in the *Colored Embalmer* to be conscientious about their appearance. He wrote, "As a professional representing dignity, cleanliness and intelligence, it is your duty to present yourself in a state of cleanliness each day. A clean collar, a clean shirt, and a pressed suit certainly add to your business influence." In most black communities, the funeral director was "the only one, other than the preacher, who wore a suit during the week . . . It was an important and visible sign of status, and although the income may have sometimes been paltry, the look was always prosperous." African American funeral directors also cultivated respectability through strong relationships with local churches. In many cases, ministers at prominent black churches endorsed a particular undertaker or, when a congregant died, directed surviving family members to a specific funeral home. Such close affiliations with church institutions not only sustained a funeral home's business but also elevated the reputation of the funeral director.[24]

Black undertakers also used advertising to project a positive image of African American culture. Despite the challenge of finding a tasteful way to market end-of-life services without appearing mercenary, starting in the mid-nineteenth century, funeral directors regularly advertised their services to the public in newspapers and other business directories. By the twentieth century, promotional funeral fans and calendars became one of the most popular forms of direct advertising in the funeral industry.[25]

In black communities, promotional funeral fans as well as funeral home calendars were more than just practical items to cool oneself or mark the days; they also provided opportunities to showcase respectable images of black family life. Beginning in the 1920s, these items consistently featured images of pious black families praying in church, young children adoring their mothers, and other idyllic scenes of black domestic life. Some fans also featured images of political leaders such as Booker T. Washington and included text that espoused Washington's accomodationist philosophy. By the 1940s, fans regularly highlighted gospel greats such as Mahalia Jackson. By the 1950s, as the modern civil rights movement began, some black funeral directors used the back of funeral fans to publish text encouraging their communities to register to vote. In all these cases, black funeral directors used the tools of modern advertising not only to promote their businesses but also to counter the racist stereotypes and patronizing portraits of black people that were the common currency of American advertising. (See photo gallery.)

Even though the funeral industry seemed uniquely well suited to promoting respectability, not all black funeral directors concerned themselves with improving the image of the race. In the urban North, especially, some used their funeral businesses to support their participation in an underworld economy of gambling, after-hours nightclubs, and other illicit pursuits. In the first half of the twentieth century, black entrepreneurs in cities such as Chicago, New York, and Detroit were regularly refused or offered minimal credit by white-owned banks. They also had to navigate capricious local zoning laws and city ward politics that were often designed to undermine minority efforts to gain a foothold in the legitimate business world. For these reasons, many black funeral directors did not hesitate to participate in gambling, bootlegging, and other unlawful activities to support their businesses and build their own political power. Such activities were most prevalent during the era of Prohibition, which began in 1918, when the illegal sale of liquor spawned a cottage industry of speakeasies, gambling dens, and other after-hours cabarets in most major American cities. When the Great Depression hit, many urban black communities came to rely on these informal and illicit economies as a primary source of revenue. Given that many black funeral directors were influential entrepreneurs in the urban economies, it is not surprising that some of them played a major role in the illegal enterprises that thrived in the 1920s and early 1930s.[26]

Among the most legendary funeral directors in the 1920s was Daniel "Dan" McKee Jackson, known as the czar of one of the largest gambling and vice syndicates in Chicago. Jackson first came to the city in

1892 when his father, Emanuel Jackson, who had founded one of the earliest black funeral establishments in Pittsburgh in 1865, decided to move his business to the Windy City. The new Emanuel Jackson Funeral Home was located at Twenty-sixth and State streets and became very successful. When Emanuel Jackson retired from the business in 1911, his son took over as president of the company. Under Dan Jackson's management, the business was reputed to be at the forefront of modern funeral service. As one article in the *Chicago Defender* noted, "Mr. Jackson . . . has kept right up to the times in the modern handling of the dead. In all of the improvements made in this exacting profession he has been the first to adopt them."[27]

By the 1920s, Dan Jackson's work as a funeral director overlapped with his career as the leader of a highly organized syndicate of gambling halls, bootlegging operations, and cabarets. Most notably, one of his undertaking parlors, located on South Michigan Avenue, operated as a front for one of his most successful gambling houses, the Dunbar Club. Politically savvy, Jackson used his power in the world of organized crime to make key alliances with the city police and top-ranking politicians, including three-time Chicago Republican mayor William "Big Bill" Hale Thompson. Jackson's close relationship to Thompson led him to a number of key political posts, including Republican committeeman of the city's Second Ward. In 1928, Governor Len Small appointed Jackson, who had already weathered several political and criminal scandals, to the Illinois Commerce Commission. As the kingpin of Chicago's black underworld economy, Jackson garnered significant political influence with the city's white politicians who sought the black vote.[28]

In the end, Dan Jackson's rise to power revealed the complicated and rather fluid interplay that existed among the black funeral industry, Chicago's informal economy of gambling and vice, and Chicago city politics in the first half of the twentieth century. On the one hand, Dan Jackson's career in the funeral business served as a counterpoint to the "respectable" funeral director perhaps best represented by Reverend Preston Taylor of Nashville, Tennessee. Jackson, like Taylor, quickly capitalized on the modern funeral business to make his fortunes, but rather than directing those fortunes to the church or other reputable public projects like Greenwood Park, Jackson parlayed his business success into domination of Chicago's black underworld economy. Through his control of gambling and vice on Chicago's South Side, however, Jackson built a substantial black political powerbase in the city that ultimately led to the 1928 election of Oscar DePriest to the U.S. House of Representatives, the first African American elected to Congress in the twentieth century. Remarkably, DePriest prevailed in the election even though he and Jackson were indicted by a grand jury in September 1928 for voter fraud. Among the charges, Jackson was accused of organizing a group of "floaters" to vote in the Second Ward in the April 1928 primary elections. When these individuals went to the polls, they gave their address as 3109 Michigan Avenue— the address of the Emanuel Jackson Funeral Home.[29]

Despite charges of political corruption, Jackson was highly regarded in Chicago's black community as a charitable businessman who was always ready to come to the aid of those in need. As one black journalist recalled, "While Jackson was in control [of South Side gambling] he donated thousands to charities, the N.A.A.C.P., working girls' homes and the like. While Jackson was in power the colored people always had a friend to go to. If some old fellow got in jail and his son came down, Jackson would sign his bond and send a note to the judge." Another admirer described Jackson as "charitable, being good to the poor, the ill, and those in dependent circumstances." Jackson's reputation as a generous philanthropist was part of a trend during the Depression era in which the "policy kings" of the gambling world became the race leaders of their respective communities. Their ability to contribute generously to the black community led many to reconsider the notion of "respectability" and social standing. Men like Jackson, who had considerable economic and political power, were advocates of the idea of "racial salvation by Negro business." Their ability to invest in legitimate business ventures, whatever the source of their capital might have been, provided some hope of a self-sufficient and independent economy within the black community.[30]

For Dan Jackson, the opportunity to merge his philanthropy with a legitimate business enterprise arose in 1925, when he co-founded the Metropolitan Funeral System Association (MFSA), a burial insurance company, with fellow entrepreneur Otto Stevenson. The MFSA focused Jackson's largesse specifically on the cause of helping the black working poor of Chicago secure a decent funeral—a goal that also supported his funeral home business. At the time, the most successful black insurance company in Chicago was Liberty Life, which catered to the city's black middle class. Jackson and Stevenson created MFSA expressly to offer the city's black working class and poor residents burial insurance policies for a minimal fifteen-cent weekly premium. While Jackson's funeral home provided the funerals for policyholders, Stevenson oversaw the sales of the policies. Unfortunately, Stevenson, who was unschooled in actuarial statistics, oversold policies to high-risk individuals, which led the fledgling company into a financial crisis. Rather than watch the company collapse, Jackson decided to take over sole ownership. In 1927, he asked Robert A. Cole, the manager of his most successful gambling club, to oversee the daily administration of MFSA. Cole soon offered to buy the company; Jackson, who was then preoccupied with his gambling empire, sold it to him for $500.00 with the stipulation that the Jackson Funeral Home would still handle all funerals from MFSA policyholders.[31]

Unlike Jackson, who began in the funeral business and moved into gambling, Robert Cole started in gambling and had no experience in the funeral industry or the burial insurance business when he took over MFSA. Wisely, he hired individuals with the requisite skills, including Ahmad A. Rayner, who was a licensed funeral director and acted as the company's vice president and treasurer. In 1929, when Cole and his board of directors had completed their reorganization of MFSA, Dan Jackson unexpectedly died of influenza. Jackson's death set off a new series of challenges for the company that revealed, once again, the complicated ethical issues involved in the merger of burial insurance firms and funeral homes. When Cole officially opened his own funeral home business, the Metropolitan Funeral Parlors, to provide funerals for MFSA policyholders, Jackson's family objected.[32]

By 1930, Cole and the MFSA faced several legal challenges from Charles Jackson, Dan Jackson's brother, who also owned a funeral home. In his lawsuit, Charles Jackson, an independent funeral director, argued that Cole wrongfully used his deceased brother's undertaking equipment and did not have legal rights to the ownership of MFSA. Although Charles Jackson's specific accusations did not hold up in court, his legal campaign raised larger questions about the relationship of burial insurance companies to their subsidiary funeral home businesses. Jackson's lawsuit against Cole also illustrated the intraracial tensions and competition within the black funeral industry. The Undertakers Association of Chicago, the city's black funeral directors association, supported Jackson's legal fight with MFSA, which it saw as an attempt to protect independent black funeral directors against burial insurance companies that tried to monopolize funeral service. Not surprisingly, Robert R. Reed, who acted as the association's executive secretary, was actively involved when the group eventually lobbied the Illinois state legislature to pass a bill in 1934 that "required burial associations to place specific cash values on policies (in lieu of offering strictly burial service) and to give the policyholders the option of employing an undertaker other than the one designated by the company." While most MFSA policyholders continued to use Cole's Metropolitan Funeral Parlors to handle arrangements for their deceased, the 1934 state legislation marked a real effort to make the relationship between burial insurance associations and funeral homes more ethical and clearly defined.[33]

After facing these legal challenges in the early 1930s, the MFSA and its subsidiary Metropolitan Funeral Parlors managed to survive the worst financial struggles of the Great Depression. In 1937, Robert A. Cole marked his tenth anniversary as president and owner of MFSA by announcing plans to build a new company headquarters as well as a separate new building for the Metropolitan Funeral Parlors. Cole's vision for this project again reflected the belief that black businesses and funeral homes should serve their communities by offering muchneeded space for public gatherings and social events. When it opened in September 1940, the new MFSA headquarters, located at 4455 South Parkway, was described by the black press as "a modern business palace [with] beautifully appointed air conditioned offices." The main floor housed the company's offices while the second floor featured the elegant Parkway Ballroom, which—like Nashville's Greenwood Park—offered local blacks an entertainment venue free from the humiliations of Jim Crow discrimination. The Parkway Ballroom not only featured entertainers such as Count Basie and Duke Ellington but also provided "first-class facilities to Bronzeville's social and cultural organizations" for meetings and other banquets. The success of the ballroom throughout the 1940s led to the opening in 1949 of the Parkway Dining Room, a fine-dining restaurant known for its courteous waiters—a significant selling point in an era in which African Americans regularly faced second-class service at most white-owned restaurants.[34]

In the end, Robert A. Cole's business empire, which began with his $500 investment in MFSA, grew to be one of the most influential and culturally significant endeavors in black Chicago. Beginning in his early years as president and owner of MFSA, Cole invested in a wide range of black cultural enterprises. In 1930, he supported early black radio when he provided the black broadcaster Jack L. Cooper with office space at MFSA headquarters to construct one of the first black-run radio studios in the country, which broadcast "The All Negro Hour." Later, in 1948, Cole made radio history when the Metropolitan-sponsored show "Here Comes Tomorrow"—touted as the "first Negro 'soap opera' in America"—was awarded second prize for best dramatic radio show by *Billboard* magazine. Describing the show's merits, *Billboard* commended Cole's sponsorship, which "has not interfered with the show's insistence upon pulling no punches placing the blame for racial intolerance." Cole and his associates at MFSA also founded Fireside Publications, which published the *Bronzeman,* one of the most popular black magazines of the 1930s. The magazine not only featured the standard fare of light fiction, sports, and entertainment stories but also promoted educational opportunities and black economic advancement in employment and entrepreneurship. Finally, Cole purchased the Chicago American Giants baseball team in 1932 in an effort to provide financial support to the Negro Leagues. Cole's investment in the Giants included renovating Schorling Park, the original stadium of the White Sox, as the team's home stadium. In all these endeavors, Cole used his resources from his funeral and burial insurance businesses to invest in and support a broad range of black cultural institutions.[35]

The story of the Metropolitan Funeral System Association, from its founding by Dan Jackson through the Robert Cole era, illustrates how black involvement in the funeral industry—from burial insurance to funeral homes—upheld the ideal of black economic prosperity, cooperation, and independence in the urban North. It also reveals how enmeshed legitimate black business enterprise was with informal economies of illegal gambling and vice. As with his predecessor, Dan Jackson, many of Cole's early business ventures, including the American Giants baseball team, were funded in part by his substantial income from gambling. Most notably, after the 1934 Illinois legislation stipulated that burial insurance companies must remain fiscally separate from funeral home establishments, Cole often used his gambling winnings to finance the Metropolitan Funeral Parlors, which had become among the most successful black funeral homes in the country. In the early 1940s, Cole's gambling money funded the construction of the new Metropolitan Funeral Parlors adjacent to the MFSA headquarters on South Parkway. He also reportedly used some gambling winnings to purchase a new fleet of Packard limousines for his funeral business. The ties between Cole's illicit earnings through gambling and his insurance and funeral businesses were known and accepted within Chicago's black community. The acceptance grew out of a shared understanding that black businessowners sometimes had to rely on illicit funding because they did not have the same access to legitimate forms of capital or accumulated wealth as white businessowners did. As a result, Robert Cole was held up as a modern Horatio Alger hero in black Chicago. His reputation as a gambler almost enhanced his image as a bold entrepreneur always ready to take financial risks in order to succeed.[36]

By the mid-1950s, Cole, popularly known in Chicago as "King Cole," had set a new standard for the public image of the black funeral director as successful entrepreneur. In September 1954, a little over a year after *Ebony* published its feature story "Death Is Big Business," the popular black monthly ran another story titled "How I Made a Million," by Robert A. Cole. In this lengthy autobiographical piece, Cole described his humble beginnings "in a four-room log cabin on a small plantation near Mt. Carmel, Tennessee," his early years as a Pullman porter, and then his decision at age forty to purchase the MFSA for $500.00. In an effort to explain how he became the "head of a multi-million dollar business," Cole did not hesitate to attribute his business success to the consequences of racial discrimination and to African Americans' strong desire for lavish burials. In terms of discrimination, Cole noted that "white companies . . . were as cold as clams about insuring Negroes, whom they believed to be poor risks." Yet because "Negroes wanted to be assured that even if they never achieved much in life, they could be buried in style," MFSA was able to flourish—even during the Depression—by insuring its black clients, most of whom were working class. Cole continued:

> For a few pennies a week, we provided burial insurance for a whole family. Any member could get a complete funeral service. We even went in for a bit of show in our funerals. We provided *steel* caskets, a sturdy grave box, two cars (Packards) to the cemetery, and, if necessary, shipment anywhere within a thousand miles. For some of our policyholders, their Metropolitan funeral was, sadly enough, the biggest, most impressive event of their lives.

Cole went on to boast that his funeral business performed more services annually "than at any other single company of its kind in the country." He also added that "visitors—white and colored—inevitably tell me that this is the most beautifully-appointed and well-equipped funeral home they have ever seen." In the end, Cole maintained that he shared his success story not "out of any desire to brag" but "to show the youth of America just what a man or group of men can do if they hold fast to their dreams and are willing to work to achieve them."[37]

Cole's "How I Made a Million" article was part of a rising trend in *Ebony* magazine coverage in the late 1940s and early 1950s that sought to lionize the black nouveau riche of postwar America. Most of these articles, including "The Ten Richest Negroes in America," published in April 1949, and "Wealthy Widows," published in August 1949, prominently featured funeral directors as among the most affluent black business people in the country. Not surprisingly, "The Ten Richest Negroes in America" described Robert A. Cole as "probably the nation's wealthiest mortician," while the "Wealthy Widows" piece included five women who inherited their fortunes from their late husbands, who were established funeral directors. Other features, such as "Death Comes to the World's Richest Negro," published in October 1950, focused on the extravagant funeral of one of the wealthiest black Americans, William "Gooseneck Bill" McDonald. McDonald's funeral included not only a 2.5-mile Cadillac-led funeral procession but also, "a $5,000 satin-finished bronze casket . . . more than $2,000 in wreaths and floral designs . . . [and burial under] a towering 55-foot granite monument costing $38,000."[38]

Ebony's May 1953 article "Death Is Big Business" stood as the culmination of this tendency to present the funeral director as a symbol of the promise of black entrepreneurship as well as the custodian of the most revered African American homegoing traditions. The *Ebony* coverage of the black funeral industry and black wealth was not without its critics, however, most notably the sociologist E. Franklin Frazier, who eventually took the publication to task in his landmark book *Black Bourgeoisie.* Frazier argued that *Ebony,* and the Negro press in general, exaggerated "the economic well-being and cultural achievements of Negroes," a practice that created "a world of make-believe into which the black bourgeoisie can escape from its inferiority and inconsequence in American society."[39]

Despite Frazier's criticism, most postwar scholarship on the subject of black business supported the claim that black funeral directors were perhaps the most successful entrepreneurs in America's segregated economy. Beginning with Gunnar Myrdal's highly influential study *An American Dilemma: The Negro Problem and Modern Democracy,* published in 1944, research confirmed that most blacks faced considerable obstacles in the business world, including strong competition from white companies, lack of credit, poor location in business districts, and a predominately impoverished base of minority consumers. Nevertheless, as Myrdal reported, "the 3,000 Negro undertakers, constituting nearly one-tenth of all undertakers in America" were a "real 'business group.'" Citing both their monopoly on handling black funerals and the tendency among black consumers "to spend relatively much on funerals," Myrdal confidently declared that "funeral homes represent one of the most solid and flourishing Negro businesses." One year later in 1945, St. Clair Drake and Horace C. Cayton published their landmark study *Black Metropolis: A Study of Negro Life in a Northern City*, a sociological analysis of black Chicago. In their chapter "Negro Business: Myth and Fact," the authors echoed Myrdal's analysis. The chapter largely recounted the "odds against the negro," including the sobering observation that "while Negro enterprises constituted almost half of all the businesses in Negro neighborhoods, they received less than a tenth of all the money spent by Negroes in these areas." Yet in a later subsection of the chapter titled "Odds to the Negro," Drake and Cayton documented the achievements of Chicago's "colored undertakers," who, along with barbers and beauticians, "operate in a closed market, competing only among themselves."[40]

While Myrdal and Drake and Cayton acknowledged that funeral directing was one of the most promising business ventures for the black entrepreneur, they also raised concerns about the ethically questionable practices of the industry. In *An American Dilemma*, Myrdal noted that "the burial business in most countries tends to be more or less of a racket, capitalizing on the reluctance of the relatives of a deceased person to economize the last time they can make any sacrifices for him." Of specific concern in black communities was the fact that the "Negro insurance men often work hand in hand with morticians," a practice that led many poor blacks to spend excessively on funerals. In a lengthy footnote, Myrdal went further:

> We have asked Negro insurance officials whether it would not be in the public interest for the insurance companies to develop policies which would set limits to the extraordinary expenses that poor Negro families incur when one of the family dies, and whether they would not start an educational campaign to teach people the importance of keeping insurance for survivors instead of spending it on funerals. The answers have, in general, been the following: (1) one should not interfere with the desires of people to use their money as they please; (2) the intense desire among even the poorest Negroes to guarantee a decent funeral after death is one of the strongest incentives for keeping up insurance, and the insurance companies should not be expected to demolish the basis for their own business; (3) even granted that the morticians artificially

stimulate in an unsocial way conspicuous consumption in luxurious funerals, and that, particularly, they exploit poor people, one business should not be expected to take a stand against another business; (4) the morticians are so powerful in the Negro community, and are so entrenched in the churches, that not even the big insurance company dares to take up a fight against them.

In *Black Metropolis,* Drake and Cayton reiterated Myrdal's central concerns about the problematic relationship between burial insurance firms and funeral homes as well as other fraudulent practices in the funeral industry. They quoted one local observer describing a black funeral director who "offers an 'All-Lincoln' funeral. He tells them they are getting a thousand-dollar funeral; what he really does costs him probably a hundred dollars. He uses cheap coffins with a lot of paint." As for legislation that required "burial associations to pay the value of the policy in cash rather than in the form of a burial," Drake and Cayton cynically noted that "funeral systems . . . have simply written this section of the policy in agate type and proceeded to continue with business as usual."[41]

From the glorification of the affluence and cultural influence of the black funeral director on the pages of *Ebony* magazine to the more grounded and sometimes critical sociological analysis of funeral directing in the black community in *An American Dilemma* and *Black Metropolis,* the late 1940s and early 1950s clearly marked a watershed in public interest and discussion about the role of the black funeral director in African American life. In response, the new leadership of the National Negro Funeral Directors Association began to step up its efforts to shape the public image of the black funeral industry. Not surprisingly, this leadership came out of Chicago, where Robert R. Reed founded the INFDA and where individuals like Robert A. Cole were setting such high standards for success.

The National Negro Funeral Directors Association was officially founded in 1940 when Robert Reed's INFDA merged with the Progressive National Funeral Directors Association, the organization that had seceded in protest from Reed and the INFDA in 1938. During the war years, the NNFDA kept a relatively low profile, centering most of its organizational activity and publications at the Atlanta College of Mortuary Service, the first accredited black embalming school. By 1948, however, Robert H. Miller, co-owner of Miller and Major Funeral Home in Chicago, announced that he had secured the rights to publish a new national trade journal for the black funeral industry, the *National Funeral Director and Embalmer*. The first edition appeared in November 1948, and in August 1949 Miller was elected the general secretary of the NNFDA at the organization's annual convention held in Atlanta. Miller served the organization in this capacity for the next thirty years until his death at the age of eighty-two in January 1979. No other individual would have as much influence over the postwar black funeral industry and the public image of the black funeral director as Robert H. Miller. His life story, like that of Robert A. Cole and others, revealed how intricately black funeral directing was interwoven with the much broader tapestry of African American culture and politics as well as with the emergent civil rights movement.[42]

Born on June 14, 1896, Robert "Bob" Miller spent his childhood in Clearwater, Florida, where his father, Columbus Miller, worked as an ice contractor. In his youth, Miller held a number of sports-related odd jobs, including caddy at the elegant Belleview Hotel golf course in Belleair, Florida, and jockey at the Green Springs racetrack in Clearwater. In 1910, when Miller was just fourteen years old, his father died unexpectedly and his mother, Lottie Miller, was suddenly left to take care of five children on her own. Faced with the challenges of single parenthood, she decided to find adoptive families for her children in order to give them a better life. In her son Bob's case, she turned to the Ackerts, an affluent white family Bob had met through his work at the Belleview Hotel. Charles Ackert had recently resigned as general manager of the Southern Railway to take a position as an executive of the Hawley Railroads based in Illinois. He and his wife, Annie La Mont Ackert, agreed to take custody of Miller. Consequently, Miller left his family in Florida and moved with the Ackerts to Chicago, where he spent the remainder of his adolescence. After he graduated from high school, the Ackerts sent Miller to State College in Orangeburg, South Carolina, where he majored in electrical engineering.[43]

In 1916, while still pursuing his college degree, Miller enlisted in the National Guard. When the United States entered World War I in 1917, Miller served in France with the 370th Regimental Combat Team and eventually became a sergeant. Upon his return from the war, he planned to resume his studies at State College, but Charles Ackert urged him to quit school and enter the workforce. Unable to resolve his conflict with Ackert, Miller left the security of his adoptive family and struck out on his own. After several failed attempts at employment, he was hired as the chauffeur of Charles M. Kittle, who eventually became the president of Sears, Roebuck and Co. in 1924. Befriended by Kittle and his family, Miller was able to work evenings as a chauffeur while pursuing his education during the day. At this time, Miller became interested in the undertaking business and enrolled in Chicago's renowned Worsham College of Embalming, where he received his diploma in 1921. After two more years of study at the Northwestern University School of Commerce and with the encouragement of Kittle, Miller established the Miller and Major Funeral Home with Howard F. Major in 1923.

Miller rose quickly as a promising new funeral director and was even featured in a profile "of the prominent members of the funeral directing profession among the Colored people of the United States," in the August 1, 1924, issue of the *Casket*. The photo spread, orchestrated by Robert R. Reed, announced an upcoming meeting in September 1924 to organize "a Nationwide organization to do for the colored mortician what the N.F.D.A. has done and is doing for the white members of the profession." Miller, then, was present at the very beginning of the INFDA and became one of the more active members of the organization. He was also a member of the Undertakers Association of Chicago, the group that represented the city's black funeral directors.[44]

For all his dedication to the funeral profession, Miller was also a Renaissance man whose varied interests led him into a number of additional entrepreneurial pursuits. Beginning in 1928, he traveled regularly to Europe with the Kittle family. While in France, he became captivated by aviation and enrolled in Farmans School of Aviation in Paris. Chicago's black press documented Miller's European adventure in an article titled "Wants to be a Lindbergh," which reported that Miller "indulged himself by participating in some activities which are closed to him in the 'land of the free' . . . [and] Mr. Miller has indicated that he intends to invest in an airline between France and Africa." Although his investment in the airline never came to pass, Miller returned to Chicago and, in 1931, opened his own aviation school known as "The Checkerboard Field." The school was active until 1933 and included an aviation club to encourage black youths to pursue a career in flying.[45]

Of all Miller's early subsidiary business activities, one best revealed his talents as an entrepreneur and had a direct connection to his funeral business: managing Mahalia Jackson's early career as a gospel singer. Jackson first migrated to Chicago from her hometown of New Orleans in 1927. As a newcomer to the city, Jackson, who worked as a maid and laundress, found comfort singing gospel songs at local churches. When Miller heard her perform at St. John Baptist Church in 1931, he offered her a job singing at his funeral home for $2.00 a funeral. For the young "Halie," the job offer was not only a welcome source of income but also a validation of her gospel singing, which was often criticized by elite blacks who looked down on her overly emotive style. Soon after she began singing at funerals, Jackson asked Miller to work as her manager. Miller agreed and used his hearse to drive Jackson to singing engagements in Chicago and surrounding areas. As Jackson recalled in her memoir *Movin' On Up*, Miller's early support was critical: "Most of the criticism of my songs in the early days came from the high-up society Negroes. There were many who were wealthy, but they did nothing to help me. The first big Negro in Chicago to help me was an undertaker and a politician. His name was Bob Miller. He was the first to present me in a concert in a high school and to raise my admission price from a dime to forty cents." Miller encouraged Jackson to make her first recordings as a marketing tool. As he would later recall, "We went down to Jackson Blvd. to one of the studios and cut the records ourselves. We didn't know about the companies at that time; we were hoping we could sell them at the National Baptist Convention."[46]

Miller's work as Jackson's first manager was prescient in that he anticipated the role the black funeral industry would play in the popularization of gospel music. As the music historian Bernice Johnson Reagon has noted, "Initially there was slight resistance to the gospel beat in some very staid, pompous churches. But ministers recognized the emotional release involved and encouraged the trend of having the gospel choir sing just before the sermon, invitation of new members, or offertory period. *Gospel music was more fully realized at funerals, where emotions were sometimes uncontrollable* [italics mine]." Not surprisingly, many black funeral directors sponsored gospel music radio shows as a way to promote the music and tastefully advertise their services. A. G. Gaston, the most successful funeral director in Alabama, sponsored gospel quartets and established "the first regular Negro radio program" in Birmingham to feature gospel music. As Gaston recalled in his memoir, "These promotions made the names of Smith & Gaston [funeral home] and the Booker T. Washington Insurance Company familiar throughout the State of Alabama and directed a large amount of business to our companies." Black funeral homes also offered lodging to gospel singers on tour who—as a result of Jim Crow discrimination—had nowhere else to stay. Even Mahalia Jackson herself ultimately combined her singing career with a foray into the funeral business when she established her own florist shop, "Mahalia's House of Flowers," to capitalize primarily on the demand for funerary floral arrangements. As she reminisced in her memoir, "My florist business did really well . . . People were always asking me to sing at funerals, and a lot of them wouldn't buy my flowers unless I promised to sing. They didn't care how the flowers looked, just so I was there to sing." Unmistakably, a synergy existed between the rising gospel music business and the black funeral industry.[47]

For Bob Miller, managing Mahalia Jackson's early career was just one of the ways he established himself as an innovative community leader and entrepreneur in Chicago's South Side in the 1930s. By 1934, the Miller and Major Funeral Home had opened three branch offices in Chicago Heights, Waukegan, and Rock Island, Illinois. As a testament to his popularity in black Chicago, Miller was elected "Mayor of Bronzeville" for two terms in 1937 and 1938. The *Chicago Defender's* very popular contest began in the early 1930s as a stunt to raise circulation of the newspaper, but it quickly became an important community event. After black citizens cast their ballots for candidates, most of whom were business leaders, the victor was honored at a festive ceremony and inaugural ball. The winner served as "a symbol of the community's aspirations . . . [who would] visit churches, file protests with the Mayor of the city, and act as official greeter of visitors to Bronzeville." Miller's two terms "in office" highlighted his popularity as one of Chicago's thriving funeral directors.[48]

When Bob Miller took over as the editor of the *National Funeral Director and Embalmer* in 1948 and as the general secretary of the NNFDA in 1949, he was able to draw on many of his life experiences and professional skills to craft his new vision for the organization and its members. Beginning with his relationship to the Ackert family and especially in his friendship with Charles Kittle, Miller had unusual access to highly successful white business executives who mentored him on effective business strategies. His travels in Europe, which sparked his interest in aviation, taught him how to break into fields that traditionally discriminated against blacks. His efforts at managing Mahalia Jackson's early gospel career helped him to master marketing and promotional techniques. All these skills would come into play as Miller became the leading public voice of black funeral directors in postwar America.

Within a few short years after Miller assumed the position of general secretary of the NNFDA, the modern civil rights movement gained momentum, beginning with the U.S. Supreme Court's 1954 decision in *Brown v. Board of Education,* which declared racial segregation in public education unconstitutional. For Miller, the NNFDA, and black funeral directors around the country, the civil rights struggle was both inspiring and threatening. The fight for racial equality and integration meant by definition that the economic insularity from which black entrepreneurs profited in a segregated group economy had to be dismantled. As a result, black funeral directors had a distinctly complex relationship to the civil rights movement, which held so much promise for their race but could ultimately endanger their livelihoods. In spite of these conflicts, many funeral directors, including Miller, took courageous action to support the civil rights cause. In doing so, they added an entirely new dimension to their public role in African American life.

The modern civil rights movement, in other words, gave added depth to funeral directors' public image as community leaders and advocates for the race. It did not, however, erase all the negative stereotypes of ruthless hucksterism that haunted the funeral profession. Black undertakers, like all individuals in the funeral industry, continued to be accused of shady business practices and ties to illicit economies. Throughout the civil rights era, however, the skill that some black funeral directors had in deception or in keeping secrets aided civil rights activists—especially when they were under direct attack. Moreover, the drama and tragedies of the civil rights struggle ultimately worked to solidify the funeral directors' pivotal role in the black community by further blurring the line between their legitimate and illegitimate activities. This situation mirrored the central argument of the civil rights movement itself, which used nonviolent civil disobedience to call into question the justice of "unjust" laws of racial segregation. For black funeral directors, the civil rights cause gave them opportunities to prove their skill at honoring the fallen dead and, behind the scenes, their ability to support the living who were fighting on the front lines.

4

A Funeral Hall Is as
Good a Place as Any

A week before the March on Washington, scheduled for August 28, 1963, James Farmer, head of the Congress of Racial Equality (CORE), traveled down to Plaquemine, Louisiana, to participate in a rally and march sponsored by local blacks to generate interest in a voter-registration drive. Farmer, who had led CORE's campaign of Freedom Rides to desegregate interstate highways, was eager to support the effort of the Louisiana black leaders and some two hundred marchers. When the protesters reached downtown Plaquemine, the police were waiting and promptly arrested everyone involved. Because the local town jail could not hold all those arrested, Farmer and others were transferred to another jail in the nearby town of Donaldsville.

Bail for each participant was set at five hundred dollars, which left Farmer, as the leader of one of the most important and active civil rights organizations in the country, facing a dilemma. On the one hand, he was scheduled to speak at the March on Washington and had the financial resources to bail himself out. On the other hand, CORE did not have the money to bail out everyone who had been jailed. If Farmer left the others in jail while he went on to Washington, he risked weakening the morale of the Plaquemine activists. In the end, Farmer decided to remain in jail, even as other national civil rights leaders pressured him to appear in Washington. Louisiana police officials ended any remaining debate about Farmer's situation when they leveled additional charges against him that precluded any possibility of bail. Consequently, Farmer was left to watch the broadcast of the

March on Washington from his prison cell on a small black-and-white television set. Three days after the march was over, as Farmer recalled, "all of us were released from the Plaquemine and Donaldsville jails. Upon my release from jail, all hell broke loose!"[1]

All hell broke loose indeed. Soon after Farmer's release, a group of Plaquemine youths decided to organize a local protest against the racial segregation of the town's public buildings. The Plaquemine activists, inspired by the resounding success of the March on Washington, soon found themselves in violent conflict with Louisiana state troopers, who were intent on ending any civil rights groundswell in their neighborhood—especially when it took the form of protests led by "outside agitators" like James Farmer. Aware of the local hostility toward outsiders, Farmer resisted all requests to lead the march himself and insisted instead that the young people rely on the leadership of local black citizens. As Farmer stayed behind the scenes at the parsonage of the Plymouth Rock Baptist Church, the Plaquemine chief of police stopped the marchers before they even reached town. Again, they were all arrested and held until the state troopers arrived. According to Farmer, the "troopers arrived on horseback, riding like cowboys, and they charged into the crowd of boys and girls as if they were rounding up a herd of stampeding cattle." The troopers, who came bearing cattle prods and billy clubs, began attacking the young students with reckless abandon. Many of the young people were injured when they fell to the ground and were trampled by horses. The wounded youths ran back to the Plymouth Rock Baptist Church for protection and first aid.[2]

The following day, a Sunday, the local black ministers of Plaquemine organized a march to protest the state troopers' brutal treatment of the young people of their town. In a repeat performance of the previous day, the state troopers violently confronted the marchers, attacking them with billy clubs and the electric shocks of the cattle prods. When the stunned and injured protesters retreated once more to the Plymouth Rock Baptist Church (quickly renamed "Freedom Rock"), the troopers surrounded the church and began bombarding it with tear gas. The trapped activists panicked and tried to escape through the back door of the parsonage. The troopers were waiting outside, however, and forced the protesters back into the church building with another volley of tear-gas canisters. The poisoned air created a scene of complete chaos. At that moment Farmer, who had been caught in the middle of the attack on the church, realized that the state troopers' main goal was to capture him. As he recounted, a couple of trapped activists overheard one of the troopers proclaim, "When we catch that goddamn nigger, Farmer, we're gonna kill him."[3]

As dusk began to fall, Farmer devised a plan: the protesters would retreat to the Good Citizens Funeral Home located about a block from the church. He sent two individuals to creep through the waist-high grass behind the church and ask the owners of the funeral home if they would shelter the group. The owners agreed, though as Farmer admitted, "I doubt they knew what they were taking on." In groups of twos and threes, the activists crawled through the tall grass to the funeral home. It took several hours before all three hundred of them were safely packed into the rather small business establishment. The state troopers, for their part, quickly figured out where the large group of activists had hidden. When one of the troopers kicked open the door of the funeral home and shouted, "Come on out, Farmer. We know you are in there. We're going to get you," Farmer was ready to surrender himself for the sake of the others, but he was stopped in his tracks. The Plaquemine activists knew that a lynch mob was waiting for him outside and refused to let him leave the building.

At the height of this life-and-death crisis, Farmer's ultimate rescue came from an unexpected but somehow appropriate source: the local funeral director. As Farmer recalled so vividly, Lizzie Powell, "who had previously held herself apart from the movement," confronted the troopers and demanded a search warrant. He continued:

> I can never know—she herself probably does not know—what inner revolution or what mysterious force plucked her from her caul of fear and thrust her forth to assert with such a dramatic and improbable gesture her new birth of freedom. A funeral hall is as good a place as any for a person to come to life, I suppose, and her action sparked a sympathetic impulse in everyone who watched as she planted herself in front of the first trooper and shook a finger in his face.

While Powell told the trooper that he could not enter her place of business without a search warrant and pushed him out the door, Farmer and the other activists began to plan his getaway. The state troopers were already busy setting up roadblocks around the town in an effort to seal off any possible escape routes.[4]

Two of the Plaquemine activists came up with the idea of using the funeral home's two hearses, which were equipped with shortwave radios, to get Farmer away from the agitated lynch mob. One hearse acted as a decoy as Farmer; Ronnie Moore, a CORE field secretary in New Orleans; and Reverend Jetson Davis, the minister of the Plymouth Rock Baptist Church, crammed into the back of the second hearse. That hearse's armed drivers then sped out through the roadblocks and back roads of Louisiana on their way to New Orleans. Aptly enough, their destination in New Orleans was another funeral home that was prepared to give the hunted activists safe haven. In another memory of the tense night, Farmer recalled, "At times during the wild ride, I thought I was already dead . . . But when at last we climbed out of the hearse into the hot New Orleans night, we were, by grace of God and the extraordinary courage of many ordinary men and women, still very much alive."[5]

James Farmer's perilous escape from the hostile lynch mob of Plaquemine, Louisiana, is an amazing story on several levels, not least because it highlights the key, though often unseen, role that African American funeral directors played in the modern civil rights movement. In the Plaquemine showdown, we witness the bravery of Lizzie Powell, whose singular act of courage in the face of a lynch mob vividly captures the unusual yet compelling relationship funeral directors often had with the tumultuous civil rights struggle. In their position as the most financially stable business leaders of their respective communities, African American undertakers often were drawn into civil rights protests even if they were not necessarily interested in leading the marches. Local activists knew they could call upon their funeral directors for bail money, to negotiate compromises with local white leaders, or—in the worst cases—to prepare the bodies of slain civil rights workers for burial. Moreover, as the James Farmer incident proves, African American funeral directors could use their funeral homes, caskets, and hearses as fronts to hide anything from civil rights meetings to weapons to protesters under attack.[6]

Indeed, black funeral directors not only regularly participated in the fight for racial equality but also made significant contributions to the cause. This involvement was part of a much longer tradition that included earlier campaigns such as Preston Taylor's battle against Jim Crow segregation in Nashville streetcars at the turn of the century and Dan Young's fight for voting rights in Georgia during the 1940s. From the mid-1950s—when the Supreme Court's decision in *Brown v. Board of Education*, the murder of Emmett Till, and the Montgomery Bus Boycott galvanized the movement—to the Freedom Rides and Birmingham campaign of the early 1960s, even more funeral directors lent their professional, financial, and political aid to the cause. Not all undertakers, of course, were ready to risk their lives or their livelihoods for the civil rights struggle. For some, especially in the Deep South, being identified as an agitator for, or simply a supporter of, local civil rights organizing could quickly lead to violent intimidation or other acts of sabotage designed to destroy one's business. As a result, some funeral directors chose to keep quiet and maintain the status quo in race relations. For many, however, including individuals like Lizzie Powell, the urgency of the movement's campaigns in local communities like Plaquemine, Louisiana, inspired them to participate in ways that even they could not have predicted.[7]

In addition to supporting civil rights campaigns in their own communities, black funeral directors continued to fight discrimination in the funeral industry. As the civil rights movement began to gain national attention in the mid- to late 1950s, the National Funeral Directors Association still maintained its racially discriminatory membership policy. By 1957, however, the National Negro Funeral Directors Association made the noteworthy decision to eliminate the word "Negro" from its name and, thereby, remove any racial qualifications from its own membership. Consequently, the organization changed its name to the National Funeral Directors and Morticians Association (NFDMA). As Robert H. Miller editorialized in the *National Funeral Director and Embalmer*, the "historic action" resulted from several motives, but "the most important was the desire on the part of the membership to make the association a really democratic organization in every sense of the word." In 1960, Miller publicly decried the NFDA's continued unwillingness to "drop the color bar" when a resolution to end the discriminatory practice was defeated at the white organization's annual convention. In his editorial column, Miller stated, "We urge the thinking members of the National Funeral Directors Association to take another look at the race resolution. I should think that they would want to end discrimination of every kind. In cemeteries, churches, chapels, and cremation. If not, they should stop burying our people."[8]

Miller's admonition that white funeral directors who practiced discrimination "should stop burying our people" echoed the racial tensions that had haunted the funeral industry since its inception. Just as Robert R. Reed had argued in the 1920s and 1930s, Miller contended that the racial discrimination that black funeral directors faced within the industry was compounded by the fact that their white counterparts continued to pursue and profit from black customers. In other words, the idea that the funeral industry had created a racially divided market that was "separate but equal" was a myth. On the contrary, black funeral directors continued to be limited in their professional advancement through their exclusion from the NFDA and restricted to their black client base through the practices of racial segregation. Aware of this reality, many black funeral directors, even those who supported the civil rights movement in principle, were resistant in practice to the idea of desegregating their business. Even after the passage of the Civil Rights Act of 1964, some white and black funeral directors were accused of maintaining an "unwritten pact" to handle funerals on a racial basis.[9]

Black capitalism, then, continued to represent a paradox in the fight for racial equality. To some, successful black capitalism still held the most potential to uplift the race and fight injustice. In the first half of the twentieth century, the well-defined lines of racial separation during the height of the Jim Crow era made a separate black economy something people could easily imagine, argue for, and, in some communities, implement. In postwar America, the civil rights movement's goal of racial integration worked in direct opposition to the central goals of a black capitalist system, which relied on its black consumer base to thrive. The conflict between these objectives came into sharpest relief in the black funeral industry simply because it was one of the most economically successful fields for black entrepreneurs. For most African American funeral directors, participating in the civil rights movement meant assuming considerable financial and personal risk for the sake of a cause that might ultimately undermine their long-term business security. Nevertheless, as we will see, many individuals stepped up to volunteer their time, to contribute their money, or to offer their professional services to the cause.

For those funeral directors willing to fight for civil rights in the postwar era, the repercussions became evident almost immediately. On May 17, 1954, the U.S. Supreme Court handed down its landmark decision in *Brown v. Board of Education*, which declared racial segregation in public education unconstitutional. In July 1954, just two months later, the first White Citizens Council (WCC) was founded in Indianola, Mississippi. As the black press reported, the WCC's goal was "to bring economic pressure on the Negro to prevent him from voting and, later, to punish any Negro who worked toward the desegregation of the schools." In December 1954, *Time* magazine reported on the quick growth of the WCC and quoted a spokesperson from the organization who claimed that members planned "to make it difficult, if not impossible, for any Negro who advocates desegregation to find and hold a job, get credit or renew a mortgage." Within two short years, the WCC claimed over sixty thousand members in Mississippi alone and had established chapters in Texas, Arkansas, Louisiana, South Carolina, Alabama, Georgia, and Florida.[10]

The emergence of the WCC had an immediate chilling effect on black businessowners, and specifically on many black funeral directors, who were active in the civil rights movement. One news report on the economic intimidation of the WCC noted that a "Negro undertaker found his burial insurance business dwindling, because he belonged to the NAACP. Business didn't pick up until he quit the organization." Another story reported that the WCC asked Johnny

Clarke, an undertaker and NAACP member in South Carolina, "to re-move his name from a petition for integrated schools promising him an enlarged business as a reward." When Clarke refused, the WCC "moved in a rival Negro undertaker in an attempt to run Clarke out of business." In addition to economic reprisals, many black activists were threatened with violence. In July 1954, the *Chicago Defender* reported that police in Fort Lauderdale, Florida, were investigating "the burn-ing of a wooden cross wrapped with gasoline-soaked linen on the lawn of a Negro undertaker's home." The undertaker, Leroy Mitzell, was "a cousin of Dr. Von. D. Mitzell, a representative of the NAACP here." Another article in December 1955 reported that William Flem-ing, "a Negro undertaker" from Manning, South Carolina, told police "that someone fired three shotgun blasts into his funeral home while he was sleeping there . . . he blamed the shooting on his work with the NAACP."[11]

Although the WCC used economic pressure as well as more aggres-sive violent intimidation throughout the South, the battle lines were most sharply drawn in Mississippi, where the group began and where local black activists were courageously beginning to fight for the right to vote. In 1951 Dr. T. R. M. Howard, a prosperous physician and en-trepreneur from Mound Bayou, Mississippi, founded the Regional Council of Negro Leadership (RCNL), a civil rights group that actively worked to register black voters and pursued other issues such as deseg-regation and police brutality. As a grassroots organization, the RCNL wanted to be seen as distinct from the NAACP in order to operate more independently. In the wake of the *Brown* decision in May 1954, the RCNL was energized—along with Mississippi's NAACP chapters —to rally local leaders and citizens to fight for civil rights.[12]

Not surprisingly, then, Howard, who served as RCNL's president and was a strong advocate of black capitalism, accepted an invitation to address the Mississippi Colored Funeral Directors and Embalmers Association when it held its twenty-eighth annual convention in Clarksdale in June 1954. Howard received a warm welcome at the meeting, as a number of the funeral directors in attendance were civil rights activists. John C. Melchor, who owned a funeral home in Clarksdale and served as the president of the association, was also an executive vice president of the RCNL and president of the Clarksdale NAACP. Robert L. Drew, another Clarksdale funeral director, was vice president of the Clarksdale NAACP. Another RCNL leader, T. V. Johnson, a funeral director from Belzoni, was active in the NAACP. Clarie Collins Harvey, director of the Frazier and Collins Funeral Home in Jackson, had been a leader in the local NAACP since her youth. Aptly, the funeral directors convention ended on an optimistic note as the association passed an official resolution expressing its enthusiasm about the *Brown* decision and all that it promised as a turning point in the civil rights struggle.[13]

The year following the *Brown* decision, however, challenged much of the hopefulness that had emerged from the Supreme Court's action—especially in the Mississippi Delta, where the WCC's concerted campaign to quell civil rights organizing had begun to take a considerable toll. Initially, the RCNL seemed undaunted by the WCC's efforts to stop their campaign for equal rights. Throughout the remainder of 1954, the WCC accelerated its crusade to use economic reprisals against anyone who supported integration or voting rights. In response, by January 1955, Dr. T. R. M. Howard and the RCNL—in collaboration with the NAACP—had devised a plan to raise money from donors across the country and deposit it in the black-owned Tri-State Bank in Memphis. The emergency funds would provide financial aid to anyone suffering economic hardship as a result of their support for civil rights. Then, on April 29, 1955, Howard hosted the RCNL's annual rally in Mound Bayou to organize local citizens for a major voter-registration drive.[14]

The RCNL political gathering, held on the grounds of Howard's private estate, was—as the black press described—a "revival meeting about American democracy." Approximately thirteen thousand people "came by mule back, wagon load, truck, car, bus, train, and air" to hear the keynote speaker, U.S. Representative Charles C. Diggs, Jr. Diggs, who had been recently elected to Congress from Michigan, held the enormous crowd spellbound with a rousing speech in which he declared that, "despite . . . seemingly insurmountable odds, if we keep up the fight to make democracy live, we will get the justice espoused by Almighty God and the Constitution of the United States." As reporters noted, "an element of drama was added to the giant meeting by the presence of Charles C. Diggs, Sr., father of the Congressman, on the rostrum," who claimed Mound Bayou as his birthplace. For the black Mississippians in attendance who were struggling just to secure the right to vote, the Diggs political and business dynasty, which originated in the Magnolia State, must have been quite an inspiration.[15]

Congressman Diggs's rise to national political office was directly connected to his father's career as a funeral director and politician. The Diggs family story not only symbolized the promise of the Great Migration but also fulfilled the most deeply held beliefs that black entrepreneurial success could be parlayed into substantial political power. Charles C. Diggs, Sr., who was born in Mississippi in 1894, moved to Detroit, Michigan, in 1913. Soon after he arrived in Detroit, Diggs Sr. opened a shoe-repair shop, but he eventually decided to pursue the more profitable mortuary business. After he completed his training at Eckle's Embalming School in Philadelphia, Diggs Sr. opened the House of Diggs Funeral Home in 1921, which became one of the most profitable black funeral establishments in the country.[16]

As a business leader, Diggs Sr. exemplified the qualities of a "race man," someone dedicated to the betterment of African Americans. In 1926, black Detroit first witnessed his commitment to the fight against racial discrimination when he founded the Detroit Memorial Park cemetery to ensure black Detroiters a decent burial. Early in his career, Diggs Sr. was an active member of the Detroit chapter of Marcus Garvey's United Negro Improvement Association, but he eventually abandoned the group to pursue his political ambitions in the Republican party. By 1932, as President Franklin Roosevelt won his first presidential election, Diggs Sr. switched his allegiance to the Democratic party. By 1936, Diggs Sr. won election as the first black Democrat elected to the Michigan State Senate.[17]

During his tenure as a Michigan State senator from 1936 through 1944, Charles C. Diggs, Sr., became known as a civil rights champion. When Diggs Sr. traveled to Lansing for his first legislative session in 1937, he attempted to rent a room at the Olds Hotel, which was located across the street from the State Capitol. When the hotel refused him because of his race, Diggs responded by introducing a civil rights bill to ban discrimination in public accommodations on the basis of race, creed, or color. As his son would later recall, "The Diggs Civil Rights Bill was passed . . . [and] was the cornerstone not only of his active political career, but the foundation of additional civil rights legislation in other states." Over the years, Diggs fought for workers' rights and advocated for better housing in his district. By 1943, he had become Michigan's senior Democratic leader and a political institution in Detroit's black community. At a testimonial dinner in April 1943 honoring his four terms in the Michigan State Senate, the evening's theme, "Reverence for the Living Rather Than for the Dead," bespoke his reputation as a funeral director turned political maverick.[18]

Diggs Sr.'s remarkable political career took an abrupt and scandalous turn, however, when in late 1943 he was accused of offering bribes in return for votes on an important banking bill. In August 1944 he, along with seventeen other defendants, was convicted of graft and ultimately served two years in prison from 1948 to 1950. Upon his release from prison in 1950, Diggs Sr. immediately ran for office to regain his seat in the Michigan State Senate. He won the election but was refused the seat by his Republican colleagues, who quickly passed a resolution banning ex-convicts from serving in the State Senate. In April 1951 his son, Charles C. Diggs, Jr., won the seat handily in a special election and took on the job his father had been denied. In 1954 Diggs Jr., with the strategic support of his father, was elected to the U.S. Congress by a wide margin, and he quickly established himself as a leading advocate for civil rights.[19]

Representative Charles C. Diggs, Jr., then, represented two generations of funeral directors who had become political and civil rights leaders—with strong Mississippi roots—when he arrived to address Dr. T. R. M. Howard's RCNL rally for voter registration in April 1955. When he sat on the rostrum that evening, Diggs Jr. was particularly impressed by one of the RCNL leaders, Reverend George W. Lee, who led four rural congregations in the Delta and was, as *Ebony* later reported, "the first Negro to qualify to vote in Belzoni since Reconstruction days." In his impassioned sermon, Lee beseeched the crowd, "Pray not for your mom and pop. They've gone to heaven. Pray that you can make it through this hell." He hoped that they, too, might vote and elect "a Negro congressman" like Diggs. The hope inspired by Lee's courageous sermon was shattered within a week when Reverend Lee was shot and killed late at night on May 7, 1955, as he was driving to his home in Belzoni. Local law enforcement immediately tried to explain the cause of Lee's death as an auto accident, even describing the buckshot found in Lee's head as loose dental fillings. Sensing a cover-up, Howard placed a call directly to Congressman Diggs, who then called the White House and demanded an FBI investigation. The assassins were never found, but the murder of George W. Lee and the publicity surrounding it became a turning point for the Mississippi freedom struggle.[20]

When the RCNL activists realized that both local law enforcement and federal investigators had little real commitment to solving the crime, they decided to use Lee's funeral to expose the atrocity of his death to the world. Tragically, the strategy of using the funeral of a civil rights martyr to heighten public awareness about the human cost of the struggle became a regular occurrence—especially in Mississippi—and one in which local funeral directors played a key role. In the case of George Lee, T. V. Johnson, Belzoni's black undertaker and an activist in the RCNL and the NAACP, prepared Lee's remains for burial. Early press coverage about the case noted that Johnson was himself a target of the WCC for his civil rights activities. The WCC had recently circulated a form letter to Belzoni tenant farmers advising them to "boycott Johnson's funeral home and patronize two undertakers in nearby Indianola who 'meet the standards' set up by the white Citizen's Council." In August 1955, *Ebony* magazine published an article about the RCNL voting-rights campaign and Lee's murder titled "The New Fighting South." The piece included photographs of eight individuals on the WCC's "Death List," including Dr. T. R. M. Howard, Medgar Evers, and T. V. Johnson, who apparently was warned to "get out of Regional Council and stop voting or get out of town." One can only imagine, then, how Johnson must have felt as he was left to the grim task of repairing Lee's severely injured corpse for burial.[21]

Noticeably, the press coverage of Lee's funeral, which drew some two thousand mourners, lingered on the details of Lee's embalmed body, which was displayed in an open casket. *Ebony*'s article featured a series of photographs including a picture of Lee in his casket with the caption, "Widow of slain minister fondly pats face as he lay in coffin. Jawbone, left side of face which was torn away by shotgun blast, was sewn back by undertaker." In the *Jet* magazine coverage of the funeral, a photograph of Lee's embalmed corpse was juxtaposed with another vibrant image of the minister when he was alive. As the historian Adam Green has commented, "coverage of this mortuary work . . . offered a powerful counterpoint to the violence with which this dignity had been wrested from Lee in the first place. Readers were led to see that, at base, the struggle against racism in postwar America was a struggle by blacks to compel recognition of their own humanity." In the wake of horrific civil rights tragedies like Lee's murder, black funeral directors were left with the complicated job of restoring the disfigured bodies of slain activists for viewing. In these situations, their use of embalming and restoration techniques to make the deceased presentable for an open casket was, on the one hand, a compassionate act on behalf of the grieving mourners. On the other hand, a flawless restoration risked visually erasing the reality of what had happened to the victim, a reality that often needed to be emphasized rather than minimized.[22]

As civil rights activists became more conscious of the power of the press to publicize the untimely deaths of individuals like George W. Lee, they paid more attention to how the appearance of a victim's body in an open casket might be interpreted by the public. No one incident illustrated these circumstances more powerfully than the murder of Emmett Till in Money, Mississippi, in August 1955. Fourteen-year-old Till, who had traveled from Chicago to Mississippi to visit relatives, was brutally killed after he was accused of flirting with a white woman, Carolyn Bryant, when he visited her country store to buy some bubble gum. When his lifeless body floated to the banks of the Tallahatchie River days after his disappearance, it was barely recognizable. Till had been severely beaten, shot, and tied to a large cotton gin fan to keep his corpse submerged in the river's waters. When the two accused murderers, Roy Bryant and J. W. Milam, were acquitted of the crime weeks later despite compelling evidence of their guilt, the horror of the murder was suddenly compounded by the clear miscarriage of justice in Mississippi's corrupt and racist legal system. As one of the most agonizing moments in the modern civil rights struggle, Emmett Till's murder has been thoroughly researched, retold, and analyzed by historians, journalists, participants, and filmmakers. Nevertheless, a careful review of the story—from the murder to the trial and its aftermath—reveals the pivotal role that funeral directors played in the case.[23]

The murder of Emmett Till became one of the most powerful collective memories in African American history primarily as the result of Mamie Till Bradley's insistence that her slain son's body be viewed in an open casket, so that—as she famously proclaimed, "the world could see what they have done to my boy." *Jet* magazine and the *Chicago Defender* fulfilled Till Bradley's wish when they published photographs of Till's horribly disfigured corpse. The widely circulated, graphic images of Till's mutilated remains stunned the American public and became a catalyst to action for an entire generation of African Americans. What many observers did not realize at the time was that these images might never have been published had it not been for the coordinated efforts of the funeral directors who handled the body.[24]

When Till's corpse was first discovered in the Tallahatchie River, Harold C. Strider, the Tallahatchie County sheriff, contacted Chester Miller, a black funeral director from the Century Burial Funeral Home in Greenwood, Mississippi, to take possession of the remains. Strider's decision to call a black funeral director to the scene of the crime later became an issue at Till's murder trial. On the witness stand, Strider and a local doctor claimed that, when Till's corpse was removed from the river, they could not tell if it was "a colored or white man." As Mamie Till Bradley later recalled, this misleading testimony was used to suggest that the body taken from the river could not be verified as Till's and that the corpse—without proper identification—could have been strategically placed by NAACP operatives as "a plot to disgrace Mississippi." For Till Bradley, Strider's decision to call Miller was all the proof she needed. As she noted,

He [Strider] too [claimed on the stand that he] couldn't tell if it [the corpse] was a colored or white man. Yet and still he called a colored undertaker. The man was black enough for nobody to wonder if he was white or black. You might not know it, but down in Mississippi you don't call a colored undertaker to handle a white body. If there is any doubt in your mind whatsoever, you call a white undertaker because a white man or a black man can get his brains blown out if he makes the mistake of giving a white corpse to a colored undertaker. That you just don't do.

Miller eventually was called to testify in the Till murder trial as a key witness and as the person who secured the only piece of evidence that the prosecution used to identify the body of the victim: the gold ring he wore on his hand, which bore the initials of Till's late father, Louis Till.[25] When Miller arrived at the river to remove the body, Sheriff Strider ordered him to bury the badly decomposed corpse immediately, possibly to avoid any further publicity about the crime. As Till Bradley later recounted, "a colored undertaker [Miller] . . . rushed to the scene with a box, a box covered with some gray flannel material. They picked up the body from the riverbank and threw it in that box. They herded it away to the cemetery." Till Bradley's uncle, Mose Wright, who knew that his niece would not want her son buried in Mississippi, drove to the cemetery in Money to stop the burial. When he got there, Till Bradley recalled, "the funeral had been preached and two men were digging a grave to bury my son's body." Wright insisted that they stop the burial proceedings so that he could "take that body up North." At this moment, Wright "had the presence of mind to call a white undertaker and ask him if he would handle that body, embalm it and fix it for shipment." Wright knew, after speaking with Chester Miller, that he had no choice but to seek the help of a white funeral director. Miller had told Wright, "I don't dare let that body stay in my establishment over night." If he did, he declared, "I wouldn't have any place in the morning and perhaps wouldn't be alive by morning." The white undertaker, C. M. "Chick" Nelson, who was also the mayor of Tutwiler, Mississippi, owned and operated the two funeral homes in the small town: Avent Funeral Home, which served the white community, and Tutwiler Funeral Home, which served the black community. Nelson agreed to prepare the body for shipment at his Tutwiler Funeral Home, but with the provision that Wright promise "that this seal will never be broken and that nobody will ever view the body." Wright then instructed Till Bradley to make arrangements with a funeral home in Chicago. She immediately contacted A. A. Rayner, one of the most respected funeral directors on the city's South Side, who then took charge of the plans to transfer Till's remains out of Mississippi.[26]

When the large wooden box containing Till's corpse arrived at Chicago's Central Station on the *City of New Orleans* train on Friday, September 2, 1955, Till Bradley was there to receive it surrounded by a crowd of curious onlookers, journalists, and photographers ready to record the moment. As she would later recall, "Finally, they unloaded the box that my son was in and placed it on a flatbed truck, a simple train-yard wagon that seemed so much like a caisson. I just lost it. I looked up, saw that box, and I just screamed, 'Oh, God. Oh, God. My only boy.' And I kept screaming, as the cameras kept flashing, in one long explosive moment that would be captured for the morning editions." Till Bradley's acute awareness of the presence of the press recording her grief at the train station must have lingered in her mind when she asked A. A. Rayner to prepare an open-casket funeral for her son. As she described so vividly in her own memoir:

> I knew that I could talk the rest of my life about what happened to my baby, I could explain it in great detail, I could describe what I saw laid out there on that slab at A. A. Rayner's, one piece, one inch, one body part, at a time. I could do all that and people still would not get the full impact . . . So I wanted to make it as real and as visible to people as I could possibly make it. I knew that if they walked by the casket, if people opened the pages of *Jet* magazine and the *Chicago Defender,* if other people could see it with their *own* eyes, then together we might find a way to express what we had seen. It was important to do that, I thought, to help people recognize the horrible problems we were facing in the South.

Given the gruesome state of Till's remains, Rayner was understandably startled by Till Bradley's request and asked her if he could retouch the body for viewing. Although she refused this offer, she later expressed appreciation that the undertaker did perform some basic restoration on the corpse before the casket was opened to the public. Even with these minor repairs to Till's remains, however, the overwhelming horror of what happened to him could never be disguised or diminished. In the end, over fifty thousand mourners came to A. A. Rayner's funeral home to pay their respects to Till and see for themselves his disfigured corpse.[27]

The national and international press coverage of the young boy's murder continued unabated when the sensational trial of his accused attackers, Roy Bryant and J. W. Milam, began in Sumner, Mississippi, on September 19, 1955. The racial tensions that fueled the crime against Till infused the staging of the trial, which included an all-white, all-male jury and a separate Jim Crow table in the courtroom for the black press and other observers, including Mamie Till Bradley and Congressman Charles C. Diggs, Jr. For Diggs, attending the trial as an "interested observer" secured his place as the leading African American member of Congress on civil rights issues. When Bryant and Milam were acquitted of all charges against them, Diggs became one of the most outspoken critics of the trial and used the press coverage of the verdict to promote his civil rights agenda in Congress. In one news report published immediately after the trial, Diggs commented on his plan to introduce legislation that would give more power to the Justice Department to intervene in civil rights cases. In his remarks, Diggs focused on the importance of securing the right of Mississippi blacks to vote. He noted that "the basis of the selection of the jury is the voter[,] and the public officials are elected by voters. An anti-lynch bill and legislation to eliminate the poll tax are the basic solutions I believe for this. I still have hope that the people will wake up to the international significance of this."[28]

While Diggs and the NAACP used outrage over the Till verdict to generate funds and public support for civil rights legislation, the situation for local black activists in the Mississippi Delta in the aftermath of the Till case did not improve but continued to worsen. The intimidation tactics used against anyone who was affiliated with RCNL, who fought for voting rights, or who even expressed support for the general civil rights cause were swift and effective in the fall of 1955. In one case, Reverend L. Terry, who led a rural church near Sumner, was forced to sell his small plantation for half its worth and move to Arkansas out of fear for his life shortly after the Till verdict was announced. During the trial, Terry drove to Sumner each day to sit in the courtroom. On one of those days, he had the opportunity to shake Congressman Diggs's hand, and the following Sunday he told his congregation that "Diggs was one of the 'smartest and most politest men' God had given him the pleasure to gaze upon." The following Wednesday, Terry told his church that he was leaving town to protect his community. For expressing his open admiration of Diggs, Terry had been threatened by "six carloads of white men with shotguns" who "told him to get out or innocent people would suffer with him." Reverend Terry's abrupt departure from Mississippi clearly illustrated the potential costs involved for any black person who simply endorsed a civil rights leader like Diggs.[29]

It was not surprising, then, when Gus Courts, president of the Belzoni NAACP and a leader in the RCNL, was critically injured in a drive-by shooting on November 25, 1955, while standing at the cash register of his own grocery store. Courts, who had worked closely with the Reverend George W. Lee, had suffered economic reprisals at the hands of the WCC for months and had been warned a few days before the shooting that an attack was imminent. Unlike Lee, however, Courts survived the attack, but only after he insisted that someone take him to Dr. T. R. M. Howard's Mound Bayou Hospital instead of Belzoni's local hospital. As he would later recall, "They [the Belzoni hospital staff] would have killed me and then announced that I died from the stomach wound."[30]

The Courts shooting ultimately signaled the symbolic end of the RCNL's activism in the Delta region. By December 1955, Gus Courts and Dr. T. R. M. Howard, who could no longer tolerate the death threats against them and their families, sold their homes and businesses in Mississippi and relocated to Chicago. T. V. Johnson, one of the few RCNL and NAACP leaders left in Belzoni, also retreated from the movement. In the minutes after he was shot, Gus Courts called Johnson to ask the undertaker to drive him to Mound Bayou for his emergency medical treatment. Johnson refused Courts the ambulance service out of fear for his own life. As Charles J. Lapidary later reported in the *New Republic,* "Mr. Johnson was one of the town's most militant leaders. Now he wants nothing more than to be left alone." Fortunately, however, Johnson's disillusionment with the civil rights struggle did not signal that all was lost either with the movement or with funeral directors' engagement with it. In fact, the fight had only just begun, and the National Negro Funeral Directors Association was about to get more directly involved.[31]

When Rosa Parks refused to give up her seat on a bus in Montgomery, Alabama, on December 1, 1955, the modern civil rights movement entered a new stage. The ensuing Montgomery Bus Boycott, which continued for 381 days, not only ended in victory with the 1956 *Browder v. Gayle* Supreme Court decision, which declared the segregation of Montgomery buses unconstitutional, but also catapulted a young Reverend Martin Luther King, Jr., into the national spotlight as the leader of the campaign. In his role as president of the Montgomery Improvement Association (MIA), the organization founded to coordinate the boycott in its earliest days, King was able to put his philosophy of nonviolent direct action into practice with striking results. In the early months of the boycott, the MIA received many financial donations to support its cause. One of the larger contributions was a $1,000 check from the National Negro Funeral Directors Association. In April 1956, Robert Miller, NNFDA executive secretary, received a personal letter of gratitude from King for the NNFDA's "faith, encouragement, and Christian generosity."[32]

As was often the case, the NNFDA's support of the Montgomery Bus Boycott emerged from the direct involvement of one of its members in the organized protest. C. W. Lee, a prominent black funeral director in Montgomery and chairman of the board of the NNFDA, was a leader and treasurer of the MIA. For his key role in the boycott, Lee was one of 114 individuals indicted in Montgomery for participation in "an alleged conspiracy to boycott the city bus lines." As chairman of the board of the NNFDA, Lee used his relationship with Robert Miller and the organization as a whole to rally funeral directors behind the cause of the bus boycott. In an editorial in the March 1956 issue of the *National Funeral Director and Embalmer,* Miller asked NNFDA members "to aid one of OUR own—C. W. Lee. We are asking each member forthwith to give financial assistance—that these citizens might be properly defended in court . . . Let's stand shoulder-to-shoulder with him as he stands trial or faces any other difficulties in trying to live like a first class American citizen should." After the $1,000 was raised for the MIA, the NNFDA's board of directors had William E. Shortridge, a leading funeral director and civil rights activist in Birmingham, present the check to Lee and Martin Luther King, Jr., at a mass meeting in Montgomery. Soon after, the NNFDA invited King to present the keynote address at its annual convention in Cleveland, Ohio, which was to be held in August 1956. King's acceptance of the invitation signaled that he and the MIA recognized that funeral directors were a key constituency that could provide both financial backing and moral support for the nascent civil rights movement.[33]

When King delivered the keynote address at the NNFDA convention on Tuesday, August 6, 1956, he described the birth of a "New Age" in race relations. In his remarks before the funeral directors, King used a death metaphor to describe the end of racial segregation. He commented that "the tired old man Segregation must now move aside and make way for the birth of The New Age . . . the rumbling you hear in the air against desegregation these days is only the death groans of the dying old man Segregation." King also acknowledged that because funeral directors had "great resources of wealth," they had a unique obligation to help the "masses . . . to speed up this coming New World." For the NNFDA members in attendance, King's appearance at their annual convention was an inspiration and marked the beginning of a "new age" for the organization in which a number of the group's leaders not only took on increasingly active roles in the organized civil rights movement but also spontaneously responded to unanticipated incidents of racial discrimination.[34]

When C. W. Lee presented his "Report of the Chairman of the Board" at the 1956 Cleveland convention, he not only thanked the NNFDA for its recent donation to the MIA's legal defense fund but also discussed another racial issue that the NNFDA had confronted.

Originally, the group had planned to hold the 1956 convention in St. Louis, Missouri. By January 1956, the NNFDA Convention Committee had determined that St. Louis did not have any major hotels willing to host a black business convention. Consequently, the NNFDA decided to move the convention to Cleveland, where the prestigious Hollenden Hotel offered to accommodate the group. As in the Montgomery Bus Boycott, the NNFDA turned its back on St. Louis to take a stand against racial discrimination in public facilities. Not surprisingly, it was at the 1956 Cleveland NNFDA convention that the NNFDA board of directors first proposed that the organization remove the word "Negro" from its name to become more "democratic." The group's new name, the National Funeral Directors and Morticians Association, was not ratified until the following year, but the political message of the name change was clear immediately.[35]

In other cases, funeral directors creatively used their own business resources to support causes like the Montgomery Bus Boycott. For example, U.S. Representative Charles Diggs, Jr., who already had political influence in Washington, used his House of Diggs Funeral Home in Detroit to raise funds for the MIA boycott. As Diggs later recalled,

In 1956, I had a twice-a-week radio program [*The House of Diggs Show*] in Detroit that was very, very popular. The Montgomery, Alabama, bus boycott had been started, and through a fund raiser sponsored by solicitations on the radio program, I collected ten thousand dollars which I took down there to give to the young preacher, who was heading the movement, at a rally at his church. His name—Reverend Martin Luther King, Jr.[36]

Notably, the House of Diggs MIA fundraiser was separate from the NNFDA's donation to the boycott because Diggs was not officially a member of the organization. The complicated nature of Diggs's relationship to the NNFDA had recently come to light in August 1955, when the NNFDA held its national convention in Detroit, Diggs's hometown. Diggs had applied for membership in the NNFDA, but the Michigan Wolverine Funeral Directors Association had refused his application for membership in its local chapter. According to the

NNFDA's constitution, Diggs was unable to be a member of the national organization without first having membership in his local chapter. Ostensibly, the reason for his denial of membership was that, as a congressman, Diggs himself was not an active funeral director but instead had his staff handle the daily operations of his funeral business.

The *Pittsburgh Courier* reported, however, that the real reason Diggs Jr. was rejected by the Michigan funeral directors association was that the state's black funeral directors had longstanding grievances dating back to his father's tenure as a state senator. According to the *Pittsburgh Courier*, when Charles Diggs, Sr., was a state senator, he had "'reneged' on a pledge to introduce legislation abolishing burial insurance companies, but [rigged] the law so as to hold onto one himself." The accusation revealed that internal tensions over unethical business practices continued among black funeral directors even as they attempted to unite in support of the national civil rights cause. Recognizing, of course, that Congressman Diggs, Jr.'s, status as a national civil rights leader could only enhance the public image of black funeral directors, the NNFDA sought a compromise: its resolutions committee "introduced a measure to amend the constitution which would permit the national body to accept Diggs as a member-at-large." To reinforce the NNFDA's commitment to civil rights, the 1955 Detroit convention ended with a pledge of sixteen lifetime memberships in the NAACP, which represented an eight thousand dollar donation to the organization.[37]

Lesser-known members of the NNFDA made equally significant contributions to the movement. Clarie Collins Harvey, who ran the Frazier and Collins Funeral Home in Jackson, Mississippi, was named the NNFDA's first "Woman of the Year" in 1955 for "her contribution to the funeral profession and to her community." Harvey's involvement with the civil rights cause began when she joined the NAACP's Youth Council as a teenager. Harvey's father, Malachi C. Collins, who fought off the Ku Klux Klan when he established the Halls and Collins Funeral Home in Hattiesburg in 1916, was one of only three founding members of the Mississippi NAACP in the 1920s. These three men, who met undercover in a different location each month to avoid possible attack by local whites, kept their activities secret but were eventually credited with saving someone from being lynched. Collins's courageous activism planted "seeds of freedom and independence" in his daughter and taught her that "you had to do something" when confronted by racism and injustice. Ironically, Harvey's experience growing up in a funeral home family shielded her from some of the daily indignities of the Jim Crow South. As she recalled in an interview, "Growing up as a 'black middleclass' I never rode the trolley cars nor buses . . . Always in Jackson, Mississippi we had some (being in the funeral business you always had some) form of private transportation and you did not use the public. So my exposure was very limited to the types of things that would make you know the painful tragic truth."[38]

Although Harvey was mostly shielded from the indignities of Jim Crow segregation as a youth, she became, in her adulthood, acutely aware of the suffering of others and the need to fight an unjust system. It was not surprising, then, when she spearheaded a campaign to support the Freedom Riders in 1961. The Freedom Rides, organized by the Congress of Racial Equality, were a nonviolent direct action used to test the 1960 Supreme Court decision in *Boynton v. Virginia*, which had declared racial segregation in railway and bus terminal accommodations to be unconstitutional and a violation of the Interstate Commerce Act. The 1961 Freedom Rides were a reprise of CORE's original freedom ride (known at the time as a "Journey of Reconciliation") conducted in 1947. That protest tested the Supreme Court's 1946 decision in *Morgan v. Virginia*, which had ruled against racial segregation in interstate public transportation. In 1947, the interracial team of CORE bus riders were arrested in North Carolina and ultimately served prison time for violating that state's Jim Crow laws, which only proved the South's unwillingness to uphold the Supreme Court's ruling on the matter. The 1961 Freedom Rides were the culmination of a fourteen-year struggle to force the South to comply with the Supreme Court's *Morgan* and *Boynton* decisions and completely desegregate interstate bus and railway transportation. The Freedom Rides officially began on May 4, 1961, when thirteen CORE activists—led by CORE's director, James Farmer—boarded a bus in Washington, D.C., with the goal of riding through the Deep South to their final destination of New Orleans.[39]

Clarie Collins Harvey's involvement in the Freedom Rides began on May 26, 1961, when Reverend E. A. Mayes, her pastor from Central Methodist Church, asked her to be part of a delegation that would witness the first court hearing of a group of Freedom Riders who had recently been arrested in Jackson for using a "whites only" restroom in a Trailways bus station. As Harvey would later recall, "It was out of this first hearing that I noticed some of the girls did not have sweaters, and when we inquired, we found that one needed a sweater—it was very cool, although it was mid-May—and our minister, Reverend E. A. Mayes . . . was kind enough to take one of my sweaters back to the jail and give it to the young lady." This incident made Harvey realize that the young protesters, who had not anticipated arrest or extended incarceration, had many basic needs for clothing and toiletries that were not being met.[40]

Just three days after this first hearing, on May 29, 1961, Harvey founded Womanpower Unlimited, an organization whose goal was to provide "all kinds of resources, food, sheets, clothes, magazines, and books, blankets and everything to help minister to the needs of the Freedom Riders." Harvey sought sponsorship from local churches and other religious social action groups, but the mainstay of the organization was a large network of several hundred volunteers from across the country who collected the much-needed supplies and clothing. As the campaign to support the Freedom Riders grew, its goals became broader. As Harvey wrote in the *National Funeral Director and Embalmer*, "Womanpower Unlimited has as its expressed goal: to mobilize all women to participate in any organized effort for good in the betterment of the community . . . In cooperation with the Voter's League, classes in registration and voting and study of the Mississippi Constitution have begun. Womanpower Unlimited's program will grow and expand."[41]

Harvey's enthusiasm for the civil rights cause, which she channeled into Womanpower Unlimited, was not always welcomed, however, by some in Jackson's black community and even a few of her own employees at the Frazier and Collins Funeral Home. In an interview about her civil rights activism, she noted, "One of my daily burdens is my own immediate staff in the office," some of whom felt that she should focus on the families of the deceased rather than participate in the movement. She described her efforts to "try to keep posted on the [office] bulletin board constantly all the things that are going on in the Movement, and whenever there's an opportunity we [the staff] do discuss these things." Nevertheless, she said, at least two members of her office staff "feel that Dr. King is doing too much, they say 'I wish Martin Luther King would just go home and tend to his own business' . . . they feel he's in it more for personal gain or merit." Despite her frustration with the views of several of her more conservative staff members, Harvey understood why some individuals—and even her own colleagues in the funeral business—did not want racial segregation to end. As she remarked,

> It's something to give up segregation. I mean there are advantages to it, definite. There's a definite advantage—well, take my business—the funeral business, for example. One of the reasons that we have been able to do as well as we have in the funeral business is because we can only serve Negroes. The Negroes weren't going to the white funeral homes, so that didn't siphon off people to the other community, but with this thing [integration] coming, who knows, maybe you can just choose your own funeral home regardless of race.

As a business leader, Harvey understood that she could choose to fight to open up new doors in a desegregated economy, but she also knew that "you've got to realize that there is a price for them being opened and it means a loss of some things to you that you've enjoyed."[42]

For Harvey, the choice was clear. She would fight. Her political activism expanded after the founding of Womanpower Unlimited. In April 1962, she was one of a select delegation of fifty American women invited to attend a "Women's Strike for Peace," held in Geneva, Switzerland. The six-day summit included representatives from seventeen countries and focused its agenda on a nuclear test ban treaty and "complete nuclear disarmament." In Switzerland, Harvey met Coretta Scott King, who was also a delegate at the event. Then, just a month after her return, Harvey filed a complaint with the Interstate Commerce Commission and the Justice Department when she herself experienced racial discrimination at a Trailways bus terminal in Gulf-port, Mississippi. When traveling from Gulfport to Jackson, Harvey decided to conduct her own freedom ride. While she was sitting in the terminal's main waiting room, a Gulfport policeman approached her and asked her nationality. When she replied, "American," the officer said, "There is a waiting room on the other side where you are sup-posed to be." When Harvey refused to move, another officer asked to speak to her on the loading ramp outside the station. Once outside, he pointed to a small rear waiting area and told Harvey to sit there. When she refused, the officer warned her not to return to the main waiting area. Harvey chose to remain on the loading ramp until the bus ar-rived. After boarding the bus, she was frustrated again to discover that she had been assigned to the last seat, even though no more than five passengers occupied the bus at any point on the journey. Harvey's for-mal complaint to the Justice Department about the Gulfport incident was one step in a growing movement in Mississippi to end racial seg-regation.[43]

In the year that followed Harvey's Gulfport bus experience, the Jackson civil rights campaign to desegregate the city gained momen-tum under the dedicated and courageous leadership of the Missis-sippi state NAACP field secretary, Medgar Evers. On May 12, 1963, the Mississippi NAACP held a meeting in Jackson to adopt a formal resolution calling for an end to segregation in all the city's public facil-ities, including restrooms, parks, playgrounds, libraries, and restau-rants. The resolution argued for fair employment opportunities and requested that the mayor of Jackson, Allen Thompson, a staunch seg-regationist, appoint a biracial committee to achieve these goals. The NAACP members involved in the initiative, including Clarie Collins Harvey, warned that if the mayor did not respond to their resolution, they would retaliate with economic boycotts and public demonstra-tions. Harvey knew the risks involved in launching boycotts: two of her funeral director colleagues, John C. Melchor and Robert L. Drew, who led the Clarksdale NAACP, were arrested in 1961 for organizing boycotts and charged with "conspiracy to injure trade." Nevertheless, Harvey became a key organizer of the Jackson boycott and founded the Council of Women's Organizations to coordinate the effort.[44]

One day after Evers announced the NAACP's resolution, Mayor Thompson held a press conference in which he rejected all the demands and declared that he would not meet with any member of the NAACP, CORE, or any other outside "agitators." Later that evening Mayor Thompson appeared on the city's local television stations to proclaim his resistance to the NAACP's agenda. After arguing to the FCC for equal time, Medgar Evers presented his own televised address on May 20 to respond to the mayor's resistance. In his remarks, Evers noted that the NAACP was not a group of "outside agitators" but had been in Jackson since 1926 and represented a longstanding commitment on the part of Mississippi's Negro citizens to "get rid of racial segregation in Mississippi life." He appealed to "the consciences of many silent, responsible citizens of the white community who know that a victory for democracy in Jackson will be a victory for democracy everywhere."[45]

Evers's public speech did reach many white Mississippians, both those who might support the civil rights cause in silence and those who vehemently opposed it. In the weeks that followed, Evers became aware that his life, which had always been in jeopardy owing to his civil rights activities, was increasingly in danger as a result of his heightened public role in the Jackson movement. Death threats were a regular occurrence in the Evers household, but after the NAACP leader made his televised speech, his fear for his and his family's safety grew. As Myrlie Evers later recalled, "Thousands of Mississippi whites who had never seen a picture of him would now be seeing Medgar on television. They would have to become familiar with his appearance. When it was over, he would be recognized everywhere: at a stop light in the city, on a lonely road in the Delta, in the light from the fuel pump at a gas station." In late May, the Evers home was attacked when unknown assailants threw a firebomb into their carport. Myrlie Evers was able to douse the flames, but there was little anyone could do to prevent a future attack.[46]

In the weeks that followed, the Jackson movement pressed on but was plagued by internal disagreements about strategy. Whereas the students on the Youth Council, who were primarily from Tougaloo College, wanted to continue with boycotts and pickets, the national

NAACP office argued for an end to the direct-action campaign and a shift back to voter-registration drives. As a result of these tactical debates, the momentum of the Jackson movement began to falter. On June 11, 1963, right after President Kennedy gave his first nationally televised speech in support of federal legislation to protect civil rights, Evers appeared at a lengthy and poorly attended mass meeting at New Jerusalem Baptist Church. At the gathering, local NAACP leaders including Clarie Collins Harvey listened to representatives from the national office make their case for a voter-registration campaign. A weary Evers left the meeting to return home just after midnight on June 12. He was shot and killed by Byron De La Beckwith as he stepped out of his car in the driveway of his home.[47]

The news of Evers's assassination shocked the nation and briefly revived the waning Jackson movement. In the days leading up to Evers's funeral, ministers and local activists in Jackson, including John Salter and Dave Dennis, led a series of mass marches in the city to keep alive the fight that Evers had championed. The energy and anger that drove these demonstrations carried over to the funeral itself, which almost ended in a full-scale race riot. On Saturday, June 15, national civil rights leaders such as Martin Luther King, Jr., and Roy Wilkins—along with approximately five thousand local mourners—attended the funeral, which was held at the Masonic Temple in Jackson. Not surprisingly, given her leadership role in the Jackson movement, Clarie Collins Harvey directed the funeral. After the service, all those in attendance joined in a march behind the Evers funeral cortege, which traveled twenty blocks from the Masonic Temple back to the Frazier and Collins Funeral Home on North Farish Street. While many walked in silent grief, others marched with defiance and shouts of "After Medgar, No More Fear!" as others joined in with choruses of "We Shall Overcome." (See photo gallery.)[48]

As the massive crowd descended on the front lawn of the Frazier and Collins Funeral Home, someone began to sing the spiritual "Oh Freedom," which defiantly proclaims, "Before I'd be a slave, I'd be buried in my grave, and go home to my Lord and be free." Almost on cue, the marchers then shouted, "Capitol Street!" and a group of several hundred black youths began to run toward the white business district on West Capitol Street, where police officers were gathered to monitor the proceedings. When the young people passed Deputy Police Chief A. L. Ray, he ordered them to disperse, but the crowd just responded with shouts of "We want the killer! We want equality! We want freedom!" Soon the Jackson police surged forward with billy clubs and police dogs to try to contain the crowd. Some of the protesters, now confronted with a direct attack by the police, retaliated by throwing bricks and bottles at the officers. Only the efforts of John Doar, a civil rights attorney from the Justice Department, averted what could have become a full-scale riot when he ran into the chaotic scene and pleaded with the youths to disperse. Even after the immediate tensions were diffused, those involved were momentarily inspired by the "massive upheaval at Farish Street," which was "the largest black protest in the history of Mississippi."[49]

Symbolically, however, the resurgence of activity that some civil rights workers hoped signaled the rebirth of the Jackson movement actually died on the lawn of the Frazier and Collins Funeral Home. In the weeks after the funeral of Medgar Evers, the Jackson movement never recovered from the loss of his leadership. The Jackson campaign was always hampered by the conflict between the young radical students from Tougaloo College, who pushed for direct-action sit-ins and boycotts, and the national NAACP, which argued for a less confrontational strategy of voter registration. Clarie Collins Harvey, who was both a black business leader and a supporter of the boycott movement, was caught somewhere in the middle of these debates. After directing Evers's funeral and transferring his remains to Washington, D.C., for burial in Arlington National Cemetery, Harvey continued her fight for racial justice through groups like Womanpower Unlimited, but the citywide movement dissolved in the months after Evers's death.

Ultimately, the 1963 Jackson campaign was overshadowed by the more organized and well publicized struggle in Birmingham, Alabama. With the strong backing of Martin Luther King, Jr.'s, Southern Christian Leadership Conference and the dynamic local leadership of individuals like the Reverend Fred Shuttlesworth, the fight to desegregate Birmingham was better able to capture the nation's attention, especially when it came up against Public Safety Commissioner Eugene "Bull" Connor's fire hoses and police dogs. As was often the case, prominent funeral directors, this time William E. Shortridge, who worked on the front lines, and A. G. Gaston, who negotiated behind the scenes with the city's white power structure, were key figures in the Birmingham campaign and bore witness to its triumphs and its tragedies.

Although the Birmingham campaign received national attention in the spring of 1963, the city's civil rights movement had been active since 1956. That year, Alabama was at the forefront of the civil rights struggle as a result of the Montgomery Bus Boycott. Then, in February 1956, Autherine Lucy won her case to integrate the state's public universities and enrolled at the University of Alabama. In an effort to quell the rising tide of civil rights activism in the state, Alabama's attorney general, John Patterson, decided to pursue a legal strategy to ban the NAACP. On June 1, 1956, Patterson's tactic succeeded when Circuit Judge Walter B. Jones issued a legal injunction forbidding the NAACP to operate in Alabama.[50]

In Birmingham, the Reverend Fred L. Shuttlesworth, minister of Bethel Baptist Church and an NAACP leader, decided that the most effective way to fight this battle was to form a new organization to replace the NAACP. Within days of the court injunction, Shuttlesworth organized a small meeting with fellow clergy and local activists at A. G. Gaston's Smith and Gaston Funeral Home, a safe haven for planning strategy. The next day, on June 5, 1956, Shuttlesworth, along with several other local ministers, held a mass meeting at the Sardis Baptist Church in Birmingham to found the Alabama Christian Movement for Human Rights (ACMHR). More than a thousand people attended this first meeting; by the end of the event, they had elected Reverend Shuttlesworth as president, Reverend R. L. Alford as vice president, Reverend Nelson H. Smith as secretary, and William E. Shortridge, another successful local funeral director, as treasurer.[51]

From its inception, the ACMHR had two major objectives: ending employment discrimination and abolishing racial segregation in public accommodations. Inspired by the Montgomery Bus Boycott, the ACMHR decided to move quickly to desegregate Birmingham's bus system. In early July 1956, Shuttlesworth and other ACMHR leaders wrote to the Birmingham Transit Company to request the removal of segregation signs on buses, the establishment of "first come, first served" seating, and the hiring of black bus drivers. Not surprisingly, the bus company and city officials completely ignored the requests. The battle to desegregate Birmingham's bus system did not fully resume until December 20, 1956, when the Montgomery Bus Boycott ended in victory as a result of the U.S. Supreme Court's decision in *Browder v. Gayle.* Buoyed by the ruling, the ACMHR moved quickly to request that the Birmingham Transit Company comply with the court order by December 26, 1956. In a written ultimatum to the bus company, Shuttlesworth warned that if the company failed to repeal its segregation ordinance by December 26, the ACMHR "would ride the buses in a desegregated fashion anyway."[52]

Shuttlesworth's aggressive stance almost cost him his life on the evening of December 25, 1956, when unknown assailants threw a bomb at his parsonage at Bethel Baptist Church. The pack of dynamite landed directly under the bedroom where Shuttlesworth was resting, and the impact of the blast completely destroyed the room. Remarkably, the mattress that Shuttlesworth was lying on protected him from the explosion and flying debris, and he escaped the attack uninjured. The religious symbolism of Shuttlesworth's miraculous survival solidified his place as the leader of the Birmingham struggle, but the attack foreshadowed the pattern of vigilante violence that would continue to haunt any effort on the part of black activists to desegregate the city. From December 1956 through September 1963, twenty bombings occurred in Birmingham's black community, earning the city the chilling epithet "Bombingham."[53]

Given these circumstances, it is important to examine more closely the role that funeral directors such as William E. Shortridge and A. G. Gaston played in the Birmingham struggle. William E. Shortridge, who owned the Shortridge Funeral Home in Ensley, Alabama, had been active in the NAACP in Alabama since the 1930s. Early on, Shortridge learned that his affiliation with the NAACP, which was actively fighting for voting rights and antilynching laws, made him a target of segregationists. In 1932, the black press reported that Shortridge was beaten "unmercifully" by an off-duty police officer on the streets of Birmingham. In 1942, Shortridge was part of a delegation of black leaders who went before local legislators to argue for voting rights, equal education, and the hiring of Negro police officers for black neighborhoods. When the ACHMR was founded in 1956, Shortridge was elected treasurer because his business acumen and relationships in the funeral industry were critical to managing the group's finances and fundraising. After Reverend Shuttlesworth's parsonage was bombed in December 1956, Shortridge quickly solicited donations from his funeral director colleagues across the state to help rebuild the church. As a member of the National Negro Funeral Directors Association board of directors, Shortridge also kept funeral directors throughout the country abreast of the situation in Birmingham. Throughout the Birmingham campaign, Shortridge was known as a "relentless fighter for civil rights" and a vocal supporter of Shuttlesworth's more confrontational approach to desegregating what Martin Luther King, Jr., eventually described as the "most segregated city in America." In one ACHMR bus boycott meeting, Shortridge quipped that he might head the organization's "physical persuasion committee," and at mass meetings Shuttlesworth liked to tease, "Bill Shortridge is not quite nonviolent."[54]

With his combative reputation, Shortridge—like Shuttlesworth—faced threats against his life. In early 1962, as a result of his prominent role in the ACMHR, Shortridge began receiving a series of threatening phone calls. In response, he tried to get a gun permit to protect his family but was refused by city officials. On March 28, 1962, an unknown assailant shot at Shortridge in a drive-by attack as he got out of his car to enter his home. Shortridge survived unharmed when he sought cover on his front porch. In the weeks after the attack, he received an anonymous phone call from a man who claimed that the gunman was a black man from Ensley who had received a $2,000 contract from Bull Connor to kill Shortridge. The caller told Shortridge that Connor believed he was "the brains of the ACMHR, and that if they got rid of him, things would improve in Birmingham." Shortridge and Shuttlesworth found the man's story plausible enough to move the ACHMR's guard detail to Shortridge's house. In spite of these threats, Shortridge never wavered in his commitment to the Birmingham campaign.[55]

A. G. Gaston's role in the Birmingham civil rights struggle was different from Shortridge's but equally significant. Gaston, whose business empire began with the founding of the Booker T. Washington Burial Society in 1923, was—by the mid-1950s—a nationally known millionaire and celebrated entrepreneur. Gaston made his fortune by aggressively pursuing the vertical integration of the black funeral industry in Alabama in the 1920s and 1930s. During this time, Gaston's Booker T. Washington Burial Society evolved into the Booker T. Washington Insurance Company, which sold burial insurance throughout the state. At the same time, Gaston founded the Smith and Gaston Funeral Home chain, which by the 1930s had thirteen branches throughout Alabama. In the late 1930s, Gaston purchased the Mt. Zion cemetery in Birmingham. When the modern civil rights movement gained momentum in the mid-1950s, Gaston owned, in addition to his funeral-related establishments, a business conglomerate including Citizens Federal Savings and Loan, the Booker T. Washington Business College, and the A. G. Gaston Motel. By the time the SCLC Birmingham campaign began in 1963, A. G. Gaston Enterprises employed more than five hundred people and had an annual payroll of over 1.5 million dollars.[56]

For Gaston, who was more conservative than Shortridge in his engagement with the civil rights struggle, there were two primary ways to support the movement: by providing financial and logistical support, and by using his authority as a financially secure black business leader to negotiate with the city's white power structure and business community. One of Gaston's earliest forays into Alabama's civil rights movement was the financial assistance he provided to Autherine Lucy when she fought to integrate the University of Alabama in February 1956. When Gaston discovered that Lucy needed employment in the middle of her legal battle, he offered her a secretarial job at the Booker T. Washington Business College. Later, when Lucy won her case and needed to drive to Tuscaloosa to register as a student, Gaston provided an upscale car from his funeral business to transport her. When Lucy attempted to attend class a few days later, a mob of white students and townspeople rioted in protest. They threw rocks and eggs at Lucy; and when she tried to escape in a car, the mob smashed the car's windows and yelled, "Let's kill her, let's kill her." To quell the violence, university officials immediately suspended Lucy from campus. In the press coverage of the attack, some accused Lucy of being "high-handed" and inciting the riot simply because "she appeared for registration well dressed, came in a Cadillac, and paid for her tuition in hundred dollar bills." In the face of this criticism, the black press both defended Lucy's courage and praised Gaston as "one of her chief financial backers." In an effort to shield her from the press frenzy surrounding her case, Lucy was "whisked . . . to a room in the A. G. Gaston motel" for "a little rest and privacy."[57]

Throughout the 1950s, Gaston inconspicuously used economic pressure to fight racial segregation. At one point, he cancelled a $100,000 order for cars and hearses for the Smith and Gaston Funeral Home because the car dealer refused to hire a Negro salesman. When he approached another dealer with the account, the new dealer agreed to hire "two Negro salesmen to keep Gaston's business and the first [dealer] hired one Negro in an effort to win Gaston back." In another instance, Gaston instructed the white-owned First National Bank to remove the "Whites Only" signs from its drinking fountain. He warned that if the sign remained, he planned to close his bank account. The bank quickly honored Gaston's request in order to ensure his patronage. In 1957, to combat racial discrimination in mortgage lending, Gaston founded the Citizens Federal Savings and Loan Association. Although he initially met with resistance from the established white lenders in Birmingham, Gaston took his case before the Federal Home Loan Bank Board in Washington, D.C., and won. He then used the business to promote homeownership in Birmingham's black community and make "it easier for our people to obtain financial assistance from other lending institutions." As a gesture of support, Martin Luther King, Jr., sent Gaston a $1,000 check in April 1958 to open a private bank account. King wrote to Gaston, "This is just a little expression of interest I have in the great work that you and your associates are doing in the area of economics." To thank King, Gaston placed him on the bank's advisory board and included his name on the company's letterhead.[58]

In addition to pressuring white-owned businesses to stop discriminating against blacks, Gaston funded business ventures like the A. G. Gaston Motel to fight the indignities of racial segregation and support the city's black community. As he commented to reporters at the motel's grand opening in 1954, "I have long regretted there was no topflight motel or resting place for Negro visitors in our city, and I was determined to make our new motel one to attract Negro tourists." For Gaston, the motel would bring black tourist dollars into the city and provide much-needed meeting facilities for the local black community. In addition, Gaston espoused an "open-door policy" at the motel whereby "no one was ever turned away simply because of his color." As early as 1956, Gaston allowed Fred Shuttlesworth and the newly formed ACMHR to use both his motel and his funeral home as gathering places to organize their early campaign to desegregate the city's bus system. By 1960, Gaston had built a new, three-story office building at the intersection of Sixteenth Street and Sixth Avenue to act as the headquarters of Gaston Enterprises. The black press made special note that "contained in the beautifully apportioned building is a 500-seat auditorium on the first floor which is to be used for community activities." In 1962, the ACMHR and SCLC rented Gaston's L. R. Hall Auditorium as well as his motel for two major gatherings. The first, in April 1962, was an interracial conference and workshop on effective civil rights protest strategies; the second, in September 1962, was the SCLC's annual convention.[59]

Gaston's willingness to allow Shuttlesworth's ACMHR and King's SCLC to use his office building and motel to hold organizational meetings did not, however, reflect his full endorsement of their strategies. On the contrary, Gaston regarded Shuttlesworth as something of a firebrand and viewed his use of direct confrontation to fight Birmingham's white power structure as potentially counterproductive. Gaston firmly believed that peaceful negotiation with white business leaders and city officials was the most effective means to change. Moreover, Gaston often saw his economic interests allied with those of the city's white power brokers. As early as September 1962, Sidney Smyer, president of the Birmingham Chamber of Commerce, invited Gaston to participate in Smyer's Senior Citizens Committee, a biracial group of business leaders. Smyer, along with most of the city's white business elite, had come to realize that Birmingham's notorious resistance to racial integration—as symbolized by Commissioner Bull Connor—had the potential to cripple the city's economy. Continued racial conflict, bombings, and demonstrations only frightened off new investors. Smyer hoped that with Gaston's involvement, the Senior Citizens Committee might lobby the SCLC to abort any plans to demonstrate against segregation during its upcoming annual convention.[60]

Gaston, in a shrewd move, used his position as the more moderate envoy of the black community's two most powerful leaders to bring the more aggressive Shuttlesworth to the bargaining table. Throughout the Birmingham struggle, Gaston's power as a negotiator derived from his ability to contrast himself with the more militant minister. Gaston let Smyer know that while he had money, "Money don't run this thing [the movement] now. He [Shuttlesworth] is the man with the marbles." Smyer then asked Gaston to invite Shuttlesworth to a meeting with the members of the Senior Citizens Committee. At the meeting, Shuttlesworth pressured the white merchants to agree to remove all segregation signs from their stores and to continue discussions about ending employment discrimination in exchange for calling off any demonstrations during the SCLC convention. At the time, the agreement was considered a significant victory for the ACMHR, but one that proved fleeting. As soon as the SCLC convention adjourned on September 28, 1962, Bull Connor moved quickly to intimidate the merchants who had participated in the voluntary desegregation to reinstate their Jim Crow signage.[61]

In the wake of this setback, Shuttlesworth renewed his campaign to bring Martin Luther King, Jr., and the SCLC to Birmingham to launch Project Confrontation, known as "Project C." After several months of meetings and delays, King and the SCLC finally decided to launch sit-ins and pickets at downtown department stores in April 1963 to capitalize on the Easter shopping season. King and Shuttlesworth agreed that Project C needed to focus specifically on an economic strategy. As

King recalled, "We decided . . . to center the Birmingham struggle on the business community, for we knew that the Negro population had sufficient buying power so that its withdrawal could make the difference between profit and loss for many businesses." The first protesters would head to lunch counters on April 3, 1963, one day after Birmingham's run-off mayoral election, which pitted the white supremacist Bull Connor against an only slightly more moderate segregationist, Albert C. Boutwell. When Boutwell won the election, the ACMHR and the SCLC proceeded with the sit-ins but were immediately criticized by the city's black middle class, who saw the demonstrations as untimely. Black elites, including Gaston, wanted to see if Boutwell would negotiate, but Shuttlesworth and the SCLC, who viewed Boutwell as "just a dignified Bull Connor," held firm to their direct-action strategy.[62]

As internal dissension grew within Birmingham's black community, King knew—as did the city's white leaders, including Smyer—that he needed the endorsement of business leaders like A. G. Gaston in order to proceed. From the beginning, Gaston's relationship to Project C was complex and reflected his unique position as the most famous black millionaire in the most segregated city in America. Gaston, who resented having "outsiders" from SCLC in Atlanta impose themselves on the racial dynamics of Birmingham, was initially reluctant to support Project C. In the middle of the first round of sit-ins, he decided to make a public statement to the press about demonstrations. In his remarks, Gaston expressed his support for the fight for "freedom and justice" but emphasized the need to work "harmoniously and together in a spirit of brotherly love." Most pointedly, Gaston stressed the need to give "due recognition to the local colored leadership among us."[63]

SCLC leaders saw Gaston's endorsement of local leadership as a clear move to discredit the group's efforts. At an SCLC mass meeting during the first week of protests, Martin Luther King, Jr., and Ralph Abernathy spoke out against the black ministers and business leaders who were reluctant to join their fight. Abernathy rallied the working-class crowd with his criticism of the "black bourgeoisie" and told the audience to threaten to withdraw their trade if black businessowners did not support the movement. Then, a few days later, Gaston was publicly branded an "Uncle Tom" in the black press when a member of his staff refused to let the SCLC hold a much-publicized fundraiser at Gaston's own L. R. Hall Auditorium—only an hour before the event was to begin. The civil rights rally was to feature the blind jazz singer Al Hibbler, who had come down from New Jersey to participate in the Project C demonstrations. After a black Masonic Temple also refused to host the event, Hibbler held an impromptu concert in Kelly Ingram Park, which was adjacent to the A. G. Gaston Motel and the A. G. Gaston Office Building. Although Gaston later claimed that the denial of the auditorium rental was a bureaucratic mix-up, the incident nevertheless left the impression that the funeral home entrepreneur was less than supportive of the SCLC campaign.[64]

Recognizing that the rising tensions between the SCLC and Birmingham's black middle class were counterproductive, Gaston hosted a meeting between King and approximately one hundred black business leaders and professionals at L. R. Hall Auditorium. During the gathering, King encouraged attendees to share their concerns about Project C, after which he made his own case for why the demonstrations should proceed. The meeting proved productive as King convinced Gaston and others that the SCLC's plan was viable. To capitalize on the goodwill from this meeting, King decided to form a Project C "Central Committee" composed of select members of the SCLC, the ACMHR, and Birmingham's black elite, including ministers, professionals, and entrepreneurs. Approximately twenty-five people joined the advisory committee, among them A. G. Gaston; William E. Shortridge; John Drew, an insurance agent; Dr. L. H. Pitts, president of Miles College; and attorney Arthur Shores. Since Gaston, Shortridge, Drew, Pitts, and Shores were also advisers to Sidney Smyer's Senior Citizens Committee, these individuals became key emissaries between the SCLC and the city's white power structure.[65]

As soon as King formed the Central Committee, the first phase of Project C hit a major crisis point when an Alabama state circuit judge issued a temporary injunction against any further demonstrations. In addition, SCLC organizers realized that they were rapidly running out of bail money to free their demonstrators who were already under arrest. On April 12, the morning of Good Friday, King asked the Central

Committee to convene a meeting in room 30 of the A. G. Gaston Motel, which had become the command center, or "war room," for Project C. King asked participants for advice as to whether he should obey the injunction and focus on raising funds for bail money, or proceed with the planned Good Friday march and face certain arrest.[66]

King was prepared to practice civil disobedience, but Gaston and other members of the Central Committee advised him against it. They argued about the need to obey the law and to initiate a cooling-off period as Easter approached. For King, the meeting proved to be a defining moment in his leadership of the movement. When he retreated for a few moments of solitude in the bedroom of the motel suite, King's mind leapt "beyond the Gaston Motel, past the city jail, past city lines and state lines, and I thought of 20 million black people who dreamed that someday they might be able to cross the Red Sea of injustice and find their way to the promised land of integration and freedom. There was no room for doubt . . . I had decided to go to jail." When King announced his decision to violate the injunction, Gaston and others made a final plea that the demonstration be aborted, but King was adamant in his decision. King and Abernathy then left the motel to lead the marchers from Zion Hill Church straight to Seventeenth Street in downtown Birmingham, where they were met by Bull Connor and his police force and promptly arrested. At the Jefferson County jail, King was put in solitary confinement, where he wrote his "Letter from a Birmingham Jail." After eight days of imprisonment, King and Abernathy were released on bail.[67]

After King and Abernathy's release, Project C entered its final and most controversial phase, which involved bringing local schoolchildren into the demonstrations to face Bull Connor's fire hoses and dogs. When King first presented the idea to his Central Committee, A. G. Gaston was one of many who adamantly opposed the tactic. Defending his opinion, Gaston later reflected, "I was convinced it was now time to use the conference table instead of the streets to try to settle differences. If wanting to spare children, save lives, bring peace was Uncle Tomism, then I wanted to be a Super Uncle Tom." Nevertheless, the SCLC decided to proceed with the plan dubbed "D-Day," which ultimately proved to be the turning point of the Birmingham campaign. From his own office window, Gaston watched as "hordes of Negro youth" streamed "into the lines of policemen waiting in Kelly Ingram Park," only to be attacked by dogs, hit by night sticks, and knocked off their feet by the sheer force of the water from the fire hoses. And yet, by the second day of the demonstrations, Gaston and others in the black community became so moved by the young people's courage in the face of the police brutality that they grew more willing to find a meaningful resolution to the Birmingham campaign.[68]

When the horrific images of the "D-Day" attacks against Birmingham's black youths were televised to the American public and also reached the international press, the White House moved with urgency to resolve the Birmingham crisis. President John F. Kennedy and Attorney General Robert Kennedy sent Burke Marshall, assistant attorney general for civil rights, to Alabama to facilitate negotiations with local leaders. On the ground in Birmingham, leaders like Sidney Smyer and A. G. Gaston met, often in secret, to begin talks to find a road to compromise. As Smyer later recalled, "He [Gaston] would sneak up this alley behind my office to see me and we would sneak off downtown somewhere to meet him."[69]

On Tuesday, May 7, 1963, 125 members of Sidney Smyer's Senior Citizens Committee met with Burke Marshall to discuss the SCLC's demands, which included the desegregation of downtown stores; increased hiring of blacks; the dismissal of all charges against jailed demonstrators; and the creation of a biracial committee to oversee further desegregation. Although the meeting began with much resistance from the white business leaders, a shift occurred over the course of the day, especially after the Jefferson County sheriff reported to the group that all local jails were full of demonstrators and noted that, if any more arrests were made, they would have to resort to placing detainees behind barbed-wire fencing. The sheriff cautioned that "pictures of that won't look very nice." Faced with the reality of another public relations disaster for their city, the members of the Senior Citizens Committee were forced to acknowledge that they needed to move toward a settlement with the SCLC.[70]

On Wednesday, May 8, in a gesture of good faith, King called a moratorium on SCLC demonstrations in order to facilitate a formal resolution with the city's white business leaders. While key black negotiators, including Gaston, supported the moratorium, King's truce infuriated Shuttlesworth, who believed it was too much of a concession and put the ACMHR and SCLC in a position of weakness. Moreover, the moratorium was immediately threatened when King and Abernathy were suddenly jailed again on charges related to their original violation of parading without a permit at the Good Friday march. The presiding judge set King's and Abernathy's bond at $2,500 each—far higher than the usual $300. Just as Shuttlesworth was about to use the arrests to end the moratorium, King and Abernathy were released from jail when A. G. Gaston posted their bail and guaranteed $160,000 of the $237,000 needed to release the other demonstrators. Some militant activists, who wanted to use King's arrest to energize the demonstrators, saw Gaston's bail payment as counterproductive. For Gaston, King's release was critical to maintaining the moratorium and was "needed to calm and control the colored community."[71]

Gaston's effort literally to bail out King and the other demonstrators was indicative of his complicated and sometimes contradictory relationship to the Birmingham campaign, a relationship that mirrored that of many other black funeral directors to the modern civil rights movement. Gaston, who had always argued for moderation in Birmingham's long struggle for racial equality, was never comfortable with Shuttlesworth's more confrontational approach. As a successful black entrepreneur, Gaston knew that he had to work with white business leaders like Smyer to maintain Birmingham's economic stability. By facilitating King's release, Gaston achieved his goal of continuing the crucial biracial negotiations that led to the announcement on May 10, 1963, of a final settlement of the Birmingham campaign. Fittingly, however, King, Abernathy, and Shuttlesworth announced the terms of the settlement in a press conference in the courtyard patio of the A. G. Gaston Motel, which had served as their headquarters throughout Project C. Gaston's willingness to allow the ACMHR and SCLC to use his motel, funeral home, and business offices to plan and implement strategy often worked directly against his own desire for a less adversarial movement. Moreover, Gaston assumed a fair amount of risk to himself and his business empire by allowing his motel to be used as the headquarters of the Birmingham campaign.

The exact risk that Gaston took in allowing Project C to encamp at his motel became apparent soon after the Birmingham settlement was declared. As King later recalled, the announcement of the "peace pact" had consumed the "segregationist forces within the city . . . with fury." Close to midnight on May 12, 1963, two bombs exploded—one at the home of Martin Luther King, Jr.'s, brother, the Reverend A. D. King, and the other aimed at room 30 of the A. G. Gaston Motel. King noted that the bomb planted at the Gaston Motel was "placed as to kill or seriously wound anyone who might have been in Room 30—my room." Although massive rioting broke out on the streets of downtown Birmingham immediately after the explosions, Birmingham's racial accord was not completely destroyed, as the segregationists had hoped. The immediate intervention of President Kennedy, who threatened to bring in three thousand federal troops to quell the violence, caused white leaders such as Sidney Smyer to publicly renew their commitment to the agreement.

A. G. Gaston, however, remained a target of local Ku Klux Klan members, who deeply resented his wealth and his willingness to shelter King during Project C. Over the summer of 1963, wild rumors also began to circulate that Gaston was using caskets to hide guns and ammunition for militant activists—an astonishing claim given Gaston's reputation as a conservative. On September 8, 1963, Klansmen threw two firebombs at Gaston's "palatial $75,000 antebellum mansion." Gaston and his wife, Minnie, had just returned to Birmingham from a trip to Washington, D.C., where they had attended a state dinner at the White House in honor of the king and queen of Afghanistan. Although the Gastons were not injured in the attack, their home suffered considerable smoke damage. In his memoir, Gaston reflected on how the attack caused him to question his critics on both sides of the racial divide:

> I kept wondering why our house had been bombed and which political faction was responsible. I had been accused by some in the white community of supporting the so-called radicals by providing motel accom-

modations and bond for civil rights demonstrators. At the same time I was being criticized by leaders of the "rights" movement because of my conservatism . . . Was there a possibility that I was being attacked by the more militant Negro leadership or the Klan?[72]

Then, just one week after Gaston's home was firebombed, Birmingham witnessed the most brutal attack of all. At 10:22 A.M. on Sunday, September 15, 1963, a bomb exploded in the basement of the Sixteenth Street Baptist Church, which had been one of the central gathering places for Project C demonstrations. The explosion instantly killed four young girls: Denise McNair, Addie Mae Collins, Carole Robertson, and Cynthia Wesley, and injured approximately twenty others. McNair, Collins, Robertson, and Wesley were in the church basement preparing for Youth Day services when the explosion occurred. Moments after the bombing, rescuers rushed to the scene to search for victims and to get them medical care as quickly as possible. The black press noted that even the rescue effort was defined by racial segregation as the victims in the attack "were taken to hospitals and a morgue in ambulances owned, operated and driven by Negroes." The story also noted that "millionaire A. G. Gaston . . . holds a contract with the city to pick up Negro accident victims [and] at least eight of Gaston's ambulances rushed to the scene of the church bombing to remove the four dead and nearly 20 injured Negroes." News reports made a point of commending Davenport and Harris Funeral Home and Poole Funeral Home for their handling of the victims' remains.[73]

The horror of the attack that ended the lives of four innocent girls reverberated with the outrage black Americans had felt when Emmett Till was murdered just eight years before. Yet stark differences marked the two tragedies and represented the evolution of the civil rights movement from 1955 to 1963. In the Emmett Till case, Mamie Till Bradley had insisted on an open casket, and her courage had energized the struggle. As Birmingham prepared to bury Robertson, McNair, Collins, and Wesley, a different, more internal despair became evident. One news story on the bombing included the headline, "No One Can View Cynthia"—a dramatic counterpoint to Till Bradley's wish for the very public exposure of her son's corpse. The report noted that

Cynthia Wesley's "head was blown off by the bomb blast. [Yet a] Birmingham Negro undertaker . . . performed such an 'embalming miracle' on her that he has joined with others here in urging that the public be allowed to view the body. Cynthia's father, however, said 'no.'" Claude Wesley's refusal to open his daughter's casket to the public reflected a deeper shift in the psyche of the national civil rights campaign. The price of the "non-violent" struggle was getting too high and the deaths (and closed caskets) of Wesley, McNair, Collins, and Robertson symbolized that cost as nothing else could have.[74]

For funeral directors like A. G. Gaston, William E. Shortridge, and others, including Congressman Charles Diggs, Jr., and Clarie Collins Harvey, the civil rights struggle would continue to prove a challenge and a mission, as well as a burden and a threat. From the 1954 *Brown* decision to the bombing at the Sixteenth Street Baptist Church, black funeral directors were consistently, though not always obviously or willingly, engaged in the fight for racial equality. Regularly called upon to act as mediators or bail bondsmen, they often interceded in local civil rights campaigns even when their influence was not immediately apparent. As the case of A. G. Gaston demonstrates, it was sometimes difficult to discern their motives for becoming involved: was it to keep the peace with white power brokers in order to maintain their own economic position, or to risk their own livelihoods in an effort to contribute—logistically and financially—to the struggle for civil rights, or was it some of both? Even when funeral directors were called upon to use their skill as embalmers to prepare the martyrs of the cause for burial, it was not always clear how they could best support the movement: should the decedent's murdered corpse be restored or left untouched to show the violence that was visited upon it? Should the casket be closed or open? There were no easy answers, and as 1963 wore on, a whole new set of challenges lay ahead for the funeral industry, the civil rights movement, and the nation.

5

The African American Way of Death

In addition to marking a turning point in the national fight for civil rights, 1963 proved a critical year for the American funeral industry. In August 1963, the same month as the March on Washington, Jessica Mitford published her book *The American Way of Death,* a scathing critique of the capitalistic excesses of the American funeral industry. For Mitford, the tasteless materialism of the American funeral—with its ornate caskets, garish floral arrangements, and penchant for embalming—represented the ultimate exploitation of the free market. The central villain in Mitford's account was none other than the funeral director, who ruthlessly capitalized on the vulnerability of grieving consumers to convince them to spend thousands of dollars on the kitschy accoutrements of the modern American funeral. With its muckraking argument, sardonic tone, and provocative content—including a vivid description of the embalming process—*The American Way of Death* became an instant sensation. As the book shot to the top of the *New York Times* bestseller list, reviewers lauded Mitford for her "savagely witty and well-documented exposé."[1]

Most significantly, Mitford's book ignited a national debate about whether the modern American funeral had real cultural value or was simply an opportunity for shrewd entrepreneurs to prey on consumers at a vulnerable moment in their lives. The question had plagued the funeral industry since the early twentieth century, but it became particularly pressing in the postwar era of consumerism. As early as May 1951, Bill Davidson published an article in *Colliers* magazine titled "The High Cost of Dying," which detailed price-fixing abuses in the funeral industry in California. Ten years later, in a June 1961 issue of the *Saturday Evening Post,* Roul Tunley wrote an article entitled "Can You Afford to Die?" which explained how local memorial societies had begun to circumvent the exorbitant costs of the modern funeral. Then, just one year before Mitford released *The American Way of Death,* Ruth Harmer wrote her book *The High Cost of Dying,* another critical study of American funeral practices.

The release of Mitford's book in August 1963, however, sparked an unprecedented national discussion about death and the American consumer. Most major newspapers reported on funeral costs in their respective communities; state legislatures held public hearings on fraudulent practices in the funeral industry; CBS broadcast an hour-long television documentary called "The Great American Funeral," based on the book's findings; and, as Mitford herself noted, "membership in the nonprofit consumer-run funeral and memorial societies rose from seventeen thousand families to close to a million." The publication of *The American Way of Death* and the public firestorm the book ignited completely transformed postwar Americans' consciousness about death and mourning.[2]

Not surprisingly, the national funeral industry's response to Mitford's attacks was vociferous and swift. Months before the book was officially published, industry leaders received word of the work in progress and used their trade journals to warn of its release with headlines such as "Mitford Day Draws Closer!" and "Who's Afraid of the Big Bad Book?" In the weeks and months following the book's release, funeral industry leaders as well as conservative politicians questioned not only Mitford's arguments but also her politics by turning her call for simpler, low-cost funerals into a communist "Red plot." Congressman James B. Utt of California described Mitford's funeral critique as a communist assault against Christianity itself. In a statement for the Congressional Record, Utt declared, "Her tirade against morticians is simply the vehicle to carry her anti-Christ attack."[3]

The public uproar over the book fed a general fear among funeral directors that the government would increase regulation of their industry. Responding to the public relations crisis caused by Mitford's work, the *Casket and Sunnyside,* the funeral industry's premier trade journal, warned its readers that "funeral service must put its house in order NOW. If it fails to do this, and QUICKLY, the various state governments or the Federal Government will attempt to do this by harsh regulations controlling funeral pricing, services and advertising claims." *Casket and Sunnyside* argued for a preemptive public relations campaign for the funeral industry, including advertisements that depicted "a real concern both for the dignity of man and for the welfare of the person planning a service as well as for the welfare of the survivors."[4]

For African American undertakers, the publication of Jessica Mitford's book was, initially, lost amid the more pressing concerns of the civil rights movement. In mid-August 1963, the NFDMA held its annual convention in Columbus, Ohio. Although the convention was ostensibly focused on business and training, the gathering was dominated by the national civil rights cause. In publicity for the conference, the NFDMA touted its plan to sponsor "a gigantic civil rights rally" on the streets of Columbus to raise funds for the Southern Christian Leadership Conference. Martin Luther King, Jr., Ralph Abernathy, and Wyatt Tee Walker were all expected to make appearances. Although King became ill and was unable to attend, William E. Shortridge stepped in to hold a special session at the convention to present updates on the Birmingham campaign to NFDMA members.

The NFDMA convention concluded with an awards banquet, which featured Dr. Benjamin E. Mays, president of Morehouse College and renowned mentor and spiritual adviser to King, as the keynote speaker. In his address, titled "An Age of Dramatic Dimensions," Mays explored the history behind the civil rights struggle and declared the "bold truth that the Negro American does not only want but is entitled to freedom now." Throughout the speech, Mays acknowledged the complicated and often unappreciated role that community leaders like funeral directors played in the movement. He described the "unfortunate" situation when "a Negro who has been acknowledged and accepted by the general community as a leader in a given field of endeavor [is] discredited and called 'Uncle Tom' because he was not a leader in the N.A.A.C.P. or the C.O.R.E." To combat this tendency, Mays argued for the importance of "diversified leadership" to guide the transition to racial integration and called on the funeral directors as members of the "Negro power structure" to organize themselves and "assume the leadership of the masses." Then, to close the convention with a final affirmation of the civil rights movement, NFDMA members passed a special resolution in support of the proposed August 28 March on Washington.[5]

In the end, African American funeral directors' engagement in the civil rights movement, which often involved considerable personal and financial risk, mitigated their reaction to the larger furor within the industry over Jessica Mitford's controversial book. Immediately after the release of *The American Way of Death*, the *National Funeral Director and Embalmer*, the trade journal of the NFDMA, reprinted rebuttals from white clergy and funeral industry leaders, but did not make its own editorial statement about the book from an African American perspective. As the impact of the book grew over time, the commentary that NFDMA members did make about Mitford's salvo was clearly driven by their experiences as minority business leaders caught in the throes of the civil rights struggle. In an NFDMA President's Report, C. W. Lee, former leader of the Montgomery Bus Boycott in 1955, took issue with Mitford's attacks against the professional integrity of funeral directors by highlighting the depth of their commitment to community service—especially in the fight for civil rights:

> A man serves his community because he loves people. He learns of their woes and sorrows and sympathizes; he helps solve their problems. He not only serves as funeral director but *he is a combination of bondsman, counselor, civic worker, church worker, political leader and social agent, contributor to every kind of cause. He is sometimes referred to as the community's burden bearer.* After all of this then comes a person who needs money and selects this humble servant of the people, this community benefactor, to attack in a book called "American Way of Death," written by one Jessica Mitford. Anyone who reads this book cannot escape the conclusion that its ultimate purpose is to downgrade the funeral director. (Italics mine.)

Taking a slightly different tack, Robert H. Miller, executive secretary of the NFDMA, eventually wrote in an editorial in the *National Funeral Director and Embalmer*, "We should know that Jessie Mitford was not writing about us." Miller's remark, which was partly a call to black funeral directors to be more competitive in the industry, suggested that the racially and economically marginalized status of black funeral directors in the national funeral industry left them somewhat removed from the main thrust of Mitford's charges of corruption.[6]

By October 1963, both the status of blacks in the funeral industry and the Mitford controversy dominated the agenda of the National Funeral Directors Association's eighty-second annual convention in Dallas, Texas. Whereas the publication of Mitford's *American Way of Death* united the members of the white funeral directors' association against a common foe, the new motion to amend the NFDA constitution "to permit membership of persons from non-white races" created clear divisions among certain NFDA state delegations. The sudden effort to end the NFDA's longstanding discriminatory membership practices seemed to reflect a desire by some in the organization to respond to the national civil rights movement, but this impulse was certainly not embraced by all. Not surprisingly, the delegates from the South fought the measure most ardently. Nevertheless, when the motion came to a vote, the NFDA representatives from Southern states were "outvoted by the necessary two-to-one majority, due to heavy voting strength found in various of the Northern and Western States."[7]

Although the motion to extend NFDA membership to nonwhites did pass, the actual terms of the agreement limited its impact on the racial makeup of the organization. In its coverage of the historic measure, the *Casket and Sunnyside* reminded its readers that "to be a member of NFDA one must belong to the association recognized by NFDA in the State, so there will be no independent NFDA membership of non-white persons." The message was clear: so long as a state chapter of the NFDA chose to continue to exclude nonwhites, the national office did not have the authority to overrule the decision and admit nonwhite funeral directors from that region as individual members. The loophole allowed the NFDA to appear to be nondiscriminatory while its state associations continued to bar black funeral directors from the organization. This was a public relations sleight of hand for an organization in desperate need of some positive press coverage.

The remainder of the convention focused on the brewing Mitford controversy, which intruded directly on the proceedings when CBS televised its documentary "The Great American Funeral" on the penultimate evening of the convention. The NFDA set up televisions at convention receptions so members could watch the broadcast, which fueled interest in pursuing an aggressive public relations campaign to defend the industry.[8]

The concurrent public debates about the state of the modern American funeral and the direction of the modern civil rights movement all came to an abrupt halt on November 22, 1963, when President John F. Kennedy was shot and killed on the streets of Dallas, Texas. Kennedy's death and funeral reminded Americans of the importance of ritual and pageantry as a legitimate means to process collective grief. For critics of the industry, the president's funeral simply proved how difficult it was—even for the White House—to avoid being taken in by the impulse to overspend in an effort to honor a loved one. In his book *The Death of a President*, William Manchester recounted Robert Kennedy's struggle when confronted by a member of the staff of Gawler's Funeral Home in Washington, D.C., about the prices of caskets:

> He [had] a clear memory of a girl who told him . . . "You can get one for $500, one for $1,400, or one for $2,000." She went on about waterproofing and optional equipment. Influenced by Mitford's book, he shied away from the high figure. He asked for the $1,400 coffin, and afterward he wondered if he had been cheap; he thought about how difficult such choices must be for everyone.

Despite Robert Kennedy's desire for a moderately priced casket, Gawler's Funeral Home convinced White House staffers to purchase its high-end mahogany model for $2,400, which, with extra charges, totaled $3,160. Gawler's fees were in addition to the $3,495 charged by Vernon B. Oneal's Oak Lawn Funeral Home in Dallas to transport the president's remains to Washington. As Jessica Mitford later reflected, "Thus, despite Robert Kennedy's laudable efforts to avoid a price gouging, he was outmaneuvered; the family ended up paying a total of $6,655 into the coffers of undertakers."[9]

The cultural meaning of President Kennedy's death and funeral was, however, much more significant than a funeral director's bill. In the immediate aftermath of Kennedy's burial, a *New York Times* editorial commented, "In time of sudden shock—such as that of this tragic weekend—we fall back naturally on traditional symbols and accustomed ceremonials. President Kennedy's funeral may well have been in many respects the most elaborate and impressive funeral a modern ruler has ever received." In addition to the national press, funeral industry leaders, clergy, and psychologists took a moment to reflect on how the president's death and funeral demonstrated Americans' psychological need for proper burial and reassuring rituals to process their grief. Reverend Ralph W. Loew, a minister from Buffalo, New York, commented:

> It is ironic that a national funeral should have interposed itself in the midst of the recent public discussions concerning the American and death. Suddenly there was played out before us the need to concern ourselves with ministering to one another in an hour of grief. It is patently true that there have been sentimentalisms and expensive actions which violate our faith. It is also truth that we have a need to express our ties of understanding.

Albert R. Kates, editor of *The American Funeral Director,* wrote a column in which he argued that the grandeur of Kennedy's funeral was "typical of the religious and sentimental manner in which virtually every other American is laid to rest, regardless of rank or degree of wealth." For Kates, Kennedy's funeral served to remind the American public that everyone could have a meaningful and well-orchestrated burial with the help of the funeral industry. Although the public praise of Kennedy's funeral did not silence industry critics like Mitford, it did provide concrete proof that the "American way of death" was not simply a business transaction but a complex matrix of religious, patriotic, cultural, and emotional forces.[10]

For African Americans, President Kennedy's death was particularly devastating. Especially in the last six months of his life, Kennedy had become increasingly willing to intervene on behalf of the national civil rights movement. The president had made his first major speech supporting the civil rights movement and detailing his plans to pursue a civil rights bill in Congress on June 11, 1963, the night before Medgar Evers was assassinated in Jackson, Mississippi. When Myrlie Evers and her children traveled with Medgar's brother, Charles, to Washington, D.C., to bury Evers at Arlington National Cemetery, President Kennedy welcomed them to the White House to express his personal condolences. Throughout the SCLC's Birmingham "Project C" campaign in the spring of 1963, President Kennedy and Attorney General Robert Kennedy regularly monitored the situation, consulted with Martin Luther King, Jr., and provided mediators from the Justice Department to broker a final resolution. And, in the immediate aftermath of the bombing of the Sixteenth Street Baptist Church, President Kennedy convened a special meeting at the White House with King and community leaders including A. G. Gaston to discuss the best federal response to the situation. After President Kennedy was assassinated, Dr. Benjamin E. Mays, who had spoken only months before at the NFDMA convention, expressed the sentiments of many black Americans when he commented, "No president in history has spoken so courageously and so forthrightly on Civil Rights as the late Mr. Kennedy . . . Negro Americans have lost their friend in high office."[11]

Although Kennedy's death was a blow to the leaders and grassroots organizers of the national civil rights campaign, they tried to take solace in President Lyndon Johnson's first address to the nation after he took office. In the speech, Johnson pledged to "put forth an end to the teaching and preaching of hate and evil and violence," a message that resonated with all who had witnessed not only Kennedy's assassination but also the recent senseless bombings in Birmingham. Johnson continued, "Nothing could honor President Kennedy's memory more than the earliest possible passage of the Civil Rights Bill for which he fought. Let us highly resolve that John F. Kennedy did not live or die in vain." True to his word, Johnson signed the Civil Rights Act of 1964 into law on July 2. The law banned racial discrimination in public accommodations, protected voting rights in federal elections, and created the Equal Employment Opportunity Commission (EEOC) to investigate complaints of employment discrimination. As the most comprehensive federal civil rights legislation passed in the nation's history, the Civil Rights Act of 1964 was a major victory for the nonviolent movement.[12]

For African American funeral directors, the period between President Kennedy's death and the passage of the Civil Rights Act of 1964 marked the beginning of a transition to a time when the American consumer marketplace would be much less clearly divided along racial lines. While the new law represented a triumph for the national civil rights campaign, its long-term consequences for black entrepreneurs —and specifically black funeral directors—were unclear and sometimes worrisome. Racial integration in the marketplace meant more choices for black consumers but a less secure base of customers for the black businessowner.

A sign of the ambiguous impact of the new civil rights age on black funeral directors came in mid-1963, when the federal government announced its campaign to end racial segregation in its handling of the dead. Specifically, the federal government decided to end the practice of racially segregating the military dead, which had traditionally involved contracting "a Negro funeral home for Negro personnel" and "an officially designated white funeral home for white soldiers." The segregation of military dead by race was a practice that an earlier generation of black funeral directors, such as Robert R. Reed, had fought to perpetuate as a means of generating business in the 1920s and 1930s. In 1963, the federal government decided to contract with one funeral home at each base, such as Ft. Hood in Texas, to handle all military deaths regardless of race.[13]

Although the decision had the potential to close off a steady stream of business to black funeral directors, the winning bid at the Ft. Hood, Texas, military base went to Mrs. B. K. Hornsby, owner of Hornsby Funeral Home, a black firm in Temple, Texas. In a news story reprinted in the *National Funeral Director and Embalmer*, Hornsby noted that "a lot of people don't know it but white funeral directors have been handling Negroes ever since they have been born. I don't see anything wrong with that, and I don't see anything wrong with it being the other way around. I don't think that we will have any trouble." Wayne Frank, the white funeral director who lost the Ft. Hood contract to Hornsby, saw the situation quite differently. Frank expressed "definite doubts as to the 'wisdom and practicality' of having a Negro firm handle all military deaths." Frank said he did not "believe that the general public is aware of this situation or the concern and ill-feeling it could cause."[14]

Frank's remarks, which could be dismissed as the resentful comments of the losing bidder in the Ft. Hood case, reflected the tensions that would continue to haunt the funeral industry and the civil rights movement for years to come. The landmark victories of the movement, such as the Civil Rights Act of 1964, illustrated how the state could intervene to enforce racial equality in America's public life. Less clear, however, was whether this type of intervention would ultimately transform or reinforce the racial politics of the private sector. For the funeral industry as a whole, the racial politics of death, which primarily revolved around the question of who buries whom, was far from resolved. Among white funeral directors, ambivalence about race was evident in the NFDA's half-hearted measure to open its membership to "non-white persons." For black funeral directors, the challenge of the civil rights age involved capitalizing on the business opportunities to which it availed them, while also working to retain their black clientele. For some, developing business in an integrated marketplace while retaining the loyalty of one's black customers was a difficult balancing act that required shrewdness and at times calculated marketing tactics. As Lincoln Ragsdale, a successful black funeral director in Arizona, eventually admitted in an interview for *Black Enterprise* magazine, "When I was losing money, I made a business decision. I took down my pictures of Martin Luther King Jr. and Booker T. Washington and put up some white folk. I hired white personnel and my business increased over 300 percent."[15]

From the mid-1960s through the 1970s, black funeral directors faced a critical period of transition. As the national civil rights campaign shifted from a nonviolent struggle for integration to a more separatist call for Black Power, they were often unsure about how best to support the cause or even whether it was worth supporting at all. On another front, they had to contend with the far-reaching influence of the Jessica Mitford controversy, which eventually led the U.S. Federal

Trade Commission to pursue increased government regulation of the funeral industry. These regulations threatened the profit margins of all funeral directors but were particularly damaging to black undertakers, who always struggled to remain competitive. Amid these challenges, black funeral directors continued to experience discrimination within the industry, which still did not fully recognize them in trade groups like the NFDA. Most immediately, however, black funeral directors found themselves on the front lines of an increasingly violent civil rights struggle as they were called upon to bury the movement's fallen.

When Congress passed the Civil Rights Act of 1964 on July 2, it was a watershed victory but only one step in the larger march to racial equality. In the months and years that followed, the civil rights struggle faced many challenges, but one of the most difficult was a pattern of increased violence against the movement's leaders and foot soldiers as a means of intimidating those fighting for the cause. The assassination of Medgar Evers, which occurred just one year earlier in June 1963, was one of the first signs of this trend. When President Kennedy was shot and killed just five months later, the shocking loss represented an ominous warning to those leading the struggle. Upon hearing the news of the president's assassination, Martin Luther King, Jr., turned to his wife, Coretta Scott King, and remarked, "This is what is going to happen to me also. I keep telling you, this is a sick society." Notoriously, Malcolm X precipitated his break from the Nation of Islam with his controversial comment that Kennedy's assassination was an example of the "chickens coming home to roost." To clarify the remark, Malcolm X explained, "I said that the hate in white men had not stopped with the killing of defenseless black people, but that hate, allowed to spread unchecked, finally had struck down this country's Chief of State." The rising tide of violence not only completely changed the spirit and direction of the civil rights movement but also illustrated how black funeral directors would continue to be critical, though relatively unseen, participants in the movement through their role directing the funerals of its martyrs.[16]

By the mid-1960s, the civil rights funeral, a tradition that had begun with Emmett Till's ceremony in 1955, became a central stage on which the dramas and internal tensions of the movement played themselves out. Most explicitly, these burial rites illustrated the lengths to which the opposition would go to thwart the cause. They revealed not only the obvious tensions between blacks and whites but also the internal divisions among black activists who were increasingly in conflict about the future direction of the struggle. Given these circumstances, the funeral directors charged with burying the martyred dead of the movement often found themselves navigating situations fraught with racial animosity and rich with political symbolism. The political theater of the civil rights burial also functioned as a striking counterpoint to Jessica Mitford's argument that the American funeral was an empty, overly commercialized ritual. Just as President Kennedy's funeral had proven, the civil rights funeral vividly illustrated that the tragedies of the times continued to reassert rather than refute the need for meaningful mourning rituals.

One such tragedy occurred right before the official passage of the 1964 act when three civil rights workers in Mississippi were reported missing on June 21, 1964. James Chaney, a black activist from Meridian, Mississippi; Mickey Schwerner, a white field organizer from the Congress of Racial Equality; and Andrew Goodman, a white volunteer from Queens College in New York, were participating in the Freedom Summer campaign to register black voters in Mississippi. The project was sponsored by a coalition of organizations including CORE and the NAACP, but the Student Nonviolent Coordinating Committee (SNCC) played the largest role in bringing white college students from the North down to the Magnolia State to work with local black activists to register black voters. Whereas Chaney and Schwerner had been working together for CORE for some time, Goodman had just arrived after completing training in nonviolent resistance in Oxford, Ohio. The three men had been investigating a church burning in Philadelphia, Mississippi, when they were arrested for speeding and put in jail. They were released on the night of June 21 and never seen again.[17]

The search for the missing men dragged on for weeks and was not resolved until a paid informant for the FBI directed investigators to an earthen dam on the grounds of a farm in Neshoba County. On August

4, the bodies of Goodman, Schwerner, and Chaney were finally located and exhumed. Autopsies revealed that Goodman and Schwerner had each been shot once in the head, and that James Chaney had been shot three times, in the head and the chest. As soon as the autopsies were completed, the victims' families proceeded with funeral arrangements that quickly became mired in the racial politics of the moment.

While Andrew Goodman's family requested that his remains be transported back to New York, Rita Schwerner, the widow of Mickey Schwerner, requested that her husband be buried next to James Chaney, his friend in the struggle, at the black cemetery in Meridian. Her request was denied, however, when James E. Bishop, the black funeral director handling Chaney's remains, refused to accept Schwerner's body. Bishop, who owned Enterprise Funeral Home in Meridian, told the Schwerners that "he feared Mississippi authorities would revoke his license—or worse—if he did." Then Rita Schwerner contacted several white undertakers to request that they transport Schwerner's remains to the black cemetery, but all of them refused. In the end, the Schwerner family arranged to have Mickey's remains cremated and transported back to New York. The Schwerners' thwarted effort to integrate one Mississippi cemetery revealed that the history of racial segregation, even in death, was fully entrenched on both sides of the racial divide.[18]

At 6 P.M. on August 7, 1964, James Chaney was buried alone—only the second person to be buried on the grounds of the newly opened Memorial Park cemetery atop Mount Barton, located a few miles outside of Meridian. The short, private burial was witnessed by approximately fifteen family members and close friends. Later that evening, hundreds of local blacks and a smaller number of white activists marched through Meridian to gather for a public memorial service for Chaney at Meridian's First Union Missionary Church. Unlike the quiet dignity of Chaney's official burial, the memorial service and the march that preceded it were charged with racial tension and dramatic confrontations. Describing the march to the service, the black press reported that "the mourners were the targets of verbal abuse and thrown bottles as they passed through a jeering gauntlet of local white residents." During the public memorial service, Dave Dennis, the CORE field secretary in Mississippi, could not contain his anger over the deaths and the racial tensions that caused them when he stood up to give his eulogy. Overcome with emotion, Dennis declared, "I don't grieve for James Chaney. He lived a fuller life than most of us will ever live. I feel that he's got his freedom and we are still fighting for it. I'm sick and tired of going to memorials! I am sick and tired of going to funerals! I've got a bitter vengeance in my heart tonight!"[19]

Dennis's angry eulogy marked a turning point in which the civil rights funeral became a more direct catalyst for activism. His bitter remarks warned mourners that it was no longer sufficient simply to bear witness to the loss of the movement's martyrs. The point of the civil rights funeral was not to wallow in grief but to take decisive action to continue the fight of those who had died for the cause. Near the end of his speech, Dennis declared, "The best thing we can do for Mr. Chaney, for Mickey Schwerner, for Andrew Goodman is stand up and demand our rights . . . Don't just look at me and the people here and go back and say that you've been to a nice service, a lot of people came . . . anything like that . . . your work is just beginning . . . If you do go back home and sit down and take it, God damn your souls!" For Dennis, continuing the fight for black voting rights was the only way to make sense out of the otherwise senseless deaths of James Chaney, Andrew Goodman, and Mickey Schwerner.[20]

The campaign for black voting rights did continue after the deaths of Chaney, Goodman, and Schwerner; and, by early 1965, it became focused on Selma, Alabama, where Martin Luther King, Jr., and the SCLC decided to join forces with the SNCC to fight for the cause. Unfortunately, the Selma campaign was quickly marred by violence and unexpected death just as the Mississippi "Freedom Summer" campaign had been. The first phase of the Selma campaign began in January 1965 with a degree of optimism. By the end of February, however, the Selma movement witnessed not only several serious death threats against its leader, Martin Luther King, Jr., but also the violent deaths and emotionally powerful funerals of two very different men, Malcolm X and Jimmie Lee Jackson, both of whom had briefly tried to support the cause.

Malcolm X's fleeting involvement in the Selma campaign was exceptional in that it was the only time the black nationalist leader had ever attempted to engage directly with the nonviolent movement led by King. Malcolm X arrived in Alabama on Wednesday, February 3, to speak at the Tuskegee Institute. He was greeted by SNCC staff from Selma, who invited him to address their organizers at a voting rights rally at Brown Chapel African Methodist Episcopal (AME) Church in Selma the next day. The young SNCC activists were struggling to reassert their role in the Selma campaign and felt that a speech from Malcolm X might energize their members. The SNCC organizers had been working on voting rights in Selma for two years and felt displaced when King and the SCLC joined the campaign in January. The national media's focus on King's involvement diverted attention away from the SNCC's longer-standing commitment to the local community. The young people were also in need of some inspiration since several hundred of their fellow activists—along with the SCLC's King and Abernathy—had been jailed since Monday for demonstrating for voting rights. Those gathered were waiting for instructions to march once again to the Dallas County Courthouse to demand their right to register to vote. They knew they would soon face off again with Selma Sheriff James G. Clark and his deputies, who "were waiting with guns, nightsticks and cattleprods."[21]

Given these circumstances, Malcolm X's appearance, which potentially threatened the local commitment to a nonviolent campaign, was controversial and not one supported by everyone. SCLC leaders Andrew Young and James Bevel met with Malcolm X briefly before he spoke and warned him not to use rhetoric that might incite violence. Never one to mute his message, Malcolm X stepped up to the lectern and told the young people gathered before him, "I don't advocate violence, but if a man steps on my toes, I will step on his . . . Whites better be glad that Martin Luther King is rallying the people because other forces are waiting to take over if he fails." For many SNCC activists, Malcolm X's speech in Selma was a formative event that prefigured the organization's shift to a more separatist philosophy of Black Power.

Although Malcolm X had hoped to visit King in jail to offer his support, he had to leave Alabama immediately for a speaking engagement in London. Malcolm X did, however, meet Coretta Scott King, who had been asked to give a short inspirational message on the importance of nonviolence to calm the crowd after Malcolm X's more provocative speech. After the rally ended, Coretta Scott King was briefly introduced to Malcolm X, who told her, "I want Dr. King to know that I didn't come to Selma to make his job difficult. I really did come thinking that I could make it easier. If the white people realize what the alternative is, perhaps they will be more willing to hear Dr. King."[22]

On Sunday, February 21, 1965, just over two weeks after his appearance in Selma, Malcolm X was assassinated at Harlem's Audubon Ballroom. Malcolm X had just begun to speak before a meeting of the Organization of Afro-American Unity, which he had founded after his break with the Nation of Islam, when a group of men charged the stage and gunned him down. The news of Malcolm X's violent death became more shocking still when reports identified his assailants as his former associates from the Nation of Islam. One of those arrested, a man identified as Norman 3X (formerly Norman Butler), was a known member of the Fruit of Islam, the Nation of Islam's security force. The killing revealed the depth of antagonism between Malcolm X and the Black Muslim movement and brought national attention to a case of black-on-black violence.[23]

The tensions that led to Malcolm X's assassination continued throughout the week after his death and resulted in one of the most high-profile and high-security funerals to be held during the civil rights era. On Monday, February 22, 1965, Malcolm X's wife, Betty Shabazz, met with Joseph E. Hall, general manager of Unity Funeral Home in Harlem, to make funeral arrangements that combined African American traditions with Muslim burial rituals. With Hall's guidance, Shabazz selected "a six foot nine inch bronze casket lined with egg-shell velvet" and decided to postpone the funeral service until Saturday. Shabazz's decision to delay the burial conflicted with Muslim beliefs about death, which held that "the sun should not set twice on a believer's body." Shabazz felt strongly, however, that the delay was necessary to enable all those who wanted to attend the service sufficient travel time—a common courtesy in African American funeral practices. Hall also worked with Shabazz to plan how Malcolm X's remains would be presented to the public. They decided on an open casket, protected by a glass cover and featuring a brass plaque embossed with Malcolm X's adopted Muslim name, El-Hajj Malik El-Shabazz. Although Hall initially dressed Malcolm X's remains in a traditional Western business suit, Sheik Ahmed Hassoun, a Sudanese Sunni Muslim, prepared his body for burial the day before the funeral service. Hassoun washed the body in sacred oil and then draped it in seven white linen shrouds known as a kafan.[24]

Unity Funeral Home assumed considerable risk when it agreed to direct Malcolm X's funeral. As soon as his remains arrived on Monday, February 22, the funeral establishment became caught in the crossfire of the very public war between Malcolm X's Organization of Afro-American Unity followers and the Nation of Islam. In the first few days after his assassination, the Nation of Islam's Mosque No. 7 in Harlem was destroyed by fire and another Black Muslim building in San Francisco was bombed. As a result, security concerns at Unity Funeral Home were extremely high. Joseph Hall had originally scheduled the viewing of the body to begin at 2:30 P.M. on Tuesday, but he was forced to postpone the event until the evening after several bomb threats were telephoned into the funeral home shortly before noon. Police had to evacuate the building twice to complete their bomb searches. At 5:15 P.M., another scare occurred when "a young Negro carrying a rifle in a canvas case was seized outside the funeral home." When guests finally entered the funeral home, they were greeted by police officers who inspected all packages, handbags, and floral arrangements. Outside the building on 126th Street, squad cars guarded the entrance to the funeral home while police sharpshooters manned the roof. Ultimately, more than two thousand people passed through Unity Funeral Home in the first four hours of the viewing alone, but the extremely high level of police protection was a vivid reminder that a black funeral home could quickly find itself on the front lines of intraracial conflicts.[25]

The threat of violence continued at the funeral service itself, which was held on Saturday, February 27, at Bishop Alvin A. Childs's Faith Temple, Church of God in Christ, at 147th Street and Amsterdam Avenue. Other large churches in Harlem, including Congressman Adam Clayton Powell's Abyssinian Baptist Church, had refused to host the funeral service out of fear of violence. As mourners entered Faith Temple, which had once housed a movie theater, police sharpshooters guarded the building from the roof. After the six hundred seats in the church's sanctuary were filled, thousands of other mourners gathered out on the street to listen to the service on loudspeakers; the overflow seating in the church's basement had to be closed owing to security concerns. During the funeral service, hundreds of police officers monitored the proceedings, including eight uniformed officers who guarded the casket and another two plainclothes officers who escorted Betty Shabazz. The Muslim service featured a stirring eulogy by the actor Ossie Davis in which he famously proclaimed Malcolm X "a Prince—our own black shining Prince—who didn't hesitate to die, because he loved us so." After the service concluded, Malcolm X's casket was placed in a "light and dark blue hearse" for a funeral motorcade, which included "seven limousines and about 20 other automobiles," to the "nonsectarian Ferndale cemetery in Hartsdale."[26]

At the graveside service, one final conflict arose when the cemetery's white gravediggers approached to bury the casket. Several of Malcolm X's followers stood in their way and declared, "No white man is going to bury Malcolm." James Hicks, a journalist from the *Amsterdam News,* interceded on behalf of the gravediggers. Joseph Hall from Unity Funeral Home reminded the protesters that the funeral procession was scheduled to depart the cemetery immediately and that they might be left behind. One of the men then replied, "We'll bury him first, man . . . We'll walk." The men then started to throw dirt on Malcolm X's casket with their bare hands. Hall and the gravediggers finally stepped aside to let the men pick up the shovels and fill the grave in silence. The defiant standoff at Malcolm X's gravesite seemed an appropriate final coda to the life of a man whose death foreshadowed a rising militancy in black America.[27]

During the week of high drama between Malcolm X's assassination and his funeral, Jimmie Lee Jackson, a young activist, died in Marion, Alabama, from complications from a gunshot wound. Jackson's death was the first official casualty of the Selma voting rights campaign. Described in the press as "an obscure Negro farm hand," Jackson could not have seemed more removed from the international celebrity that

Malcolm X had achieved in his lifetime. Nevertheless, the two men were connected through the closeness in time of their violent deaths and through the public attention given to their respective funerals. Just twenty-six years old at the time of his death, Jackson was known in Marion, Alabama, as a mature young man devoted to his family; his only claim to fame was having been appointed the youngest deacon at St. James Baptist Church. He worked as a farmer and supplemented his income as a pulpwood logger in the pinewoods of Perry County. As soon as he graduated from high school, Jackson left Alabama to move in with his uncle and cousin in Fort Wayne, Indiana, but he had to return just weeks later when his father died unexpectedly in a car accident. His noticeable maturity stemmed from his ability to assume the responsibilities of head of his family's household at such a young age.[28]

Jackson's involvement in the black voting rights campaign in Alabama began in 1962, when he participated in a black voter-registration drive organized by the Perry County Civic League, which was centered in Marion. At the time, only 150 of Perry County's 5,000 eligible black citizens were registered to vote. In December 1962, Jackson; his mother, Viola; and his eighty-year-old grandfather, Cager Lee, were among the 300 potential registrants who appeared at the Perry County courthouse with a federal court injunction demanding their right to register. When Perry County registrars defied the injunction, the Civic League organized a mass letter-writing campaign to the federal judge in Mobile, Alabama, in protest. In the prolonged court battles that ensued, Jimmie Lee Jackson emerged as a devoted local organizer—drafting letters to the court and faithfully attending local mass meetings and demonstrations. Although Jackson's mother, Viola, eventually won the right to register in July 1963, Jackson and his grandfather continued to be denied up through early 1965, when Martin Luther King, Jr., arrived in Selma to lead the SCLC voting rights campaign.[29]

When King traveled to Alabama on January 2, 1965, to officially launch the SCLC campaign, he announced to the press that the movement included not only Selma, which was located in Dallas County, but also all ten counties in Alabama's Black Belt region—including

Perry County, where Jimmie Lee Jackson and others in Marion had been leading the fight. At the time, the highly energized Marion movement met every Tuesday night for freedom rallies. By February, Marion activists began holding their meetings nightly at Zion Chapel Methodist Church to plan demonstrations and boycotts in response to increased resistance from Marion's white community.

On the evening of February 18, hundreds of local blacks—including Jimmie Lee Jackson, his mother, Viola, and his grandfather, Cager Lee—arrived at Zion Chapel to hear Reverend C. T. Vivian, one of King's closest advisers at the SCLC, speak. When the rally ended at around 9:30 P.M., hundreds of participants streamed out of the church onto the streets of Marion only to be confronted by local police and state troopers, who immediately ordered them to disperse. Just as the demonstrators were deciding how to respond, all the streetlights in the town square went out. The sudden darkness created an instant sense of chaos as troopers began assaulting demonstrators and reporters with nightsticks. In the melee that ensued, Jimmie Lee Jackson and his family ran into a local diner, Mack's Café, in search of safety but instead ran directly into the state troopers. In an effort to protect his mother, Viola, from being beaten, Jackson began tussling with several troopers, one of whom shot him in the stomach at close range. On February 26, 1965, eight days after the shooting, Jackson died from a massive infection at Good Samaritan Hospital in Selma, Alabama.[30]

The plans for Jackson's funeral quickly became the main news story out of the Selma campaign. To honor Jackson properly and accommodate all mourners, SCLC officials and local leaders in Marion held not one but two funeral services for the slain activist on March 3—one in Selma and one in Marion. Appropriately, Hampton D. Lee, owner of Lee's Funeral Home in Marion, directed both services. Lee was one of the most respected black leaders in Marion, a longstanding member of the NAACP, and one of Jimmie Lee Jackson's political mentors. The first service in Selma was held at Brown's Chapel AME Church, where Malcolm X had spoken before SNCC activists just one month earlier. To underscore the political significance of the event, SCLC organizers described the proceedings as a "freedom funeral" and emphasized that Jackson would be "buried in blue denim overalls, a blue denim jumper, white shirt and necktie—the uniform of the Southern Christian Leadership Conference headed by Dr. King." As the approximately 3,000 mourners arrived at Brown Chapel for the service and began singing "We Shall Overcome," Selma activists hung a large banner over the church entrance that boldly proclaimed, "Racism Killed Our Brother." In the sanctuary, Reverend Ralph Abernathy offered a stirring eulogy in which he praised Jackson as a martyr of the movement who "takes his rightful place among Abraham Lincoln, John Brown, Medgar Evers and Emmett Till."[31]

After the Selma service, Lee's Funeral Home transported Jackson's casket to Zion's Chapel Methodist Church in Marion for the second funeral, which featured a eulogy by Dr. Martin Luther King, Jr. King arrived at Jackson's funeral under a cloud of concern for his own personal safety. In the week that had passed between Jackson's shooting and his death, King had announced publicly that a "high official in the government" had notified him of "a plot taking place in Selma and Dallas County and Perry County to take your life." Although King had grown somewhat accustomed to death threats, the specificity of the Alabama plot—especially in the immediate wake of the assassination of Malcolm X—was clearly worrisome. Just days before Jackson's funeral, King flew to Los Angeles for a brief SCLC fundraising trip and, again, had to appear under heavy guard. When news surfaced about a serious bomb threat at one of King's Los Angeles speaking engagements, journalists questioned the civil rights leader about the security concerns and his reaction to the assassination of Malcolm X. After expressing his condolences about Malcolm X, King remarked, "One has to conquer the fear of death if he is going to do anything constructive in life and take a stand against evil. I am prepared to face anything that comes." Just days later, King echoed these sentiments in his eulogy of Jackson when he commented, "Jimmie Lee Jackson is speaking to us from the casket and he is saying to us that we must substitute courage for caution."[32]

Similar to Dave Dennis's eulogy at James Chaney's funeral, King's eulogy of Jackson both criticized those responsible for Jackson's death and instigated more action for voting rights. In a repeated refrain, King blamed Jackson's murder on "the brutality of every sheriff who practices lawlessness in the name of the law; the irresponsibility of every politician . . . who has fed his constituents the stale bread of hatred and the spoiled meat of racism; [and] the cowardice of every Negro who passively accepts the evils of segregation and stands on the sidelines in the struggle for justice." Most provocatively, King singled out "the timidity of a Federal Government that is willing to spend millions of dollars a day to defend freedom in Vietnam but cannot protect the rights of its citizens at home." King's remarks on Vietnam were his first public criticism of U.S. foreign policy and a clear effort to push President Lyndon Johnson to act more forcefully in support of voting rights legislation. In conclusion, King declared, "We are going to march the length of Alabama until we can vote . . . You [Jackson] died [so] that we can vote and we will vote." King's call to march echoed the sentiments that his colleague James Bevel had expressed at a mass meeting the day that Jimmie Lee Jackson died. At that meeting Bevel had declared, "The blood of Jackson will be on our hands if we don't march. Be prepared to walk to Montgomery. Be prepared to sleep on the highways." More than any other impetus, Jackson's death and funeral inspired the Selma-to-Montgomery March for voting rights.[33]

From Jimmie Lee Jackson's burial on March 3 to the conclusion of the Selma-to-Montgomery March on March 25, the Selma campaign continued to be plagued by violence and death, but organizers nonetheless persevered. On Sunday, March 7, just days after Jimmie Lee Jackson's funeral, the Selma activists made their first attempt to march to Montgomery. The demonstration, ultimately named "Bloody Sunday," ended quickly when Alabama state troopers attacked the marchers with nightsticks and tear gas as they tried to cross the Edmund Pettus Bridge in Selma. Just days later, Reverend James Reeb, a white Unitarian minister who had traveled from Boston to lend support to the voting rights campaign, was beaten to death outside a Selma café by a group of white supremacists. The national outrage over Reeb's death became the final impetus behind President Lyndon Johnson's decision to go before Congress on March 15 and announce his plans for a federal Voting Rights Act. For those who followed the Selma campaign closely, Johnson's speech before Congress, in which he appropriated the movement's rallying cry, "We Shall Overcome," was a historic moment, but it also contained a critical oversight: the president cited Reeb's murder rather than Jimmie Lee Jackson's death as the first casualty of the Selma campaign.[34]

When the Selma-to-Montgomery March finally commenced—after several court injunctions failed to stop it—on Sunday, March 21, few observers were aware that local black funeral directors from Alabama's central Black Belt region played a significant role in managing the logistics of the fifty-four-mile walk and its immediate aftermath. Randall Miller, owner of Miller's Funeral Home in Selma, provided his hearses for emergency ambulance service throughout the five-day march. Birmingham's A. G. Gaston offered the demonstrators his family-owned farm, located off U.S. Route 80 midway between Selma and Montgomery, as a safe haven for demonstrators to camp. Many other funeral directors, including Marion's Hampton D. Lee and Robert H. Miller, executive secretary of the NFDMA, also participated in the march. Most notably, a group of black funeral directors coordinated an "unusual demonstration" on the Montgomery State Capitol after Viola Liuzzo, a white supporter from Detroit, was shot to death by Ku Klux Klan members while she was driving back to Selma after the march ended on March 25. Selma activists decided to hold a brief memorial service for Liuzzo at the spot on U.S. Route 80 where she was slain and then lead a motorcade to the State Capitol in order, as the national press reported, "to stage a simulated burial of [the] ten civil rights workers who have died violently in Alabama during Governor Wallace's term." The "ten make-shift caskets" that represented the victims were made from the crates "used to pack regular caskets" and were provided and delivered "by Negro undertakers in the Black Belt counties in nearby rural areas."[35]

On the surface, the symbolic burial of the ten martyrs of the Alabama civil rights movement appeared to be a small footnote in the much larger story of the Selma Voting Rights campaign that finally ended in victory on August 6, when President Johnson signed the Voting Rights Act of 1965 into law. Yet when understood in the context of the history of the civil rights funeral, the simulated burial of Alabama's civil rights martyrs marked the end of a distinct period in which funerals—both actual and simulated—were effectively used as a type of political theater to dramatize the cause of the movement and energize its followers. In many ways, the passage of the Voting Rights Act in August 1965 marked the final major legislative achievement of the nonviolent civil rights movement. After the Selma campaign, the leaders of the nonviolent struggle confronted one of the more striking consequences of the death of Malcolm X: the rise in popularity of the Black Power movement and an increased willingness on the part of many disenfranchised blacks to embrace the more militant vision of the martyred black nationalist leader. In the two years after Selma, the increasingly fractured civil rights movement also confronted an epidemic of urban uprisings in cities from Watts to Detroit to Newark, a development which revealed that economic inequality coupled with police brutality were defining the struggle far more than the earlier battles to end racial segregation and secure the vote.

The final major funeral of the modern civil rights era did not take place until 1968, when Martin Luther King, Jr., was laid to rest after his assassination on the balcony of the Lorraine Motel in Memphis, Tennessee, on April 4. At the time of his death, King was in Memphis to support a local garbage collectors' strike, which reflected his deepening commitment to fighting for the rights of the poor through the SCLC's Poor People's Campaign. During his visit to Memphis, King's only security protection came from a local funeral home, R. S. Lewis and Sons, which provided him with a chauffeured limousine whenever he was in town. When the civil rights struggle became increasingly violent in the mid-1960s, civil rights leaders and activists often relied on local black funeral directors to provide inconspicuous transportation to and from demonstrations and rallies. On the evening of King's assassination, Solomon Jones, King's chauffeur from R. S. Lewis and Sons Funeral Home, was one of the last people to speak to King before he was shot and thus was an eyewitness to the murder. As soon as King was felled, Jones jumped into his limousine and tried to chase the shooter, but to no avail.[36]

When news of King's death spread across the country that night, riots broke out in more than sixty cities. For many, it seemed that the vision of a meaningful nonviolent movement had died with its leader.

Unlike earlier civil rights deaths, which seemed to inspire the movement to press ahead, King's assassination—and the subsequent assassination of Senator Robert Kennedy just months later—marked the symbolic end of the modern civil rights era.[37]

On April 9, 1968, approximately 150,000 mourners gathered in Atlanta for King's funeral, which—similar to Jimmie Lee Jackson's funeral in 1965—included two services: one smaller service in the morning at King's Ebenezer Baptist Church and a second, more public, gathering in the afternoon on the grounds of Morehouse College, King's alma mater. The first service at Ebenezer, which had limited seating, was relatively brief in accordance with King's wishes, which he had recently declared in a sermon at Ebenezer in February 1968. There King had remarked, "If any of you are around when I meet my day, I don't want a long funeral. And if you get somebody to deliver a eulogy, tell them not to talk too long." The service, officiated by the Reverend Ralph Abernathy, included selected scripture readings from the Old and New Testament and a selection of King's favorite hymns, including "When I Survey the Wondrous Cross" and "In Christ There Is No East or West." The service concluded with the recording of King's February sermon at Ebenezer in which he had requested that any eulogist at his funeral not dwell on his life's accomplishments but simply remember that "Martin Luther King Jr. tried to give his life serving others."[38]

After the Ebenezer service concluded, King's casket was placed on a mule-drawn farm wagon, a symbol of his commitment to the poor, and escorted five miles to the grounds of Morehouse College. Over 100,000 mourners participated in the funeral procession from Ebenezer to Morehouse College, a journey that Coretta Scott King described as King's "last great march" for justice and freedom. The memorial service included tributes from Rosa Parks, the Reverend Joseph E. Lowery, and Andrew Young, and a eulogy from King's lifelong mentor, Morehouse President Dr. Benjamin Mays. Mays focused his remarks on King's desire "to give dignity to the common man." The musical highlight of the service was Mahalia Jackson's performance of the famous gospel hymn "Precious Lord, Take My Hand." Immediately following the Morehouse service, King's remains were taken to a private burial ceremony. Appropriately, King was buried "among poor people" at Atlanta's South View cemetery, as he had requested. As the press reported, South View cemetery "was founded in 1886 by Negroes who resented having to use a back entrance to the city's downtown cemetery."[39]

The struggle for racial equality continued in the years after King's death, but the national campaign for African American civil rights would never again be as unified as it was under King's leadership. For African American funeral directors, King's funeral only reinforced the value of their calling to provide a proper homegoing service to console black America at a time of tremendous loss. They used the public response to the funerals of King and other activists to defend their business practices against funeral-reform advocates such as Jessica Mitford. By the late 1960s and early 1970s, as public interest in regulating the funeral industry grew, black funeral directors held fast to their defense of the African American "way of death" and also to their intention to keep the memory and dream of Martin Luther King, Jr., alive.[40]

In the immediate years after King's death, the National Funeral Directors and Morticians Association began to fight racial discrimination in the funeral industry more directly. The NFDMA won a major victory on this front in October 1970, when the National Funeral Directors Association finally passed a resolution to completely ban racial discrimination in its membership. The 1970 resolution declared that the NFDA would "revoke the charter" of any state or territorial association that limited its membership on the basis of "race, color, creed or religious belief." The wording of the resolution was a direct effort to close the loophole in the organization's 1963 resolution that opened its national membership to "non-white persons" but allowed state associations to set their own rules on the matter. In 1970, only one state delegation—from Texas—protested the measure and argued that the resolution was an encroachment of a "state's rights" to make the decision itself. The dissent from Texas was quelled quickly, however, when the NFDA's general counsel explained that the association operated "under a federal consent decree" and so its membership policies needed to comply with federal law if it was to maintain its status as a not-for-profit, tax-free organization.[41]

Not surprisingly, the NFDMA welcomed the news of the NFDA's more comprehensive nondiscriminatory membership policy. In a brief article about the change and the Texas delegation's resistance to it, Robert H. Miller commented that NFDA members should not "have anything to fear nationally by associating with Negro membership." He continued, "There are over one thousand towns and villages in the United States where Negroes have only white funeral directors to serve them, but there are very few towns where there are only Negro funeral directors that serve white."[42]

Miller's observation about the competitive advantage that white funeral directors held over black funeral directors was only one example of racial inequality in the funeral industry. By the early 1970s, the NFDMA also began a campaign to force funeral service suppliers including casket companies and hearse manufacturers to increase minority hiring. In a column about the problem, Miller proposed that "funeral directors of our association withhold their business from those companies who refuse to hire Blacks in responsible positions." The threat of these informal boycotts did produce change. The Batesville Company, the leading casket manufacturer in the country, began to hire its first black salespeople in direct response to boycott threats. In a related initiative, the NFDMA encouraged its members to patronize black-owned and -operated funeral suppliers such as Bondol Laboratories, Inc., "one of the largest manufacturers of embalming chemicals in the nation." As the *National Funeral Director and Embalmer* reported, Bondol was owned by the black entrepreneur Dr. Charles J. Latimer and epitomized "'Black Power' in business." Not surprisingly, the NFDMA's endorsement of Bondol emphasized that the company offered "employment for many Blacks in a field from which they might otherwise have been shut, thus providing them with both skill and purchasing power."[43]

Despite the persistence of racial disparities in the funeral industry into the early 1970s, one cause—the fight against government regulation—united the industry against a common foe: the Federal Trade

Commission (FTC). In 1973, the FTC's Bureau of Consumer Protection announced that it was launching an investigation of pricing policies at funeral homes in the District of Columbia. The FTC's Washington, D.C., investigation was only the first stage in what would become an intensive two-year study of funeral industry practices that included additional investigations, public hearings in other cities, and eventually a proposed "trade rule" for regulating the funeral business. The FTC's original proposal for a trade-regulation rule would have required funeral directors to make the costs of a funeral transparent through itemized price lists; to quote prices over the telephone; and to display openly their least expensive caskets. Moreover, it would have not only prohibited them from misrepresenting the legal requirements for embalming but also encouraged them to offer alternatives such as cremation. Much to the dismay of the funeral industry, when the FTC published its final public report on its findings in 1978, the agency acknowledged that its staff—not consumer complaints—had initiated the investigation.[44]

The real impetus behind the FTC's interest in monitoring and regulating funeral trade practices was the growing consumer advocacy movement led by Ralph Nader. Nader first sparked a national debate about consumers' rights in 1965, when he published *Unsafe at Any Speed*, a book that condemned the auto industry's complacency regarding vehicle safety. In 1970, Nader wrote a report criticizing the FTC for its failure "to carry out its mission as a watchdog in the marketplace" and protect "consumers from abusive practices." In response, the FTC began hiring staff members to defend the "beleaguered consumer." After some staff read Jessica Mitford's *American Way of Death* along with Ruth Harmer's *High Cost of Dying*, the agency decided to focus its energies on reforming the funeral industry.[45]

As with its criticism of Mitford's book in 1963, funeral industry leaders considered the FTC investigations on funeral pricing and its proposed "trade rule" not simply as an attack on their profession but as a menace to American democracy and values. An editorial in the *American Funeral Director* described the FTC hearings as "a Soviet-style set piece." When asked to testify at an FTC hearing in New York, John C. Curran, past president of the New York State Funeral Directors Association, called the FTC's proposed funeral trade rule "a threat to the American way of life" that tampered "with the soul of America." In a similar vein, an editorial in *Mortuary Management* claimed that "FTC staff are trying to force their agnostic, atheistic ways on God-fearing, traditional family-oriented America."[46]

If white funeral directors saw the FTC's investigation and proposed trade rule as a threat to the American way of life, black funeral directors saw it as a threat to the African American way of death. In 1973, ten years after the original publication of Mitford's book, Robert Miller published his first editorial arguing that black people had a unique allegiance to funeral rituals that could not be economized. His column was a response to an article published in Florida's *St. Petersburg Times* that criticized the funeral industry and advocated for quick, low-cost funerals. In his rebuttal, Miller wrote:

> One group of Americans, which I feel I can safely go on record in describing as being opposed to the churchless, empty burial proposals advocated in the *Times* article, are Black Folks. I am sure they want no part of them. Blacks definitely want to respect and dignify their dead out of deep religious conviction. And . . . they want no part of an extension in death of the disrespect and abuses heaped upon them during their lifetime.[47]

After the FTC officially launched its price investigations of the funeral industry, Miller deepened his argument about black people's distinct reverence for proper burial, which he saw as a cultural response to the racial discrimination and poverty many blacks experienced in life. In an article titled "Blacks Have Traditional Respect for the Dead," Miller explained:

> In years past . . . when there were no mobile hearses, no fancy chapels, or even money, Black people used to get together, pool their meager resources and saw to it that their loved ones got a decent and respectful burial. Even those Blacks who were victims of lynchings were able to enjoy the dignity of a respectful burial. For once the racists had laid low their victims, they had absolutely no interest in what happened to them

after death. As a result, the surviving Blacks were left unmolested to bury the victims reverently.

For Miller, African Americans had the right to a dignified, well-orchestrated funeral, a ritual that for black America was directly connected to America's long history of racism and discrimination. He viewed any attempt by the federal government to regulate the funeral industry to protect the consumer as a potential threat that might infringe on African Americans' ability to celebrate their cherished homegoing rituals.[48]

From 1974, when the FTC began its investigation of Washington, D.C., funeral homes, through 1976, when a large number of NFDMA members testified about their business practices at the FTC hearings, black funeral directors repeatedly returned to Miller's original arguments about the sacred role of the funeral in African American life. Time and again they stressed black people's preference for embalming over the more economical process of cremation. In defense of embalming, A. A. Rayner, the Chicago funeral director who had embalmed Emmett Till in 1955, testified that chemically preserving the corpse was a necessity in his business. In his statement to the FTC in a hearing on May 18, 1976, Rayner noted that embalming facilitated the African American tradition of waiting for mourners to travel to the funeral. As he colorfully described, "By the time Aunt Sisie and cousin Joe arrive from Jackson and Uncle Bill gets here from Atlanta, a minimum of five days has elapsed; we must embalm when 80 to 90 degree temperatures abound."[49]

Black funeral directors also took issue with the FTC's efforts to regulate and set a standard price for funerals. The problem was that the FTC's proposed regulation did not take into account the impact of economic inequality on the business practices of black funeral homes. Leon Harrison, NFDMA member and owner of Harrison and Ross Funeral Home in Los Angeles, explained to FTC commissioners:

It is common knowledge that we [black funeral directors] are . . . at the bottom of the economic pole, as are the people we serve. The National average spent per death with Funeral Homes has been set at $1,128.32.

The average for Black Funeral Homes would be $890.00 by our estimate
... [As for itemization,] I do not think any member of our association
fails to give customers full details of costs, for we are always aware that
our people have limited means to pay such costs and that to oversell
would result in a loss for the operator.[50]

Throughout the FTC ordeal, African American funeral directors
felt both that they were unfairly targeted in the commission's price investigations and that they were too often ignored when the commission sought industry experts to testify at its hearings. When the FTC
first began its price investigation of funeral homes in Washington,
D.C., in 1973, the NFDMA took issue with the commission's choice of
the District of Columbia since the majority of funeral homes there
were owned by African Americans. When the findings of the Washington, D.C., investigation led to a proposed city ordinance to regulate
the charging practices of funeral homes in the District of Columbia,
Robert Miller and the NFDMA lobbied city officials heavily and defeated the measure. By 1975, when the FTC hearings first began, Robert Miller wrote an editorial in which he criticized the FTC for ig-
noring the NFDMA when it initially sought feedback from industry
leaders about improving funeral service. He continued:

We weren't even invited to express our views in connection with the
formulation of price guidelines. Naturally, we feel we should have been
invited, since we are an established, bona fide, functioning national organization representing Black funeral directors across the land, who in
turn, represent a large segment of the funeral service profession.

In 1976, the FTC responded to these complaints by inviting a larger
number of NFDMA members to testify at its regional hearings. Unfortunately, even these efforts to rectify any racial bias in the hearings
were flawed. In early 1977, several officials of the NFDMA traveled to
Washington, D.C., to testify before the U.S. Senate Judiciary Committee regarding their claim that the FTC had discriminated against black
funeral directors during the agency's hearings on its proposed trade
regulation. In their testimony, the NFDMA officers claimed that "the
FTC doled out thousands of dollars to various white organizations for

appearances at its hearings, but without allocations to the NFD&MA, as required by FTC law. The FTC did not inform the NFD&MA that the funds were available."[51]

In the end, the FTC investigation of the funeral industry in the 1970s illustrated the paradoxical relationship that black funeral directors had to the federal government. Throughout their participation in the civil rights movement in the 1960s, black funeral directors had seen the federal government as an ally with the power to end racial segregation and promote racial equality through legislation such as the Civil Rights Act of 1964 and the Voting Rights Act of 1965. By the 1970s, however, black funeral directors found themselves at war with the federal government and its efforts to protect the consumer from corruption in the funeral industry. These shifts revealed that the conflicts inherent in the relationship between racial freedom and free enterprise had yet to be resolved.

On January 14, 1979, Robert H. Miller, executive secretary of the NFDMA, died at the age of eighty-two. Miller, a man who had dedicated his life to the black funeral industry, passed away just a few steps from his daughter's Chicago home on Martin Luther King, Jr., Drive when he collapsed in the snow after suffering a heart attack. When he died, Miller was on his way to speak on a local black radio station to solicit funds to build a permanent memorial in front of Brown Chapel AME Church in Selma, Alabama, to commemorate the Selma-to-Montgomery March and to honor the lives of Martin Luther King, Jr., Jimmie Lee Jackson, James Reeb, and Viola Liuzzo.

The memorial to King and the Selma campaign was Miller's idea, which he first presented to the NFDMA board of directors in April 1978, exactly ten years after King's death. In his original proposal, Miller argued that the NFDMA should be the memorial's lead sponsor by contributing the first $5,000 of the $30,000 needed to complete the monument. Miller's argument to justify the sponsorship was simple: "We Black funeral directors have always been close to the people and to the civil rights movement. We should, therefore, be proud to be able to play a leading role in the shaping of a bit of our history . . . Our members have been a part of the movement since the beginning." Miller's decision to spearhead the Selma Memorial campaign in the last year of his life was logical given that his commitment to the civil rights movement was as deep as his devotion to the black funeral industry. Throughout his thirty-year tenure as executive secretary of the NFDMA, Miller had always personally supported the goals of the national civil rights campaign, but he had also used his role as a leader in the NFDMA to galvanize the organization's membership to fight for the cause.[52]

On August 5, 1979, the NFDMA convened its forty-second annual convention in Atlanta, Georgia, the first gathering of the organization without the presence of Miller. Appropriately, then, the grand finale of the week's activities involved a two-day bus trip to Selma, Alabama, to dedicate the organization's Selma Memorial in front of Brown Chapel and to complete Miller's final project. The two-day trip—scheduled to begin on Friday, August 10—included a tour of the Tuskegee Institute, a prayer breakfast at King's Dexter Avenue Baptist Church in Montgomery, and finally the dedication ceremony in Selma.

These well-laid plans were threatened, however, when news arrived at the convention that the Alabama Ku Klux Klan had announced a plan to hold its own Selma-to-Montgomery March for "White Power" on Thursday, August 9. When KKK Imperial Wizard Bill Richardson made his prediction that 2,000 people would join the white supremacist demonstration, NFDMA members back in Atlanta began to reconsider their plans to dedicate their memorial out of concern for their safety. News reports that the Klan planned to be armed with high-powered weapons made "black morticians [fear] a confrontation [with the Klan] when they passed the marchers on their way to Selma." When only 60 Klan supporters showed up for the first 14-mile leg of the march, two church leaders from Brown Chapel flew on a private plane to Atlanta to persuade the NFDMA members to continue with their planned dedication of the Selma Memorial, which was also expected to draw 2,000 participants.[53]

By Saturday, August 10, the NFDMA decided to proceed with its planned dedication, though some of the excitement about the ceremony had been diffused by the tensions surrounding the Klan march. The memorial included a detailed description of the historic signifi-cance of the Selma-to-Montgomery March and specifically noted that in the years since the passage of the Voting Rights Act of 1965, "black voters increased from 1,463,000 to 3,845,000 and black elected officials from 72 to 2,368 in the states affected." The fact that the dedication of the NFDMA Selma Memorial was almost cancelled as a result of a Ku Klux Klan march for "White Power" stood as a testament to how tense race relations in Alabama still were fourteen years after the Selma cam-paign had ended. Given the circumstances, the need to remember the victories and victims of the civil rights movement seemed all the more necessary. In the end, black funeral directors were among the first in-dividuals to recognize the importance of memorializing the move-ment as a reminder that the fight for racial equality was not over.[54]

Just two years later, a similar opportunity arose on September 11, 1981, when approximately 900 mourners gathered at the Community Church of New York for the funeral of Roy Wilkins, one of the most influential leaders of the modern civil rights movement, who had died at the age of eighty. Wilkins first came into national prominence when he was appointed executive secretary of the NAACP in 1955, just as the civil rights movement first began to capture the attention of the American public through the Emmett Till case and the Montgom-ery Bus Boycott. Throughout his twenty-two-year tenure as executive secretary of the NAACP, Wilkins maintained a politically moderate approach to civil rights advocacy that emphasized legal-action over direct-action protest. He was admired as a skilled power broker whose political clout on Capitol Hill and at the White House facilitated the passage of the Civil Rights Act of 1964, the Voting Rights Act of 1965, and the Fair Housing Act of 1968.

Wilkins's funeral service reflected his stature as a civil rights leader who had earned deep respect over his lifetime. Many political and civil rights luminaries attended, including Vice President George Bush, Su-preme Court Justice Thurgood Marshall, Senator Edward Kennedy, Bayard Rustin, the Reverend Jesse Jackson, Jr., and Benjamin Hooks, who offered one of the eulogies. Hooks noted that Wilkins possessed "a personal charm and magnanimous grace that were powerful nonviolent weapons in the pursuit of justice." Press coverage of the funeral made special note of the ecumenical service, which was officiated by "two Protestant bishops and a minister, a rabbi and a Roman Catholic cardinal [and] the Rev. Donald S. Harrington, pastor of the Unitarian-Universalist Church." After the service concluded, the renowned soprano Leontyne Price led mourners who had gathered outside the church in a rendition of "We Shall Overcome" as pallbearers receded with Wilkins's casket, which was then taken for burial in a private ceremony at Pinelawn Cemetery in Farmingdale, Long Island.[55]

Wilkins's funeral, which at first appeared a flawless tribute to a civil rights icon, actually sparked an unexpected protest. As the black press reported, throughout the service, a small group of "independent Black morticians," dressed in black and wearing purple armbands as symbols of protest, walked a picket line to object that "the funeral services of Roy Wilkins [were] being held in a White church, with a White undertaker in charge." The leader of the group, Lonnie A. Evans, Jr., told reporters that his group was "not here to demean Mr. Wilkins . . . [as] he was one of the greatest heroes Black people could ever have." Rather, Evans and the other protesters questioned why Wilkins's service was not held in one of the historic black churches in Harlem, such as Abyssinian Baptist Church. Most important, Evans noted, "we feel that Wilkins, in his fight for our civil rights, belongs to the Black community and his body should have been entrusted to Black undertakers." To emphasize their indignation, Evans and the other demonstrators told the press that "they [planned] to file a formal protest to the NAACP" about the funeral arrangements.[56]

The deep irony that the NAACP would receive a formal complaint about the funeral of its former executive secretary revealed the long and complex history of African American funeral directing and its relationship to the civil rights movement. Although the participants of the 1981 Wilkins protest were unaware of it at the time, their demonstration reenacted a similar blockade of a funeral procession staged by "race chauffeurs" in Jacksonville, Florida, in 1918. In both incidents, the demonstrators were attempting to express their outrage that a prominent black family would hire a white funeral director when black funeral directors were available to serve them. The key difference between the two events, of course, was the sixty-three years that had passed between them. In the decades between 1918 and 1981, American society had been completely transformed by the modern civil rights movement and leaders like Roy Wilkins and Martin Luther King, Jr. When the race chauffeurs staged their blockade in 1918, they could never have envisioned a world without Jim Crow racial segregation. At Wilkins's funeral in 1981, the protesters lived in a country where racial integration and civil rights were protected by law.

Ideally, then, the Wilkins family's decision to hire a white funeral firm and hold their service at a Unitarian-Universalist Church could be interpreted as a victory of the civil rights movement. Viewed from this perspective, Wilkins's funeral proved that American death practices had finally moved beyond race. Clearly, however, the black funeral directors marching outside the church did not see it that way. For them, "race patronage" still mattered and African American homegoing traditions demanded loyalty to the black funeral director. In the end, Roy Wilkins's funeral symbolized both how much the modern civil rights movement had achieved as well as how deeply entrenched the racial politics of death and funerals remained in America.

In the 1980s and 1990s, the racial politics of the funeral industry took a new turn when black funeral directors had to confront the rise of white-owned corporate conglomerates in the funeral industry such as Service Corporation International (SCI), the Loewen Group, and Stewart Enterprises, which were described by some as "the Wal-Mart[s] of the funeral home and cemetery business." These multinational corporations, which sought to buy out locally owned funeral homes in an effort to control the national funeral market, were particularly drawn to African American businesses, whose clientele were known to prefer high-end funerals as opposed to lower-cost cremations. A 1997 *Wall Street Journal* report titled "Death Watch? Black Funeral Homes Fear a Gloomy Future as Big Chains Move In" featured remarks from Hugh Winstead, Jr., owner of G. C. Williams Funeral Home in Louisville, Kentucky, who was fighting to keep his clientele as

SCI and the Loewen Group launched aggressive advertising campaigns for low-cost funerals in his neighborhood. Winstead expressed concern that the conglomerates were targeting Louisville's black neighborhoods and noted that "overnight, they're trying to take away what it's taken us generations to do." The report also included remarks from O'Neil D. Swanson, Sr., a prominent funeral director in Detroit, Michigan. In commenting on the conglomerate threat, Swanson remarked, "It actually frightens me. Before integration, every major city had a black hotel that we could be proud of. And all of those businesses were just killed off by chains. That just might happen to us."[57]

For many black funeral directors in the mid-1990s, the rise of funeral corporations offered the stark choice of either being owned by a white-owned conglomerate or being forced out of business. Some, fearful about survival, joined up. Others, unwilling to hand over family businesses they had cherished for generations, did not. The threat of the multinational conglomerates also developed an intraracial dynamic when it was announced in 1996 that the National Baptist Convention, the nation's largest organization of African American churches, had signed an exclusive sales and marketing contract with the Loewen Group to sell the company's cemetery products, including graves, vaults, and tombstones, directly to congregants in exchange for a sales commission for the affiliated churches. The deal outraged African American funeral directors across the country who saw it as a clear threat to their market share as well as their long-established relationship with local black churches. When the NFDMA publicly voiced its criticism of the deal, the National Baptist Convention renegotiated the terms of the contract to ensure that the Loewen Group could not use the arrangement to sell its funeral services in addition to cemetery products.[58]

At the beginning of the twenty-first century, the funeral conglomerates became the victims of their own business failings, falling stock prices, and legal problems; as a result, they posed much less of a threat to local funeral homes. African American funeral directors' ability to weather the storm of the multinational conglomerates is yet another testament to the strength of the institution of the funeral home in African American life. As the history of black funeral directing has shown, the funeral home, which continues to be a fixture in the black community, will always be something more than simply a place to honor the dead. Today, African American funeral directors continue to serve the living while burying the dead; in so doing, they continue to remind us of the role that death and funerals have always played in the long quest for freedom.[59]

Epilogue

She Has Gone Home

Rosa Parks, the iconic mother of the modern civil rights movement, died at her home in Detroit, Michigan, on October 24, 2005, at the age of ninety-two. Parks's death came almost exactly fifty years after she was arrested on December 1, 1955, for refusing to give up her seat on a segregated bus in Montgomery, Alabama. Although many accounts of her legendary arrest emphasize physical exhaustion as a contributing factor to her act of defiance, Parks took pains throughout her life to refute that claim. As she wrote in her autobiography, "Some people think I kept my seat because I'd had a hard day, but that is not true. I was just tired of giving in." For many, the power of Parks's act of civil disobedience was rooted in its simplicity and in her humble circumstances. Parks, who was working as a department store seamstress at the time of her arrest, demonstrated that revolutions begin when ordinary people decide to take a stand. As civil rights activists have often declared, when Rosa Parks sat down, "the world turned around."[1]

Whereas Parks's life was defined by her unassuming courage, her death was characterized by extraordinary honors usually reserved for heads of state. In the ten days that elapsed between her death on October 24 and her burial in Detroit on November 2, 2005, Parks was remembered at three separate funeral services, in Montgomery, Alabama; Washington, D.C.; and Detroit, Michigan. The first service, on October 30, was held at St. Paul African Methodist Episcopal (AME) Church in Montgomery and commemorated her early life in the city that inspired her activism. Civil rights luminaries including the Reverends Jesse Jackson, Al Sharpton, and Joseph E. Lowery attended. Condoleezza Rice, also a native of Alabama, spoke at the memorial service and publicly credited Parks with paving the way for her own achievement as the first African American woman to serve as secretary of state.

Immediately following the Montgomery service, Parks's body was flown to Washington, D.C., where, according to a congressional resolution, it was to lie in state in the Capitol Rotunda. Parks was the first woman and only the second African American in the nation's history to receive this honor. An estimated 40,000 people, including President George W. Bush and First Lady Laura Bush, came to the Capitol Rotunda to pay their respects. At 1:00 P.M. on October 31, approximately 2,500 mourners—including Defense Secretary Donald Rumsfeld, Homeland Security Secretary Michael Chertoff, Labor Secretary Elaine L. Chao, Senate Majority Leader Bill Frist, and Senate Minority Leader Harry M. Reid—crowded into Washington, D.C.'s, Metropolitan AME Church for Parks's second funeral service, which included tributes from NAACP Chairman Julian Bond, Oprah Winfrey, and actress Cicely Tyson.[2]

Parks's remains were finally flown back to Detroit for burial at 9:00 P.M. on Monday, October 31, under the escort of a United States military honor guard. When the airplane arrived at Detroit Metropolitan Airport, O'Neil Swanson, Jr., owner of Swanson's Funeral Home, arranged to have two white hearses drive out onto the tarmac: one to carry Parks's casket and the other to hold the floral arrangements from the president, the House of Representatives, and the Senate. As Swanson later recalled, "We formed a cortege right there at the airport. There were 20 cars. It was amazing. Some were law enforcement. We had police escort everywhere we went." Swanson then directed the cortege to the Charles H. Wright Museum of African American History in downtown Detroit. After briefly touching up the body, Swanson put Parks's remains on display at the museum for a final viewing, which lasted through Wednesday morning and drew more than 75,000 visitors. On the morning of November 2, Swanson and his staff arrived at the museum in a vintage 1940 white LaSalle hearse to transport Parks's casket to the Greater Grace Temple of the Apostolic Faith Church, where her final funeral was scheduled to begin at noon.[3]

Parks's Detroit funeral proved to be the most elaborate, well attended, and lengthy of the three services held in her honor. Four thousand mourners gathered in the enormous sanctuary of Greater Grace Temple to participate in the event. Originally scheduled for three hours, the funeral service lasted for more than seven hours as thirty-seven politicians and civil rights dignitaries rose to eulogize the modest woman who had ignited the modern civil rights movement. Speakers included former president Bill Clinton; Senator Hillary Rodham Clinton; Senator John Kerry; the Reverend Bernice King, daughter of Martin Luther King, Jr.; and U.S. Representative John Conyers, for whom Parks had worked for more than twenty years. Mezzo-soprano Brenda Jackson's rendition of "The Lord's Prayer" and Aretha Franklin's performances of "The Impossible Dream" and "I'll Fly Away" were among the many musical tributes offered. As one attendee, Bishop T. D. Jakes, later remarked, "That funeral was so long that I can hardly remember it!"[4]

After the funeral service ended, Parks's casket, which was draped with an American flag, was placed in an antique, horse-drawn hearse and driven to the Woodlawn cemetery to be entombed in the soon-to-be renamed Rosa L. Parks Freedom Chapel. Just before the final burial, doves were released and Parks, who was not a veteran, received military honors, including a twenty-one-gun salute, the playing of "Taps," and the presentation of the American flag. Reflecting on the ten days of honors, O'Neil Swanson, Jr., commented, "I think this is probably the largest funeral service in U.S. history. Not even John F. Kennedy or Martin Luther King Jr. or Ronald Reagan went to three different cities. The atmosphere was very, very charged. As we brought the remains to the church, we were astounded to see the massive crowds, chanting, 'Rosa, Rosa, Rosa.'"[5]

Just three months after Rosa Parks's death and her three illustrious funerals, Coretta Scott King, the widow of Martin Luther King, Jr., died on January 30, 2006, at the age of seventy-eight. Although not quite as complicated geographically as Parks's final farewell, Scott King's homegoing celebration, which lasted several days, was magisterial in its own right and reflected the national stature she had achieved in her lifetime as one of the most highly respected matriarchs of the modern civil rights movement. Beginning on Saturday, February 4,

Scott King became the first woman and the first African American to lie in state at the Georgia State Capitol, where Georgia Governor Sonny Perdue and Atlanta Mayor Shirley Franklin hosted a special ceremony to commemorate her life. Then, on Monday, February 6, Scott King lay in repose at Atlanta's Ebenezer Baptist Church, which held its own memorial concert to celebrate Scott King's life. Between the first viewing of the casket at the Georgia State Capitol and the second viewing at Ebenezer Baptist Church, more than 150,000 people paid their respects to Scott King. Finally, at noon on Tuesday, February 7, her funeral was held at New Birth Missionary Baptist Church, a large church just outside Atlanta with seating for 10,000 mourners.

As with Rosa Parks's funeral in Detroit, Scott King's funeral drew an impressive array of politicians, dignitaries, and luminaries, including "four presidents, three governors, three planeloads of Congress members, celebrities, gospel stars and leading figures of the civil rights movement." The six-hour service, televised live on cable news channels, was a mass-media spectacle that combined sacred religious ritual with a no-holds-barred political rally punctuated with interludes of "humor, interpretive dance, gospel and classical music, shouting and testifying." As former president George H. W. Bush commented, "I come from a rather conservative Episcopal parish, and I haven't seen anything like this in my life."[6]

The funerals of Rosa Parks and Coretta Scott King were remarkable on a number of levels. Most immediately, they firmly established that the African American homegoing tradition—with all its resplendent glory—was alive and well in the twenty-first century. More strikingly, these services illustrated that the spirit of the modern civil rights movement, which symbolically died in April 1968 after the assassination of Martin Luther King, Jr., could be brought back to life through the deaths of these two icons of the struggle. The timing of the deaths of Parks and Scott King, which both occurred just months after the devastation of Hurricane Katrina in August 2005, heightened the sense of political urgency that was evident at the funerals. For African Americans, who were disproportionately affected by Katrina's wrath, the federal government's gross mishandling of the natural disaster— from FEMA's delayed and incompetent response to President Bush's noticeable detachment—was a defining moment in twenty-first-century race relations in America. Moreover, of all the searing images of despair and hopelessness that Katrina produced, none were more devastating to African Americans than those depicting the abandoned corpses of Katrina victims who were left on the streets of New Orleans without proper burial. Given these circumstances, it is not surprising that the most notable feature of both Parks's and Scott King's funerals—beyond their grandeur—was their politically charged and prophetic tone.

Among the many politicians invited to offer a eulogy at Rosa Parks's final funeral service in Detroit was the junior senator from Illinois, Barack Obama. Although Obama's brief remarks did not contain political commentary, his later reflections on Parks's funeral did. In his book *The Audacity of Hope,* Obama recalled:

> Indeed, the magnificent church, the multitude of black elected officials, the evident prosperity of so many of those in attendance, and my own presence onstage as a United States senator—all of it could be traced to that December day in 1955 when, with quiet determination and unruffled dignity, Mrs. Parks had refused to surrender her seat on a bus . . . And yet, as I sat and listened to the former President and the procession of speakers that followed, my mind kept wandering back to the scenes of devastation that had dominated the news just two months earlier, when Hurricane Katrina struck the Gulf Coast and New Orleans was submerged.

In the weeks after Katrina hit, Obama used his position as a U.S. senator to secure relief funds and to push through Congress proposed legislation to assist the victims. Also, in a racially conciliatory move, Obama made appearances on the Sunday morning talk shows to refute the idea, as he later recalled, "that the [Bush] Administration had acted slowly because Katrina's victims were black—'the incompetence was color-blind,' I said—but insisting that the Administration's inadequate planning showed a degree of remove from and indifference toward, the problems of inner-city poverty that needed to be addressed." In the end, Obama described Parks's funeral as an unsettling experience that left him "entombed in nostalgia" and wondering "what Rosa Parks would make of all this—whether [commemorative] stamps or statues could summon her spirit, or whether honoring her memory demanded something more."[7]

If Obama felt that honoring the memory of individuals like Parks "demanded something more" politically, then he need look no further than Coretta Scott King's funeral, which was much more politically charged than Parks's services. The stage was set for high drama when President George W. Bush and First Lady Laura Bush decided to attend Scott King's funeral. Some commentators believed that President Bush made a special effort to attend the funeral in an attempt to bolster his battered image with African Americans who were bitter about his administration's handling of Katrina. Any hopes of repairing his relationship with African Americans were quickly dashed, however, when other speakers, including former president Jimmy Carter and the Reverend Joseph E. Lowery, used their eulogies as an opportunity to publicly criticize President Bush's domestic and foreign policies. In his tribute to Scott King, Carter reminded listeners, "We only have to recall the color of the faces of those in Louisiana, Alabama and Mississippi, those who were most devastated by Katrina, to know that there are not yet equal opportunities for all Americans."[8]

Nor did the Reverend Joseph E. Lowery, a founding member of King's Southern Christian Leadership Conference, let his close proximity to the president deter him from directly criticizing the Bush administration throughout his eulogy. Lowery began his remarks with a question, "Will words become deeds that meet needs?" which was a direct challenge to all those who came to honor Scott King—including the president—to do more than simply praise her legacy. Lowery then reminded listeners that Coretta Scott King had opposed the war in Iraq. Using a boisterous, crowd-pleasing rhyme, Lowery continued, "She deplored the terror inflicted by our smart bombs on missions way afar. We know now there were no weapons of mass destruction over there. But Coretta knew, and we knew, that there are weapons of misdirection right down here. Millions without health insurance. Poverty abounds. For war, billions more, but no more for the poor." To some conservative commentators, Lowery's pointed criticism of the

Bush administration—delivered while Reverend Lowery stood directly in front of the president—was out of line, but for those who understood the history of the civil rights movement, his verbal tirade was part of a longstanding tradition of "speaking truth to power."[9]

Although he was not invited to speak at Coretta Scott King's funeral, Senator Barack Obama attended the service, which he later admitted to one of his aides was "pretty intimidating." Obama's presence at the funerals of both Rosa Parks and Coretta Scott King was prophetic and served as a reminder that in African American history, funerals were often the place where the seeds of political freedom were sown. Reverend Bernice King addressed this fact in her eulogy of her mother when she commented on a small controversy that had arisen concerning the location of the funeral. Some people felt strongly that the service should have been held in the historic, though much smaller, Ebenezer Baptist Church, where Martin Luther King, Jr., his father, and his maternal grandmother had all been preachers. Bernice King told the 10,000 people gathered at New Birth Missionary Baptist Church, where she was an Elder, that God, who wanted "new birth," divinely chose the location of her mother's funeral. She continued, "I said, 'God, why here?' He said, 'It's time for the world to be born again.' . . . God is not looking for Martin Luther King or Coretta Scott King. The old has passed away; there is a new order emerging." A hint of this new order came during the funeral service, when Ethel Kennedy, the widow of Robert Kennedy, leaned over to Obama and whispered, "The torch is being passed to you." Caught off guard by the remark, Obama later confessed, "A chill went up my spine."[10]

If the age of Obama was born at the funeral of Coretta Scott King, then it was just one more striking example of how death and funerals have always been an essential and transformative part of African Americans' long struggle for freedom. In many ways the shadow of death was a constant presence throughout Obama's historic campaign to become the first African American president of the United States. As the press regularly noted, Obama received Secret Service protection earlier than any other previous presidential candidate owing to the high number of death threats he received during his quest for the White House. Most poignantly, just one day before he was elected, Obama's beloved maternal grandmother, Madelyn Dunham, died. Obama announced the passing of Dunham, whom he affectionately called "Toot," at a final campaign rally in Charlotte, North Carolina, on Monday, November 3. Standing before a crowd of 25,000, Obama choked up as he announced his grandmother's death with a simple declarative statement, "She has gone home." His choice of words powerfully evoked the African American concept of death as a homegoing, an event that was celebrated so dramatically at the funerals of Rosa Parks and Coretta Scott King. When Barack Obama was finally sworn into office as president of the United States on January 20, 2009, he invited the Reverend Joseph E. Lowery to offer the benediction at the inauguration ceremony. Lowery was given this honor as an acknowledgment not only of the legacy of his generation's courage in the civil rights struggle in the 1960s but also for his continued political leadership in the twenty-first century, which was so powerfully evident in his incisive eulogy at Coretta Scott King's funeral.[11]

Viewing Barack Obama's successful presidential campaign in the context of the funerals of Rosa Parks and Coretta Scott King offers a compelling narrative of the linear progression of the modern civil rights struggle. In this story, Obama's victory is, as Bernice King claimed, a "new birth" that could come into being only when the old order—symbolized by figureheads like Parks and Scott King—had died away. Much of the historic power of Obama's election to the presidency seemed drawn from a belief that it did indeed mark the beginning of a new era in American history, which may not completely transcend race, but certainly changed the way race influences the political process. The actual twists and turns of Obama's campaign, however, revealed that even this triumphant narrative is perhaps too simplistic and overly optimistic. For many, the fact that the most significant race-related crisis Obama faced during his campaign revolved around his relationship to the Reverend Jeremiah Wright, his own minister and spiritual mentor at Trinity United Church of Christ in Chicago, illustrated that the intraracial tensions of American politics were sometimes as challenging as any interracial issues. Moreover, if President Obama's election does signal that America has entered a new age with regard to race, it is still not entirely clear what this means for the day-to-day realities of life *and* death for many African Americans.[12]

Throughout African American history, the funeral home—a place to honor death—has also acted as a bellwether for the most pressing challenges facing African Americans in life. In March 2008, the same month that Barack Obama made his highly regarded speech on race on the campaign trail in Philadelphia, the *Wall Street Journal* published a disturbing article titled "Deadly Business: Violence Roils Black Funeral Parlors." The report describes a rise in violence at African American funeral homes that correlates with a rise in the African American homicide rate. According to statistics from the Federal Bureau of Investigation, murders among African Americans—often the result of black-on-black violence—rose 11 percent, from 6,680 to 7,421, between 2004 and 2006. Most troubling, this rise occurred "when the rate for other groups has been flat or falling." Although experts including criminologists, sociologists, and law enforcement officials cannot pinpoint a specific cause for the increase, they note that many of the killings are drug- or gang-related and illustrate the difficult transition many ex-felons face when attempting to reenter society. The violence has driven many African American funeral directors to spend increasing time, energy, and funds trying to protect their business establishments from literally getting caught in the crossfire. Some of these measures, including "concealed-weapons, pre-funeral intelligence briefings, [security] cameras, panic buttons and armed security," have become "as much a part of [African American funeral] services as the eulogy."[13]

Although not all black funeral homes directly confront the problem of rising violence at services, the trend has become pronounced enough to be a pressing topic of discussion at the professional level, especially since increased security measures are a significant business expense. When the National Funeral Directors and Morticians Association held its annual convention in Philadelphia in 2007, organizers devoted one panel to the topic of violence at funeral homes. Given that many of the shootings at funeral establishments are gang-related, some experienced undertakers have recommended that any funeral service that involves a homicide case and may present "the possibility of 'drama'" not be publicized. But even these precautions cannot prevent a tragedy.[14]

On May 21, 2006, mourners gathered at A. D. Porter and Sons Funeral Home in Louisville, Kentucky, for a wake honoring Frank Sherley, Jr., who died of natural causes at the age of seventy. During the viewing, two gunmen arrived in the funeral home parking lot and opened fire in what local officials later determined to be a completely random attack. One person was killed and four others were wounded. As the Louisville *Courier-Journal* reported, the shooting at A. D. Porter and Sons appeared to be part of a larger trend in the rise of homicides in the city, which had already witnessed twenty other murders that year—four of which occurred just one week before the funeral home attack. The fact that this shooting took place on the grounds of a black funeral home, which has long represented sacred public space, hit the local community particularly hard. When the attack began, John Curd, an employee at A. D. Porter and Sons, called 911 and remembered thinking, "This isn't supposed to be happening at a funeral home."[15]

Although it is easy to sympathize with Curd's horror and his sentiment that a random shooting isn't "supposed to be happening at a funeral home," perhaps the most profound lesson to take away from the history of African American funeral directing is that almost *anything* can happen at a black funeral home. From the earliest slave funerals in the New World and into the antebellum period, the hush harbors served as the first "funeral home" for African Americans. In these wooded, secluded spots, usually under the cover of night, African Americans not only buried their dead with dignity but sometimes conspired to resist their enslavement. By the end of the nineteenth century and into the beginning of the twentieth century, the hush harbors were replaced by actual funeral parlors, which signaled the rise of the modern funeral industry.

This development occurred parallel to the rise of Jim Crow segregation, and African American funeral directors were quick to use their funeral homes in imaginative ways. Some offered them as elegant social gathering places to lessen the stinging indignities of Jim Crow laws that denied their communities access to white establishments. By the Prohibition era, others used their funeral homes as fronts for illegal gambling houses or speakeasies and then funneled the proceeds into their communities or used them to build political power. In 1946, Dan Young offered his funeral home not only as a safe place for local blacks in Monroe, Georgia, to process their grief over the victims of the Moore's Ford lynching, but also as a venue to organize a campaign for black voting rights. By the 1950s and early 1960s, black funeral directors used their funeral establishments and hearses to hide and protect activists under attack and facilitate community movements from behind the scenes. Most poignantly, they directed the funerals of the martyrs of the movement, events that often became a form of protest in their own right and, in some instances, the site of violent conflict. No event illustrated this phenomenon better than the funeral of Malcolm X in 1965. When Harlem's Unity Funeral Home opened its doors for Malcolm X's viewing, some people came bearing their grief. Others came bearing guns. Throughout its history, therefore, the black funeral home has stood as both a refuge for the black community *and* the stage upon which its most challenging problems—from lynching to black-on-black violence—have played out.

The history of A. D. Porter and Sons Funeral Home, site of the May 2006 shooting and one of the oldest black funeral homes in Louisville, exemplifies the multidimensional role of the funeral home in African American life. When A. D. Porter first opened his funeral business in 1907, he quickly established himself as a community leader and "race man" who was willing to fight the injustices of Jim Crow legislation. By the end of his first decade in business, Porter had become Louisville's leading black undertaker and one of its most respected race leaders. In 1921, he joined with a cadre of other young, assertive black leaders in Louisville to found the Lincoln Independent Party (LIP), which sought to disrupt the Republican party's dominance over city politics and black voters. The founders of the LIP felt that the Republican party had fostered political corruption and crime in the city's black community and, despite the loyalty of black voters, had done little to reward the community with any political patronage. Nor did the

LIP members see any hope in the Democratic party, which was led by white supremacists intent on disenfranchising black voters entirely. As A. D. Porter explained at one of the first LIP meetings, "This condition of political slavery has placed us in the very unenviable position of being owned by the Republicans and hated by the Democrats."[16]

When A. D. Porter announced his candidacy for mayor of Louisville on the LIP ticket for the November 1921 election, he quickly came under attack—particularly from local black leaders who directly benefited from the Republican party's control of city politics. His main adversary was Harvey Burns, a rival black funeral director and leader of the city's black underworld economy of gambling and speakeasies. Burns's reputation as the kingpin of Louisville's black organized crime syndicate earned him the respect of many in the city's black community, who were awed by his wealth and by his clout with Louisville's police force. Because of his position among local African Americans, white Republican politicians relied on Burns to use his considerable influence to get out the black vote on election day. In return, Burns received the municipal contract to be the city's funeral director, and police officials agreed to turn a blind eye to his illegal bootlegging and gambling activities. The formation of the LIP threatened Burns as well as other established elites in Louisville's black community, who decided to thwart the party's 1921 campaign in any way possible.[17]

The first signs of trouble occurred when black hecklers began to disrupt LIP campaign meetings. At one political rally the protest turned violent when a shot was fired into a crowd of party supporters. When the police arrived at the scene to investigate, they blamed the LIP candidates for causing the disturbance and ordered them to leave. As the LIP members departed, another group of black onlookers—later identified as accomplices of Harvey Burns—began throwing rocks and eggs at them. In the final weeks before the election, vandals attacked A. D. Porter's Funeral Home in three separate incidents. At one point, gunshots were fired into Porter's home. When Porter asked city police for protection, they told him they would not help him so long as he remained the LIP mayoral candidate. In a final attempt to end Porter's candidacy, a group of black ruffians armed with clubs and guns attacked his funeral home on election day. As the local press reported, "Negroes [broke] out the plate glass of his large front window, [destroyed] the furniture and fixtures and [tore] up his high priced books and valuables."[18]

The 1921 attack on A. D. Porter and Sons Funeral Home served its purpose and illustrated the depth of resistance to the LIP's campaign from the Republican party and from blacks who, like Harvey Burns, directly benefited from the Republicans' control of Louisville's city hall. As might be expected, the LIP lost the 1921 election by dramatic margins. Porter received only 274 votes in his race for mayor compared with the Republican candidate's 63,332 votes and the 56,199 votes cast for the Democratic candidate. Porter and other LIP members disputed the final vote tallies with a claim that "Republican henchmen had dumped some of their votes in the Ohio River." Even W. E. B. Du Bois, who admired the LIP campaign, weighed in on the election results in an editorial in the NAACP's magazine *The Crisis*. Du Bois wrote, "The party was credited with 274 votes at the polls but as they were not represented at the counting of the ballots and were beaten away from the polls by the police, this probably does not represent one-tenth of the actual votes cast."[19]

Despite its resounding defeat at the polls, the LIP marked the beginning of a new era of black politics in Louisville. The Republican party, which eventually admitted to spending approximately $200,000 in its efforts to quash the LIP's 1921 campaign, began hiring blacks not only for white-collar jobs in city government but, more significantly, for positions in the city fire department and police force. In 1927 LIP leaders, including A. D. Porter, renewed their campaign to fight the Republican party's control of the city's black vote and made more progress. By the 1930s, Louisville's black vote was no longer guaranteed for the Republicans, and both parties had to work to win the allegiance of the black electorate.[20]

In the end, the history of A. D. Porter and Sons Funeral Home offers a provocative final coda to the larger history of African American funeral directors and their efforts to serve the living while burying the dead. On the one hand, A. D. Porter provides an affirming story of the funeral director as local political hero who risks all—including his life and livelihood—to fight for change and to uplift the race. Porter clearly believed that Louisville's black community deserved better political representation and launched his own courageous, independent campaign to make it happen. On the other hand, Porter was thwarted from within the black community by Harvey Burns, a competing funeral director whose fortunes were tied to the Republican party and its willingness to allow him to rule Louisville's black underworld in exchange for votes. Burns's story, though not as heroic as Porter's, nevertheless reveals the way some black funeral directors were able to bridge their legal and illegal activities and gain considerable local clout. Although the conflict between Porter and Burns illustrated that Louisville's black community was far from unified in its political agenda in 1921, it did show that the political life of any black community often was found—and fought over—at the local black funeral home.[21]

The 1921 battle between Porter and Burns also encapsulates the central tensions that have animated African American funeral directing throughout its history. The impulse to fight for racial equality, which drove many funeral directors like Porter to political action, often ran directly counter to the more self-interested drive to reap the financial rewards of a racially segregated economic system. Harvey Burns clearly went to great lengths to maintain his control over Louisville's black underworld economy and to keep his job as the city's undertaker—even if it meant giving political support to the white Republicans and abetting in the destruction of another black-owned funeral home. The violent conflict between Porter and Burns reveals the difficult balancing act between fighting for racial justice and political enfranchisement and maintaining a foothold in the local segregated economy.

During the modern civil rights era, African American funeral directors continued to wrestle with how to remain competitive in the funeral industry while serving their local communities. In 1961, A. D. Porter's son, Woodford R. Porter, was elected as Louisville's first black chairman of the local Board of Education. The national press took note of Porter's accomplishment because it occurred during a time of racial tension in Louisville that was heightened by "recent sit-down demonstrations by Negroes protesting segregation in [the city's] eating places." In an interview about his accomplishment, Porter acknowledged the delicate balance he had to strike throughout his career to navigate the racial politics of his city. When he first ran for the board in 1958, he severed his ties with the NAACP because he intended "to be the representative of all citizens, not just the colored ones." Yet by 1961, he did not hesitate to voice his support "for total integration of all phases of local life"; and by 1962, he had used his leadership position to expose racial bias in employment in the Louisville public school system. Not surprisingly, Porter acknowledged his father's earlier political battles as inspiration for his own motivations toward public service.[22]

In many ways, the remarkable history of A. D. Porter and Sons Funeral Home only underscores the senselessness of the fatal shooting that took place on its premises in May 2006. The random attack is a sobering commentary on the way African American communities have disproportionately suffered from the violent consequences of economic inequality—violence that does not stop at the doors of a funeral home. And yet if the history of African American funeral directing teaches us anything, it is that from the depths of the most unspeakable tragedies and death, those who served the living—and those they served—persevered. The political fights of previous generations —for emancipation, for the right to vote, to hold office, to live a life of equal opportunity and personal safety—never die but continue to be born anew.[23]

Notes

Acknowledgments

Index

Notes

PROLOGUE

1. Bob Kemper, "'Justice Can't Just Forget': Long-ago Racial Killings," *Atlanta Journal-Constitution,* September 13, 2006; Philip Jacobson, "The Unforgotten Evil," *Sunday Times,* July 2, 2006.

2. Kemper, "'Justice Can't Just Forget.'"

3. Laura Wexler, *Fire in a Canebrake: The Last Mass Lynching in America* (New York: Scribner, 2003), 1–14.

4. Ibid., 24–25; Eugene M. Martin, Letter to Walter White, August 24, 1946, NAACP Papers, Part II, Box A412, Library of Congress, Manuscript Division.

5. Wexler, *Fire in a Canebrake,* 45–55; Joseph L. Bernd, "White Supremacy and the Disenfranchisement of Blacks in Georgia, 1946," *Georgia Historical Quarterly,* vol. 66, no. 4 (Winter 1982): 492–513; "American Lidice: An Editorial," *Chicago Defender,* August 3, 1946; Tom O'Connor, "Lynch Law Back in Georgia—Four Murdered," *P.M. Magazine,* July 28, 1946.

6. Wexler, *Fire in a Canebrake,* 67–83.

7. Walter White, "Press Bulletin, July 26, 1946," NAACP Papers, Part II, Box A413, Library of Congress, Manuscript Division; Walter White, *A Man Called White: The Autobiography of Walter White* (Athens: University of Georgia Press, 1995), 322.

8. John LeFlore, "On-the-Scene Story of Butchery," *Chicago Defender,* August 3, 1946; Wexler, *Fire in a Canebrake,* 82–83.

9. Wexler, *Fire in a Canebrake,* 86–90.

10. Eugene M. Martin, Letter to Walter White, July 27, 1946, NAACP Papers, Part II, Box A412, Library of Congress, Manuscript Division.

11. Eugene M. Martin, Letter to Walter White, August 8, 1946, and Thomas W. Johnson, Letter to Walter White, July 28, 1946, NAACP Papers, Part II, Box A412, Library of Congress, Manuscript Division.

12. Eugene M. Martin, Letter to Walter White, August 24, 1946, NAACP Papers, Part II, Box A412, Library of Congress, Manuscript Division.

13. "Talked-a-Plenty, But It Didn't Mean a Thing," *Pittsburgh Courier*, May 27, 1939.

14. Booker T. Washington and W. E. B. Du Bois, *The Negro in the South* (Philadelphia: George W. Jacobs, 1907), 99.

15. "Truman Orders Probe," *Pittsburgh Courier*, August 3, 1946; "'Decent People of Georgia Humiliated'—Gov. Arnall," *Pittsburgh Courier*, August 3, 1946.

16. "Memorial Service Held for Mob-Lynch Victims," *Pittsburgh Courier*, August 17, 1946; "Lynch Victims Mourned Here," *Pittsburgh Courier*, August 10, 1946; "Services Held for Ga. Mob Victims," *Pittsburgh Courier*, August 10, 1946; "Undertakers Condemn Mobs; Elect Officers," *Pittsburgh Courier*, August 24, 1946.

17. "Monroe Lynchers Unknown," *Pittsburgh Courier*, December 28, 1946.

18. Stephen G. N. Tuck, *Beyond Atlanta: The Struggle for Racial Equality in Georgia, 1940–1980* (Athens: University of Georgia Press, 2001), 66–76.

19. "Non-Partisan Group out to Up Negro Vote," *Pittsburgh Courier*, August 21, 1954; "Ga. Voters League to Discuss Registration," *Chicago Defender*, October 18, 1958.

20. In July 2008, descendants of Roger Malcom protested that year's reenactment, which included a ceremony in which Representative Tyrone Brooks symbolically named the unborn child of Dorothy Malcom "Justice Malcom." In the decades after the crime, the local rumor that Malcom was seven months pregnant when she was killed had become an accepted fact. Yet none of the historical documentation or news reports from 1946 about the Moore's Ford lynching investigation mention that Malcom was pregnant. In their public statement, Malcom's family members urged "all who write or speak about the Moore's Ford lynching to acknowledge that it simply is not known whether or not [Dorothy Malcom] was pregnant at the time of her death." Adam Thompson, "More Questions Remain about Lynching," www.onlineathens.com, August 3, 2008.

21. "GA Authorities Probe 1946 Unsolved Lynchings," *USAToday.com*, July 2, 2008.

1. From Hush Harbors to Funeral Parlors

1. Levi Coffin, *Reminiscences of Levi Coffin, the Reputed President of the Underground Railroad* (Cincinnati: Western Tract Society, 1876; reprint, New York: Augustus M. Kelley, 1968), 305.

2. Ibid., 306.

3. Ibid., 307–310.

4. For a detailed analysis of death and the Atlantic slave trade, see Vincent Brown, *The Reaper's Garden: Death and Power in the World of Atlantic Slavery* (Cambridge, Mass.: Harvard University Press, 2008).

5. W. E. B. Du Bois, *The Souls of Black Folk* (Boston: Bedford Books, 1997), 191.

6. Poem is from Janheinz Jahn, *Muntu: An Outline of the New African Culture*, trans. Marjorie Grene (New York: Grove Press, 1961), 108.

7. For further discussion of the conception of death and rebirth in African society, see ibid., 109–114. See also Margot Astrov, "Death in Africa," *New Mexico Quarterly*, vol. 30, no. 2 (Summer 1960): 115–126; John S. Mbiti, *African Religions and Philosophy* (New York: Praeger, 1969), 83–91, 149–165; Melville J. Herskovits, *The Myth of the Negro Past* (Boston: Beacon Press, 1958), 197–198; and Langston Hughes and Arna Bontemps, eds., *The Book of Negro Folklore* (New York: Dodd, Mead, 1958), 106.

8. Philip D. Curtin, *The Atlantic Slave Trade: A Census* (Madison: University of Wisconsin Press, 1969), 157, 228–229. See also Joseph E. Holloway, "The Origins of African-American Culture," in *Africanisms in American Culture*, ed. James E. Holloway (Bloomington: Indiana University Press, 1990), 6–7; Mechal Sobel, *Trabelin' On: The Slave Journey to an Afro-Baptist Faith* (Princeton, N.J.: Princeton University Press, 1988), 23–25; Albert J. Raboteau, *Slave Religion: The "Invisible Institution" in the Antebellum South* (New York: Oxford University Press, 1978), 7; Wyatt MacGaffey, "The West in Congolese Experience," in *Africa and the West: Intellectual Responses to European Culture*, ed. Philip D. Curtin (Madison: University of Wisconsin Press, 1972), 51–55.

9. Fukiau kia Bunseki, *N'Kongo ye Nza Yakun' zungidila* (1969), as translated in John M. Janzen and Wyatt MacGaffey, eds., *An Anthology of Kongo Religion: Primary Texts from Lower Zaire* (Lawrence: University of Kansas Publications in Anthropology, no. 5, 1974), 34.

10. Elizabeth A. Fenn, "Honoring the Ancestors: Kongo-American Graves in the American South," *Southern Exposure*, vol. 13, no. 5 (September–October 1985): 43; Robert Farris Thompson, *The Flash of the Spirit: African and*

Afro-American Art and Philosophy (New York: Vintage Books, 1984), 103–116; Newbell Niles Puckett, *Folk Beliefs of the Southern Negro* (New York: Negro Universities Press, 1968), 94; Sobel, *Trabelin' On*, 198.

11. Ancient forms of embalming involved the use of special herbs to preserve the body. Modern embalming fluids did not come into use in West Africa until the late nineteenth and early twentieth centuries. Ako Adjei, "Mortuary Uses of the Ga People of the Gold Coast," *American Anthropologist*, vol. 45, no. 1 (January–March 1943): 86–91.

12. Adjei, "Mortuary Uses of the Ga People," 86–91; Brown, *The Reaper's Garden*, 66–69.

13. Adjei, "Mortuary Uses of the Ga People," 91–95. For an additional overview of African funeral rituals and the distinction between natural and unnatural death, see J. H. Nketia, *Funeral Dirges of the Akan People* (New York: Negro Universities Press, 1969), 5–18. For descriptions of dancing and drumming around the grave, see Robert Sutherland Rattray, *The Tribes of the Ashanti Hinterland* (Oxford, England: Clarendon Press, 1932), 194; Melville Herskovits and Frances Herskovits, *Rebel Destiny* (New York: Whittlesey House, 1934), 3; and David Livingstone, *Missionary Travels and Researches in South Africa* (New York: Harper and Bros., 1858), 467.

14. Arthur Glyn Leonard, *The Lower Niger and Its Tribes* (New York: Macmillan, 1906), 159–160; Brown, *The Reaper's Garden*, 69–74.

15. Robert Farris Thompson, *The Four Moments of the Sun: Kongo Art in Two Worlds* (Washington, D.C.: National Gallery of Art, 1981), 27, 186–187, 198; Thompson, *The Flash of the Spirit*, 132–135, 138–139; Fenn, "Honoring the Ancestors," 43. For additional discussion of water symbolism in grave decoration, see John Michael Vlach, *The Afro-American Tradition in Decorative Arts* (Cleveland: Cleveland Museum of Art, 1978), 143.

16. Fenn, "Honoring the Ancestors," 43–44; Thompson, *The Flash of the Spirit*, 142; E. J. Glave, "Fetishism in Congo Land," *Century Magazine* 41 (1891): 835; Raboteau, *Slave Religion*, 83–85; and Dorothy Jean Michael, "Grave Decoration," *Publications of the Texas Folklore Society* 18 (1943): 131.

17. For mortuary practices in other world cultures, see Peter Metcalf and Richard Huntington, *Celebrations of Death: The Anthropology of Mortuary Ritual* (New York: Cambridge University Press, 1991); and Philippe Ariès, *The Hour of Death* (New York: Knopf, 1981). For retention of African funeral practices in the New World, see Brown, *The Reaper's Garden*, 63–66; and Ross W. Jamieson, "Material Culture and Social Death: African-American Burial Practices," *Historical Archaeology*, vol. 29, no. 4 (1995): 39–58.

18. "Lay Dis Body Down" (also known as "Lay This Body Down") is one of the most revered African American slave spirituals. Thomas Wentworth Higginson, an abolitionist and Union soldier, transcribed and published this version of the lyrics in his book *Army Life in a Black Regiment* (New York: Penguin Classics, 1997), 160. For additional analysis of the spiritual, see John Lowell Jr., *Black Song: The Forge and the Flame* (New York: MacMillan, 1972), 192–193.

19. David R. Roediger, "And Die in Dixie: Funerals, Death, and Heaven in the Slave Community, 1700–1865," *Massachusetts Review* 22 (1981): 163–183; Sobel, *Trabelin' On*, 187–200; Raboteau, *Slave Religion*, 230–231; Ira Berlin, *Many Thousands Gone: The First Two Centuries of Slavery in North America* (Cambridge, Mass.: Belknap Press of Harvard University Press, 1998), 60–63, 158.

20. Eugene D. Genovese, *Roll Jordan Roll: The World the Slaves Made* (New York: Random House, 1974), 195–196; Roediger, "And Die in Dixie," 163–168; Norman Yetman, *Life under the "Peculiar Institution": Selections from the Slave Narrative Collection* (New York: Holt, Rinehart and Winston, 1970), 262; Marcus Rediker, *The Slave Ship: A Human History* (New York: Penguin Books, 2007); Joseph Carroll, *Slave Insurrections in the United States, 1800–65* (New York: Negro Universities Press, 1968), 16–17, 30, 32; Herbert Aptheker, *American Negro Slave Revolts* (New York: International Publishers, 1963), 250.

21. Roediger, "And Die in Dixie," 164; Genovese, *Roll Jordan Roll*, 194; Edgar J. McManus, *Black Bondage in the North* (Syracuse: Syracuse University Press, 1973), 82; John H. Weeks, *Among the Primitive Bakongo* (London: Seeley, Service and Co., 1914), 270.

22. Douglas R. Egerton, *Gabriel's Rebellion: The Virginia Slave Conspiracies of 1800 and 1802* (Chapel Hill: University of North Carolina Press, 1993), 64; Gerald W. Mullin, *Flight and Rebellion: Slave Resistance in Eighteenth-Century Virginia* (New York: Oxford University Press, 1972), 148; Works Progress Administration, *The Negro in Virginia* (New York: Hastings House, 1940), 77; and John Hurd, *The Law of Freedom and Bondage in the United States*, vol. 2 (New York: Negro Universities Press, 1968), 9.

23. "Robert Shepherd, Ex-Slave, age 91," from *Born in Slavery: Slave Narratives from the Federal Writers' Project, 1936–1938, Georgia Narratives*, vol. 4, part 3, 251–252; Roediger, "And Die in Dixie," 169–170; Georgia Writers Project, *Drums and Shadows: Survival Studies among Georgia Coastal Negroes* (Athens: University of Georgia Press, 1940), 67, 218; Mrs. Henry Schoolcraft,

Plantation Life (New York: Negro Universities Press, 1969), 162; Elizabeth Ware Pearson, ed., *Letters from Port Royal Written at the Time of the Civil War* (Boston: W. B. Clark, 1906), 252–253. For more on the sounds of the slave funeral, see Shane White and Graham White, *The Sounds of Slavery: Discovering African American History through Songs, Sermons, and Speech* (Boston: Beacon Press, 2005), 11–19.

24. George P. Radwick, ed., *The American Slave: A Composite Autobiography*, supplement, series 1, vol. 8, Mississippi Narratives, part 3 (Westport, Conn.: Greenwood, 1977), 1273; Elaine Nichols, *Last Miles of the Way: African American Homegoing Traditions, 1890–Present* (Columbia: Commissioners of the South Carolina State Museum, 1989), 17.

25. Herskovits, *The Myth of the Negro Past*, 205; Howard Thurman, *Deep River* and *The Negro Spiritual Speaks of Life and Death* (Indiana: Friends United Press, 1975); Raboteau, *Slave Religion*, 230–231; White and White, *The Sounds of Slavery*, 15–16; Dennis Wilson Folly, "'You Preach Your Funeral While You Are Living': Death in Afro-American Folklore" (M.A. thesis, University of California–Berkeley, 1976), 39.

26. Puckett, *Folk Beliefs of the Southern Negro*, 92–94; William E. Hatcher, *John Jasper: The Unmatched Negro Philosopher and Preacher* (Fleming H. Revell, 1908; reprint 1969, New York: Negro Universities Press), 36–37; Genovese, *Roll Jordan Roll*, 255–279; Michael A. Plater, *African American Entrepreneurship in Richmond, 1890–1940: The Story of R. C. Scott* (New York: Garland Publishing, 1996), 110–111.

27. Georgia Writers Project, *Drums and Shadows*, 54; Ernest Ingersoll, "Decoration of Negro Graves," *Journal of American Folklore*, vol. 5, no. 16 (January–March 1892): 68–69.

28. Robert W. Haberstein and William M. Lamers, *The History of American Funeral Directing*, 5th ed. (Brookfield, Wis.: Burton and Mayer, 2001), 257–290.

29. For the most recent scholarship on the way the Civil War transformed Americans' relationship to death, see Drew Gilpin Faust, *This Republic of Suffering: Death and the American Civil War* (New York: Knopf, 2008). See also Gary Laderman, *The Sacred Remains: American Attitudes toward Death, 1799–1883* (New Haven: Yale University Press, 1996), 104–105.

30. Interestingly, Holmes requested that he not be embalmed after his own death. Haberstein and Lamers, *The History of American Funeral Directing*, 205–218. For more on the history of embalming, see Michael Sappol, *A Traffic of Dead Bodies: Anatomy and Embodied Social Identity in Nineteenth-Century America* (Princeton, N.J.: Princeton University Press, 2002).

31. James J. Farrell, *Inventing the American Way of Death, 1820–1920* (Philadelphia: Temple University Press, 1980), 147. For additional details about Cornelius's role in Polk's funeral, see Todd W. Van Beck, "The Death and Funeral of James K. Polk," *American Funeral Director* (September 2002): 80–88; Edward C. Johnson and Gail R. Johnson, "Prince Greer: America's First Negro Embalmer," *Liaison Bulletin,* FIAT-International Federation of Thanatopractic Association (April 1973).

32. Greer worked for Cornelius for the remainder of his life. Johnson and Johnson, "Prince Greer: America's First Negro Embalmer"; and Haberstein and Lamers, *The History of American Funeral Directing,* 211. For a reference to another early African American embalmer, Pierre Casenave, who was from New Orleans and advertised that he had invented a "secret embalming process," see Juliet E. K. Walker, "Racism, Slavery, and Free Enterprise: Black Entrepreneurship in the United States before the Civil War," *Business History Review,* vol. 60, no. 3. (Autumn 1986): 363.

33. For a more detailed description and analysis of Lincoln's funeral, see Laderman, *The Sacred Remains,* 157–163.

34. Burton Bledstein, *The Culture of Professionalism: The Middle Class and the Development of Higher Education in America* (New York: W. W. Norton, 1978), 4–5; Farrell, *Inventing the American Way of Death,* 150–152.

35. Charles R. Wilson, "The Southern Funeral Director: Managing Death in the New South," *Georgia Historical Quarterly,* vol. 67, no. 1 (Spring 1983): 67. Other evidence of African American students in early embalming schools can be found in the early graduation pictures of the Renouard Training School for Embalmers; see private photograph collections of Scarborough Funeral Home, Durham, North Carolina, and Lee Funeral Home, White Plains, New York.

36. Robert G. Mayer, *Embalming: History, Theory, and Practice* (New York: McGraw-Hill, 2006), 483–486; Haberstein and Lamers, *The History of American Funeral Directing,* 225; Farrell, *Inventing the American Way of Death,* 157–159.

37. Mayer, *Embalming,* 484; Seabury Quinn, "Who Was the Father of Modern Embalming?" *American Funeral Director,* vol. 67, no. 5 (May 1944): 27–29.

38. Haberstein and Lamers, *The History of American Funeral Directing,* 171–175, 310; Farrell, *Inventing the American Way of Death,* 148–150; and Gary Laderman, *Rest in Peace: A Cultural History of Death and the Funeral Home in Twentieth-Century America* (New York: Oxford University Press, 2003), 15.

39. W. E. B. Du Bois, *The Negro in Business* (Atlanta: Atlanta University Press, 1899), 5.

40. Abram L. Harris, *The Negro as Capitalist: A Study of Banking and Business among American Negroes* (New York: Haskell House, 1970), 20–21. For more information on Prince Hall and the black Masonic movement, see William A. Muraskin, *Middle-Class Blacks in a White Society: Prince Hall Freemasonry in America* (Berkeley: University of California Press, 1975); and Arthur Diamond and Nathan I. Huggins, eds., *Prince Hall: Social Reformer* (New York: Chelsea House, 1992).

41. Robert L. Harris, Jr., "Early Black Benevolent Societies, 1780–1830," *Massachusetts Review,* vol. 20, no. 3 (Autumn 1979): 613–618; James B. Browning, "The Beginnings of Insurance Enterprise among Negroes," *Journal of Negro History,* vol. 2, issue 4 (October 1937): 417–432; Plater, *African American Entrepreneurship in Richmond, 1890–1940,* 109.

42. Carter G. Woodson, "Insurance Business among Negroes," *Journal of Negro History,* vol. 14, no. 2 (April 1929): 203–204; Edward Nelson Palmer, "Negro Secret Societies," *Social Forces,* vol. 23, no. 2 (December 1944): 209.

43. August Meier, *Negro Thought in America, 1880–1915* (Ann Arbor: University of Michigan Press, 1963), 136–138; Woodson, "Insurance Business among Negroes," 211–213; W. E. B. Du Bois, *Economic Co-operation among Negro Americans* (Atlanta: Atlanta University Press, 1907), 92–109. For the history of North Carolina Mutual Life Insurance Company, see Walter B. Weare, *Black Business in the New South: A Social History of the North Carolina Mutual Life Insurance Company* (Durham: Duke University Press, 1993).

44. Hortense Powdermaker, *After Freedom: A Cultural Study in the Deep South* (New York: Atheneum, 1969), 122.

45. W. E. B. Du Bois, *Some Efforts of American Negroes for Their Own Social Betterment* (Atlanta: Atlanta University Press, 1898), 17; James Weldon Johnson, *Negro Americans, What Now?* (New York: Viking Press, 1938), 33; Booker T. Washington, *Black-Belt Diamonds* (New York: Negro Universities Press, 1969), 41.

46. Booker T. Washington, *The Story of the Negro: The Rise of the Race from Slavery* (Philadelphia: University of Pennsylvania Press, 2005; original pub. New York: Doubleday, Page, 1909), 168–169, 200.

47. Booker T. Washington, *The Negro in Business* (Boston: Hertel, Jenkins, 1907), 95–96, 107–108.

48. Booker T. Washington and W. E. B. Du Bois, *The Negro in the South* (Philadelphia: George W. Jacobs, 1907), 99.

2. THE COLORED EMBALMER

1. "Race Chauffeurs Block a Funeral Procession," *Cleveland Advocate*, November 16, 1918.

2. Clarie Collins Harvey, oral history transcript, interviewers: John Dittmer and John Jones, Mississippi Department of Archives and History (Accession Number: OH 83–04, Acquisition Date: April 23, 1981), 8; Neil R. McMillen, *Dark Journey: Black Mississippians in the Age of Jim Crow* (Urbana: University of Illinois Press, 1989), 193; and "Frazier and Collins Funeral Home Observes 50th Anniversary," *Jackson Daily News*, December 17, 1953, 14.

3. For more on the history of these tensions, see Robert H. Kinzer and Edward Sagarin, *The Negro in American Business: The Conflict between Separatism and Integration* (New York: Greenwood, 1950).

4. August Meier, *Negro Thought in America, 1880–1915: Racial Ideologies in the Age of Booker T. Washington* (Ann Arbor: University of Michigan Press, 1966), 125.

5. *Report of the Seventeenth Annual Session of the National Negro Business League* (Chattanooga, Tennessee, 1917), 105.

6. W. E. B. Du Bois, *The Negro in Business* (Atlanta: Atlanta University Press, 1899), 50.

7. *Proceedings of the First Annual Session of the National Negro Business League* (Boston, Massachusetts, 1900), 7; John H. Burrows, *The Necessity of Myth: A History of the National Negro Business League, 1900–1945* (Auburn, Ala.: Hickory Hill Press, 1988), 32–38.

8. *Proceedings of the First Annual Session of the National Negro Business League*, 171; *Proceedings of the Fifth Annual Session of the National Negro Business League* (Indianapolis, Indiana, 1904), 91–92.

9. *Proceedings of the Twelfth Annual Session of the National Negro Business League* (Little Rock, Arkansas, 1911), 67.

10. *Proceedings of the Fourteenth Annual Session of the National Negro Business League* (Philadelphia, Pennsylvania, 1913), 224–225; italics added.

11. National Funeral Directors Association Constitution, adopted October 4, 1912, NFDA Library at NFDA Headquarters, Milwaukee, Wisconsin, 239.

12. *Proceedings of the Thirty-first Annual Convention, National Funeral Directors Association* (October 4, 1912), 66, NFDA Library at NFDA Headquarters, Milwaukee, Wisconsin.

13. *By-Laws of the National Funeral Directors Association of the United*

States, Inc. (adopted October 1926), 207, NFDA Library at NFDA Headquarters, Milwaukee, Wisconsin. For early discussion of the decision to incorporate the NFDA, see "Incorporation," *Casket,* October 1, 1923.

14. "Colored Members Barred," *Casket and Sunnyside,* November 1, 1926, 42.

15. *Proceedings of the Sixteenth Annual Session of the National Negro Business League* (Boston, Massachusetts, 1915), 127; *Proceedings of the Eighteenth Annual Session of the National Negro Business League* (Chattanooga, Tennessee, 1917), 98–99, 101.

16. *Proceedings of the Nineteenth Annual Session of the National Negro Business League* (Atlantic City, New Jersey, 1918), 312; *Proceedings of the Twenty-second Annual Session of the National Negro Business League* (Atlanta, Georgia, 1921), 89.

17. Steven Hahn, *A Nation under Our Feet: Black Political Struggles in the Rural South from Slavery to the Great Migration* (Cambridge, Mass.: Belknap Press of Harvard University Press, 2003), 154–155; John Hope Franklin and Alfred A. Moss, Jr., *From Slavery to Freedom: A History of African Americans* (New York: McGraw-Hill, 2000), 250–251.

18. Leon F. Litwack, *Trouble in Mind: Black Southerners in the Age of Jim Crow* (New York: Vintage Books, 1999), 229–238. For more on railroads as the first battleground of Jim Crow, see Barbara Young Welke, *Recasting American Liberty: Gender, Race, Law, and the Railroad Revolution, 1865–1920* (New York: Cambridge University Press, 2001). For the broader history of Jim Crow, see C. Van Woodward, *The Strange Career of Jim Crow* (New York: Oxford University Press, 1955); Grace Elizabeth Hale, *Making Whiteness: The Culture of Segregation in the South, 1890–1940* (New York: Vintage Press, 1999); and Howard N. Rabinowitz, *Race Relations in the Urban South, 1865–1890* (Urbana: University of Illinois Press, 1980). For details on *Plessy,* see Charles A. Lofgren, *The Plessy Case: A Legal-Historical Interpretation* (New York: Oxford University Press, 1987); and Keith Weldon Medley, *We as Freemen: Plessy v. Ferguson* (Gretna, La.: Pelican, 2003), 89, 125–126.

19. Medley, *We as Freemen,* 126–127; Rebecca J. Scott, *Degrees of Freedom: Louisiana and Cuba after Slavery* (Cambridge, Mass.: Belknap Press of Harvard University Press, 2005), 88–93; Shirley Elizabeth Thompson, *Exiles at Home: The Struggle to Become American in Creole New Orleans* (Cambridge, Mass.: Harvard University Press, 2009), 99–101.

20. Medley, *We as Freemen,* 186; Rodolphe Lucien Desdunes, *Our People and Our History* (Baton Rouge: Louisiana State University Press, 1973), 96;

"Family Proud of 126-year-old Business Tradition," *Times-Picayune*, August 23, 1998, 10–11.

21. Not surprisingly, a large percentage of the funds raised to support the Citizens Committee came from local benevolent societies and burial societies. For more specific details about the Citizens Committee and its members, see Medley, *We as Freemen*, 111–137.

22. James T. Haley, *Afro-American Encyclopedia; or the Thoughts, Doings, and Sayings of the Race* (Nashville, Tenn.: Haley and Florida, 1896), 215–216; William Newton Hartshorn, *An Era of Progress and Promise, 1863–1910* (Boston: Priscilla, 1910), 445.

23. Haley, *Afro-American Encyclopedia*, 220. For more on the relationship between the black church and the funeral business, see Karla F. C. Holloway, *Passed On: African American Mourning Stories* (Durham, N.C.: Duke University Press, 2002), 22–23. Before Taylor opened Greenwood Cemetery, Nashville's black citizens were buried either at the City Cemetery, which had a "Negro section," or at Mt. Ararat Cemetery, which was the first black cemetery in the city.

24. Haley, *Afro-American Encyclopedia*, 220.

25. August Meier and Elliott Rudwick, "The Boycott Movement against Jim Crow Streetcars in the South, 1900–1906," *Journal of American History*, vol. 55, no. 4 (March 1969): 770–771.

26. "Nashville's Revolt against Jimcrowism," *Voice of the Negro*, vol. 2, no. 12 (December 1905): 827. For additional discussion of the conservative nature of the protest, see "Fighting 'Jim-Crowism' in Nashville," *Literary Digest*, vol. 31, no. 15 (October 7, 1905); Meier and Rudwick, "The Boycott Movement against Jim Crow Streetcars," 760–761.

27. "Nashville's Revolt against Jimcrowism," 830. Notably, the Union Transportation Company did not discriminate against white riders, but instead welcomed all passengers regardless of race. Don H. Doyle, *Nashville in the New South, 1880–1930* (Knoxville: University of Tennessee Press, 1985), 117–120; Lester C. Lamon, *Black Tennesseans, 1900–1930* (Knoxville: University of Tennessee Press, 1977), 20–36.

28. "Union Transportation Co.'s Interesting Meeting Monday Night at Nat'l Baptist Chapel," *Nashville Globe*, April 12, 1907; "Union Transportation Co. Sold Eight of Its Large Electric Automobiles," *Nashville Globe*, May 3, 1907; Lamon, *Black Tennesseans, 1900–1930*, 34; Lena R. Marbury, "Nashville's 1905 Streetcar Boycott" (M.A. thesis, Tennessee State University, 1985), 52–54; Meier and Rudwick, "The Boycott Movement against Jim Crow Streetcars," 766.

29. "Union Transportation Co. Sold Eight of Its Large Electric Automobiles," *Nashville Globe*, May 3, 1907; Marbury, "Nashville's 1905 Streetcar Boycott," 54.

30. For more history on racial segregation in cemeteries, see Angelika Krüger-Kahloula, "On the Wrong Side of the Fence: Racial Segregation in American Cemeteries," in *History and Memory in African-American Culture*, ed. Geneviève Fabre and Robert O'Meally (New York: Oxford University Press, 1994); and Roberta Hughes Wright and Wilbur B. Hughes III, *Lay Down Body: Living History in African American Cemeteries* (Detroit: Visible Ink Press, 1996).

31. For more details about the career of Charles C. Diggs, Sr., see Richard W. Thomas, *Life for Us Is What We Make It: Building Black Community in Detroit, 1915–1945* (Bloomington: Indiana University Press, 1992), 265–269; Roberta Hughes Wright, *Detroit Memorial Park: The Evolution of an American Corporation* (Southfield, Mich.: Charro Book Company, 1993), 19.

32. Hughes Wright, *Detroit Memorial Park*, 5, 24–25.

33. Ibid., 25–28, 55–56.

34. For more specific details on the crises at the NNBL after Washington's death, see Burrows, *The Necessity of Myth*, 73–125.

35. James J. Farrell, *Inventing the American Way of Death, 1820–1920* (Philadelphia: Temple University Press, 2002), 156–157; "Souvenir Program of the Independent National Funeral Association," Fourth Annual Session (Philadelphia, Pennsylvania, June 26–28, 1929), 17; Gary Laderman, *Rest in Peace: A Cultural History of Death and the Funeral Home in Twentieth-Century America* (New York: Oxford University Press, 2003), 19; William M. Lamers, *A Centurama of Conventions: A Review of all the Conventions of NFDA Focusing on the Words and Deeds of Funeral Service Practioners* (Milwaukee, Wis.: National Funeral Directors Association, 1981), 31.

36. Robert W. Haberstein and William M. Lamers, *The History of American Funeral Directing* (Milwaukee, Wis.: Bulfin, 1962), 439; "Popularizing the Funeral Home," *Casket and Sunnyside*, March 1, 1925; Farrell, *Inventing the American Way of Death*, 172–177; Laderman, *Rest in Peace*, 3–8.

37. "Negro Nationals Meet," *Casket*, September 1, 1924.

38. Robert R. Reed, "The Negro Funeral Director," *Casket and Sunnyside*, September 15, 1925; Editorial, "The Awakening," *Colored Embalmer*, vol. 1, no. 1 (1926): 4; Robert R. Reed, "The Name of the Association," *Colored Embalmer*, vol. 2, no. 9 (April 1929): 4.

39. "Colored Organization Perfected," *Casket and Sunnyside*, n.d.; "Col-

ored Executives Meet," *Casket and Sunnyside,* May 15, 1925, 35–36; Editorial, *Colored Embalmer,* vol. 2, no. 4 (April 1928): 8, 10–11, 14–15, 21.

40. "Our 1929 Program," *Colored Embalmer,* vol. 2, no. 8 (February 1929): 4.

41. "Funeral Directors Best Organized," *Colored Embalmer,* vol. 2, no. 9 (April 1929): 17.

42. "Southern White Funeral Director Still Seeks to Bury Negro Soldiers from Tuskegee Hospital, a Letter by Editor Reed," *Colored Embalmer,* vol. 2, no. 4 (April 1928): 9; "Secy. Reed Goes after Colored War Camp Work for Colored Funeral Directors," *Colored Embalmer,* vol. 2, no. 10 (May 1929): 2.

43. R. R. Reed, "Viewed from the Sidelines," *Colored Embalmer,* vol. 2, no. 10 (May 1929): 17; R. E. Hartley, "Annual Address of President R. E. Hartley at Savannah," *Colored Embalmer,* vol. 2, no. 11 (June 1929): 8.

44. Green P. Hamilton, *Beacon Lights of the Race* (Memphis: E. H. Clarke and Brother, 1911), 233–237; Green P. Hamilton, *The Bright Side of Memphis* (Memphis, Tenn., 1908), 279. For more information on Wilkerson's political ambitions, see Lamon, *Black Tennesseans, 1900–1930,* 56–57.

45. "Wayman Wilkerson Is Suicide Victim: Prominent Negro Politician Takes His Own Life," *Memphis Commercial Appeal,* July 2, 1928, 1–2; "Memphis Banker a Suicide," *Chicago Defender,* July 7, 1928, 1. For additional details on the Memphis banking scandal, see Lamon, *Black Tennesseans, 1900–1930,* 193–197.

46. Editorial, *Colored Embalmer,* vol. 2, no. 4 (April 1928): 10–11.

47. Personal diary entry from December 20, 1940, John Turner Miles Collection, 1922–1976, Kenneth Spencer Research Library, Kansas Collection, University of Kansas.

48. Ralph J. Bunche, *Extended Memorandum of the Programs, Ideologies, Tactics and Achievements of Negro Betterment and Interracial Organization,* June 7, 1940, 315; Abram L. Harris, *The Negro as Capitalist: A Study of Banking and Business among American Negroes* (New York: Haskell House, 1970), 177.

49. Robert F. Himmelberg, *The Origins of the National Recovery Administration* (New York: Fordham University Press, 1995); Ellis W. Hawley, *The New Deal and the Problem of Monopoly: A Study in Economic Ambivalence* (New York: Fordham University Press, 1995); and Leverett S. Lyon, *The National Recovery Administration: An Analysis and Appraisal* (New York: Da Capo Press, 1972).

50. "Funeral Directors Take Part in Drafting Code under National Indus-

trial Recovery Act," *Colored Embalmer,* vol. 4, no. 10 (July 1933): 18; "Codification Is Discussed," *Casket and Sunnyside,* vol. 64, no. 9 (August 1, 1933): 12–13, 32.

51. "T. M. Fletcher, Mortician, Gets High Post: Chosen a Member of Code Authority," *Chicago Defender,* June 23, 1934, 2.

52. For details about the INFDA infighting and Reed's ouster, see "Undertakers Open Cincinnati Meet," *Chicago Defender,* August 22, 1936; "Funeral Men Unanimously Re-Elect All," *Chicago Defender,* August 29, 1936; "Undertakers Pick Morsell as President," *Chicago Defender,* August 28, 1937; "Morticians Organize Anew after Convention Clash," *Chicago Defender,* July 9, 1938; "Undertakers Give Support to R. R. Reed," *Chicago Defender,* July 30, 1938; "Reed Pleads for Unity of Undertakers," *Chicago Defender,* June 1, 1940.

53. "52 Conventions Cancelled on Request of ODF Chief," *Chicago Defender,* May 8, 1943; "A Statement of History and Purpose of Epsilon Nu Delta," *National Funeral Director and Embalmer,* vol. 12, no. 9 (September 1959): 8.

3. My Man's an Undertaker

1. For a recording of the song, see *Dinah Washington: The Queen of the Blues,* Leroy Kirkland and Mamie Thomas, "My Man's an Undertaker," Mercury Records, 1953.

2. "Death Is Big Business," *Ebony,* vol. 8, no. 7 (May 1953): 17–18, 25, 30–31. In his book *Black Bourgeoisie,* E. Franklin Frazier cites the *Ebony* article as an example of the way the black press glorifies the acquisition of wealth in black America. See E. Franklin Frazier, *Black Bourgeoisie* (New York: Free Press, 1997 edition), 185.

3. Robert R. Reed, "The Negro Undertaker," *Casket and Sunnyside,* September 15, 1925. For an example of early press coverage of unethical black funeral directors, see "Slick Negro Undertaker Fleeced Augusta Board of Charities of Considerable Amount," *Atlanta Constitution,* December 6, 1907.

4. "Annual Address of President Kelsey L. Pharr before the Florida State Meeting at Miami, June 25, 1928," *Colored Embalmer,* vol. 2, no. 8 (March 1929): 3.

5. Gary Laderman, *Rest in Peace: A Cultural History of Death and the Funeral Home in Twentieth-Century America* (New York: Oxford University Press, 2003), 31–32, 54–59; John C. Gebhart, *Funeral Costs: What They Average; Are They Too High? Can They Be Reduced?* (New York: G. P. Putnam's Sons, 1928), 42–43.

6. For more on African American funeral rituals, see Elaine Nichols, ed., *The Last Miles of the Way: African-American Homegoing Traditions, 1890–Present* (Columbia: Commissioners of the South Carolina State Museum, 1989); Charlotte Lewis McGee and Phyllis Pitts Scoby, *A Comparative Study of Current Practices of Secular Mortuary Chapel Funeral Services of Black and White Families* (M.A. thesis, California State University, Dominguez Hills, 1981); Karla F. C. Holloway, *Passed On: African American Mourning Stories* (Durham, N.C.: Duke University Press, 2002), 163–188; Elizabeth H. Pleck, *Celebrating the Family: Consumer Culture and Family Rituals* (Cambridge, Mass.: Harvard University Press, 2000), 198–206; Charlton McIlwain, *Death in Black and White: Death, Ritual and Family Ecology* (Cresskill, N.J.: Hampton Press, 2003).

7. Holloway, *Passed On,* 165–166; Nichols, *The Last Miles of the Way,* 21; Roi Ottley, "Trace Negro Burial Societies, Rituals to Pre-Civil War Roots," *Chicago Daily Tribune,* September 18, 1955.

8. McIlwain, *Death in Black and White,* x. For more on the history of the jazz funeral, see Leo Touchet and Vernel Bagneris, *Rejoice When You Die: The New Orleans Jazz Funerals* (Baton Rouge: Louisiana State University Press, 1998); Helen A. Regis, "Blackness and the Power of Memory in the New Orleans Second Line," *American Ethnologist,* vol. 28, no. 4 (November, 2001): 752–777.

9. McGee and Scoby, *A Comparative Study,* 38–45.

10. James Van Der Zee, Owen Dodson, and Camille Billops, *The Harlem Book of the Dead* (Dobbs Ferry, N.Y.: Morgan and Morgan, 1978). For analysis of the role of memorial photographs of the dead, see Jay Ruby, *Secure the Shadow: Death and Photography in America* (Cambridge, Mass.: MIT Press, 1995).

11. "A. N. Johnson," *Nashville Globe,* February 11, 1910.

12. Michael A. Plater, *African American Entrepreneurship in Richmond, 1890–1940* (New York: Garland Publishing, 1996), 28, 39. For more discussion of the role of hearses and limousines in African American funeral pageantry, see Holloway, *Passed On,* 47–48. Holloway notes that many funeral homes would purchase vehicles in one recognizable color as an advertising technique and to promote customer loyalty.

13. Robert R. Reed, "Concerning the Negro Funeral Director," *Casket and Sunnyside,* December 1, 1925, 31; "What We Shall Contend For," *Colored Embalmer,* vol. 1, no. 1 (1926): 4.

14. Robert R. Reed, "Burial Leagues and the Negro Funeral Director," *Casket and Sunnyside,* February 15, 1926, 29. Some black funeral directors estab-

lished burial societies to fight competition from white funeral directors and their burial leagues. For details see "Undertakers Flay Burial Societies," *Chicago Defender*, May 6, 1933. For additional commentary on the trend of black funeral directors' establishing burial associations, see St. Clair Drake and Horace R. Cayton, *Black Metropolis: A Study of Negro Life in a Northern City* (New York: Harper and Row, 1962), 456–460.

15. James J. Farrell, *Inventing the American Way of Death, 1830–1920* (Philadelphia: Temple University Press, 1980), 172–177.

16. "Popularizing the Funeral Home," *Casket and Sunnyside*, March 1, 1925; "The What Not Column," *Colored Embalmer*, vol. 2, no. 4 (April 1928): 7.

17. Plater, *African American Entrepreneurship in Richmond*, 12.

18. Ibid., 9, 12, 26.

19. "You and Your Friends Are Most Cordially Invited to Attend Our Grand Formal Re-Opening on Friday, January 1, 1909," *Nashville Globe*, December 25, 1908.

20. For more on Johnson's theater, see Lester C. Lamon, *Black Tennesseans, 1900–1930* (Knoxville: University of Tennessee Press, 1977), 168.

21. "Fourth of July at Greenwood Park," *Nashville Globe*, July 12, 1907; "First Fair a Grand Success: Tennessee Colored State Fair Meets Approval of Public," *Nashville Globe*, September 25, 1908. For more on Greenwood Park and its racial politics, see Craig Allan Kaplowitz, "A Breath of Fresh Air: Segregation, Parks, and Progressivism in Nashville, Tennessee, 1900–1920," *Tennessee Historical Quarterly*, vol. 57, no. 2 (Fall 1998): 132–149; and Bobby L. Lovett, *The African-American History of Nashville, Tennessee, 1780–1930* (Fayetteville: University of Arkansas Press, 1999), 123–125.

22. "Beautiful Greenwood Park: Struck Down by Class Legislation," *Nashville Globe*, April 12, 1907; "Greenwood Park," *Nashville Globe*, April 19, 1907; "Record Breaking Crowd Expected at the Greenwood Dedication Saturday," *Nashville Globe*, August 7, 1908; Kaplowitz, "A Breath of Fresh Air," 141.

23. For more discussion of these cultural trends, see Grace Elizabeth Hale, *Making Whiteness: The Culture of Segregation in the South, 1890–1940* (New York: Vintage Books, 1998), 151–168; Michael Rogin, "'The Sword Became a Flashing Vision': D. W. Griffith's *The Birth of a Nation*," *Representations*, no. 9 (Winter 1985): 150–195; Melvin Patrick Ely, *The Adventures of Amos and Andy: A Social History of an American Phenomenon* (Charlottesville: University of Virginia Press, 2001); and Patricia Turner, *Ceramic Uncles and Celluloid Mammies: Black Images and Their Influence on Culture* (Charlottesville: University of Virginia Press, 2002).

24. "The What Not Column," *Colored Embalmer,* vol. 2, no. 4 (April 1928): 7; Holloway, *Passed On,* 22–23; Drake and Cayton, *Black Metropolis,* 457.

25. Robert A. Armour and J. Carol Williams, "Image Making and Advertising in the Funeral Industry," *Journal of Popular Culture,* vol. 14, no. 4 (Spring 1981): 701–710; Charles R. Wilson, "The Southern Funeral Director: Managing Death in the New South," *Georgia Historical Quarterly,* vol. 67, no. 1 (Spring 1983): 61.

26. Julius J. Adams, "Policy, Once a Big Industry, Hits Skids: *Defender* Reporter Spills the 'Inside' Dope on Rise and Fall of Numbers," *Chicago Defender,* April 22, 1933, 11; Drake and Cayton, *Black Metropolis,* 437–453, 470–494; Gunnar Myrdal, *An American Dilemma: The Negro Problem and Modern Democracy* (New York: Harper and Brothers, 1944), 330–332; Victoria W. Wolcott, *Remaking Respectability: African American Women in Interwar Detroit* (Chapel Hill: University of North Carolina Press, 2001), 93–126.

27. Harold F. Gosnell, *Negro Politicians: The Rise of Negro Politics in Chicago* (Chicago: University of Chicago Press, 1935), 130–131; "Undertaking Concern Established in 1865 Still in Lead," *Chicago Defender,* November 14, 1914; "Emanuel Jackson Turns Farmer," *Chicago Defender,* November 18, 1911; "The Negro in Chicago's History," *Chicago Defender,* February 19, 1949; "Negro Funeral Home Owner to Be Buried," *Chicago Daily Tribune,* October 1, 1962.

28. In the last year of his life, Jackson faced charges of voter fraud and was indicted by a grand jury for conspiracy to protect gambling. For details about Jackson's political influence and scandals, see Gosnell, *Negro Politicians,* 132–133; Charles Russel Branham, "The Transformation of Black Political Leadership in Chicago, 1864–1942" (Ph.D. diss., University of Chicago, 1981), 235–237; "Indict Jackson and DePriest: Well Known Politicians Hit in Probe," *Chicago Defender,* October 6, 1928.

29. "Dan Jackson Faces Quiz in Clean-Up," *Chicago Defender,* July 28, 1928; "Indict Jackson and DePriest: Well Known Politicians Hit in Probe," *Chicago Defender,* October 6, 1928; "Indictment of Two Quashed by Court's Order," *Chicago Defender,* May 25, 1929. For more background information on the scandal, see Gosnell, *Negro Politicians,* 180–185; Dianne M. Pinderhughes, *Race and Ethnicity in Chicago Politics* (Urbana: University of Illinois Press, 1987), 148–150.

30. Gosnell, *Negro Politicians,* 132; Cora A. Graham, "Mrs. Graham Pays Tribute to Memory of Statesmen," *Chicago Defender,* June 1, 1929; Drake and Cayton, *Black Metropolis,* 487, 548. Gunnar Myrdal echoed these sentiments in *An American Dilemma* when he wrote about the respect given to "policy

kings" in black communities. He noted that this communal admiration came from the fact that "policy 'kings' are wealthy, and that they are generous in a poor community." Myrdal, *An American Dilemma*, 331.

31. Robert E. Weems, Jr., *Black Business in the Black Metropolis: The Chicago Metropolitan Assurance Company, 1925–1985* (Bloomington: Indiana University Press, 1996), 2–4.

32. Ibid., 5–8.

33. Ibid., 8–9. For details about the legislation, see "Good Insurance Aim in Illinois, Palmer Asserts," *Chicago Tribune,* October 20, 1934; "Burial Associations Hold Conference," *Chicago Defender,* April 27, 1935; "New Insurance Code Is Given to Assembly," *Chicago Tribune,* May 7, 1935; "Insurance Bill Passes House Little Changed," *Chicago Tribune,* June 13, 1935.

34. Deton J. Brooks, Jr., "From Cabin to Riches Is Cole Success Story," *Chicago Defender,* December 19, 1942; Weems, *Black Business in the Black Metropolis,* 23, 67–68.

35. Weems, *Black Business in the Black Metropolis,* 56–70; "Insurance Firm's Radio Drama Wins National Radio Honors," *Chicago Defender,* December 18, 1948; Hillard J. McFall, "Story of Chicago Met—A Company on the Go," *Chicago Defender,* April 28, 1962.

36. Weems, *Black Business in the Black Metropolis,* 22; "Fear 'King' Cole Kidnapped: Police and Private Detectives Search for Business Man," *Chicago Defender,* December 27, 1930; "Metropolitan Buys New Funeral Cars," *Chicago Defender,* June 8, 1940; Albert Barnett, "Metropolitan Mutual: Titan of the Business World," *Chicago Defender,* March 31, 1951; "Robert A. Cole, Object Lesson," *Chicago Defender,* July 30, 1956.

37. Robert A. Cole, "How I Made a Million," *Ebony,* 9 (September 1954): 43–52. *Ebony* also covered the Metropolitan story a year earlier in a shorter piece that noted the company's twenty-fifth anniversary; see "Insurance Anniversary: Metropolitan Mutual of Chicago Marks 25th Year," *Ebony,* 8 (January 1953): 79.

38. "The Ten Richest Negroes in America," *Ebony,* vol. 4, no. 6 (April 1949): 13–15; "Wealthy Widows," *Ebony,* vol. 4, no. 10 (August 1949): 52–55; "Death Comes to the World's Richest Negro," *Ebony,* vol. 5, no. 12 (October 1950): 66–70.

39. "Death Is Big Business," *Ebony,* vol. 8, no. 7 (May 1953): 17; Frazier, *Black Bourgeoisie,* 174. For additional analysis of *Ebony* and its presentation of the black bourgeoisie, see Adam Green, *Selling Race: Culture, Community, and Black Chicago, 1940–1955* (Chicago: University of Chicago Press, 2006), 129–177.

40. Myrdal, *An American Dilemma,* 309–310; Drake and Cayton, *Black Metropolis,* 430–467.

41. Myrdal, *An American Dilemma,* 1262–1263n29; Drake and Cayton, *Black Metropolis,* 458–460.

42. "Chicagoan to Publish Morticians' Journal," *Chicago Defender,* October 2, 1948.

43. The main source for Bob Miller's biography is a transcript of the testimonial speech given at a dinner titled "Through the Years with Bob Miller," held in March 29, 1957. The speech includes the story of Bob Miller's adoption by the Ackert family, but I have found no evidence that this "adoption" was ever legal. Nevertheless, when Miller does ultimately have a conflict with Charles Ackert and decides to leave the family, the transcript notes that Miller "was advised not to leave since he was mentioned in [the family's] Will." See Odas Nicholson, "Through the Years with Bob Miller," Transcript of Testimonial Dinner, Grand Ballroom, Chicago, Illinois, March 29, 1957, in author's possession.

44. Photo essay, *Casket,* August 1, 1924, 24–25.

45. Nicholson, "Through the Years with Bob Miller," 6; "Wants to be a Lindbergh," *The Light: America's News Magazine,* vol. 4, no. 45 (September 29, 1928): 1; "In Memoriam: Robert H. 'Bob' Miller, 1896–1979," *The National Green Book of Funeral Directors, Embalmers, and Florists,* 13th ed., 1979–1980.

46. Mahalia Jackson with Evan McLeod Wylie, *Movin' On Up* (New York: Hawthorn Books, 1966), 66; Laurraine Goreau, *Just Mahalia, Baby* (Gretna, La.: Pelican, 1984), 58–59.

47. Bernice Johnson Reagon, ed., *We'll Understand It Better By and By: Pioneering African American Gospel Composers* (Washington, D.C.: Smithsonian Institution Press, 1992), 293; A. G. Gaston, *Green Power: The Successful Way of A. G. Gaston* (Birmingham, Ala.: Southern University Press, 1968), 71; Gayle F. Ward, *Shout, Sister, Shout!: The Untold Story of Rock and Roll Trailblazer Sister Rosetta Tharpe* (Boston: Beacon Press, 2007), 85; Jackson, *Movin' On Up,* 80.

48. "Four in Chicago Bronzeville Mayoralty Race," *Chicago Defender,* September 10, 1938; Drake and Cayton, *Black Metropolis,* 383.

4. A FUNERAL HALL IS AS GOOD A PLACE AS ANY

1. James Farmer, *Lay Bare the Heart: An Autobiography of the Civil Rights Movement* (New York: Arbor House, 1985), 244–245. Farmer first published an account of this incident in his 1965 memoir *Freedom When?* (New York: Random House, 1965), 3–22.

2. Farmer, *Lay Bare the Heart*, 246.

3. Ibid., 247–248.

4. Ibid., 249.

5. Ibid., 252.

6. For additional examples (and legends) of funeral directors' using caskets to protect civil rights activists or to hide weapons, see David T. Beito and Linda Royster Beito, *Black Maverick: T. R. M. Howard's Fight for Civil Rights and Economic Power* (Urbana: University of Illinois Press, 2009), 142–144, 182; "Arrington High as Told to Marc Crawford, *Jet* Exclusive: I Escaped Mississippi in a Casket," *Jet* 13 (February 27, 1958): 11–13; and Timothy Tyson, *Radio-Free Dixie: Robert F. Williams and the Roots of Black Power* (Chapel Hill: University of North Carolina Press, 1999), 282.

7. For one recent local study of a funeral director's involvement in civil rights activism, see Matthew C. Whitaker, *Race Work: The Rise of Civil Rights in the Urban West* (Lincoln: University of Nebraska Press, 2005).

8. Robert H. Miller, "From the Editor's Desk," *National Funeral Director and Embalmer*, vol. 10, no. 8 (August 1957): 6; Robert H. Miller, "From the Editor's Desk," *National Funeral Director and Embalmer*, vol. 13, no. 12 (December 1960).

9. Robert G. Kaiser, "Undertakers Have 'Unwritten' Pact to Handle Funerals on Racial Basis," *Washington Post and Times Herald*, February 24, 1967.

10. Horace R. Cayton, "World at Large," *Pittsburgh Courier*, May 19, 1955; "The Bite," *Time*, 64 (December 20, 1954), 54; Neil R. McMillen, *The Citizens' Council: Organized Resistance to the Second Reconstruction, 1954–64* (Urbana: University of Illinois Press, 1971).

11. "From Fiery Cross . . . to Economic Squeeze!" *Pittsburgh Courier*, September 1, 1956; "The Tale Ends," *Chicago Defender*, October 22, 1955; "Fla. Mortician Threatened by Burning Cross," *Chicago Defender*, July 3, 1954; "Shooting at Mortuary Laid to NAACP Foes," *Washington Post and Times Herald*, December 1, 1955.

12. For a more detailed discussion of the RCNL and Dr. T. R. M. Howard, see Beito and Beito, *Black Maverick*.

13. John Dittmer, *Local People: The Struggle for Civil Rights in Mississippi* (Urbana: University of Illinois Press, 1994), 33; David T. Beito and Linda Royster Beito, "T. R. M. Howard: Pragmatism over Strict Integrationist Ideology in the Mississippi Delta, 1942–1954," in *Before Brown: Civil Rights and White Backlash in the Modern South*, ed. Glenn Feldman (Tuscaloosa: University of Alabama Press, 2004), 68–95.

14. "NAACP Strikes Back in Miss. Economic Battle," *Chicago Defender*,

January 1, 1955; "Cash, Clothes, Food Aid Victims of Economic War," *Chicago Defender,* February 8, 1956; "Gifts Pour in for Squeeze Victims, Aid Thousands in Mississippi," *Chicago Defender,* February 18, 1956.

15. "Rep. Diggs Rouses Mississippi Rally," *Chicago Defender,* May 14, 1955. Historical records list two other Mississippi birthplaces for Charles Diggs, Sr.: Tupelo and Tallula. I could find no official verification that he was born in Mound Bayou. In any case, the salient point remains that Diggs was a Mississippi native.

16. Richard W. Thomas, *Life for Us Is What We Make It: Building Black Community in Detroit, 1915–1945* (Bloomington: Indiana University Press, 1992), 265–269.

17. "Across the Years" editorial, *Michigan Chronicle,* April 10, 1943. For a definition of a "race man," see St. Clair Drake and Horace R. Cayton, *Black Metropolis: A Study of Negro Life in a Northern City* (New York: Harper and Row, 1962), 394–395; Thomas, *Life for Us Is What We Make It,* 265–269.

18. "Transcript of Charles Diggs Interview (1991)," Elaine Lanzman Moon Collection, Archives of Labor and Urban Affairs, Walter P. Reuther Archives, Wayne State University; "Pay Tribute to Diggs at Testimonial," *Michigan Chronicle,* April 10, 1943; Thomas, *Life for Us Is What We Make It,* 265–269.

19. Thomas, *Life for Us Is What We Make It,* 265–269; "Michigan's First Negro Congressman Elected," *Los Angeles Times,* November 4, 1954; "Michigan Elects Negro to Congress," *Christian Science Monitor,* November 4, 1954; "Charles Diggs Becomes 3rd Negro Congressman," *Chicago Defender,* November 20, 1954.

20. For a detailed account of Lee's murder, see Jack Mendelsohn, *The Martyrs: Sixteen Who Gave Their Lives for Racial Justice* (New York: Harper and Row, 1966), 1–20; "The New Fighting South: Militant Negroes Refuse to Leave Dixie or Be Silenced," *Ebony* (August 1955): 69–74; "Mississippi Gunmen Take Life of Militant Negro Minister," *Jet,* vol. 8, no. 3 (1955): 8–11.

21. "The New Fighting South."

22. Adam Green, *Selling the Race: Culture, Community, and Black Chicago, 1940–1955* (Chicago: University of Chicago Press, 2007), 195.

23. For more information and analysis of the Till case, see Stephen J. Whitfield, *A Death in the Delta: The Story of Emmett Till* (New York: The Free Press, 1988); Mamie Till-Mobley and Christopher Benson, *Death of Innocence: The Story of the Hate Crime That Changed America* (New York: Random House, 2003); Christopher Metress, ed., *The Lynching of Emmett Till: A Documentary Narrative* (Charlottesville: University of Virginia Press, 2002); Ruth Feldstein, "'I Wanted the Whole World to See': Race, Gender, and the Con-

struction of Motherhood in the Death of Emmett Till," in *Not June Cleaver: Women and Gender in Postwar America, 1945–1960*, ed. Joanne Meyerowitz (Philadelphia: Temple University Press, 1994), 263–303; Keith Beauchamp, "The Untold Story of Emmett Louis Till," DVD, ThinkFilm Company, 2006.

24. For more on the long-term impact of the Till case on African American collective memory, see Metress, *The Lynching of Emmett Till*, 226–349.

25. Mamie Till Bradley, "I Want You to Know What They Did to My Boy," speech given at Bethel AME Church, Baltimore, Maryland, October 29, 1955, reprinted in *Rhetoric, Religion and the Civil Rights Movement, 1954–1965*, Davis W. Houck and David E. Dixon, eds. (Waco, Tex.: Baylor University Press, 2006), 144–145; Metress, *The Lynching of Emmett Till*, 72–73, 76. See also the Federal Bureau of Investigation, Prosecutive Report of Investigation, *State of Mississippi v. J. W. Milam and Roy Bryant*, September Term 1955, Appendix A: Transcript, 64–80.

26. Bradley, "I Want You to Know What They Did to My Boy," 135–136; and Metress, *The Lynching of Emmett Till*, 79–80.

27. In her memoir, Mamie Till-Mobley recounts the specifics of Rayner's restoration, including his decision to remove the swollen tongue that hung from Till's mouth, to sew pieces of his scalp back together, and to remove Till's one remaining eye, which was dangling from its socket. Till-Mobley and Benson, *Death of Innocence*, 132–140. For press coverage of the funeral, see Carl Hirsch, "50,000 Mourn at Bier of Lynched Negro Child," *Daily Worker*, September 10, 1955, reprinted in Metress, *The Lynching of Emmett Till*, 31–34.

28. Mattie Smith Colin, "Till's Mom, Diggs Both Disappointed," *Chicago Defender*, October 1, 1955. For further coverage of Diggs's role as a civil rights spokesperson after the trial, see "100,000 Across Nation Protest Till Lynching," *Chicago Defender*, October 8, 1955; John LeFlore, "2,000 in Mobile Hear Diggs Rip Dixie Terror," *Chicago Defender*, November 12, 1955.

29. Bayard Rustin, "Fear in the Delta," in *Time on Two Crosses: The Collected Writings of Bayard Rustin*, Devon W. Carbado and Donald Weise, eds. (San Francisco: Cleis Press, 2003), 72.

30. Eddie Madison, Jr., "Miss. Racist Victim Raps State's New Lynching," *Chicago Defender*, April 30, 1959.

31. Charles J. Lapidary, "Belzoni, Mississippi," *New Republic* (May 7, 1956): 12–13.

32. Robert H. Miller, "Aid for a Righteous Cause," *National Funeral Director and Embalmer*, vol. 9, no. 4 (April 1956): 6.

33. Robert H. Miller, "An Open Letter to Fellow Members of the National

Negro Funeral Directors Association," *National Funeral Director and Embalmer,* vol. 9, no. 3 (March 1956): 6.

34. Robert H. Miller, "Our Cleveland Convention," *National Funeral Director and Embalmer,* vol. 9, no. 9 (September 1956): 4; "Tribute to Martin Luther King Jr.," *National Funeral Director and Embalmer,* vol. 32, no. 4 (July/August 1979): 11.

35. C. W. Lee, "Report of the Chairman of the Board," *National Funeral Director and Embalmer,* vol. 9, no. 9 (September 1956): 6; "Undertakers to Change Name at St. Louis Confab," *Chicago Defender,* August 3, 1957.

36. Elaine Latzman Moon, *Untold Tales, Unsung Heroes: An Oral History of Detroit's African American Community, 1918–1967* (Detroit: Wayne State University Press, 1994), 57.

37. "Funeral Directors Still Bar Diggs," *Pittsburgh Courier,* August 20, 1955; "Morticians Give NAACP $8000," *Pittsburgh Courier,* August 20, 1955; "Morticians Join NAACP," *Chicago Defender,* September 3, 1955.

38. Robert H. Miller, "Clarie Collins Harvey Named 'Woman of the Year,'" *National Funeral Director and Embalmer,* vol. 9, no. 1 (January 1956): 4; Clarice T. Campbell and Oscar Allan Rodgers, Jr., *Mississippi: The View from Tougaloo* (Jackson: University Press of Mississippi, 1979), 186; Clarie Collins Harvey, Oral History transcript, Interviewers: John Dittmer and John Jones, Mississippi Department of Archives and History (Accession Number: OH 83-04, Acquisition Date: April 23, 1981), 6–7; Clarie Collins Harvey, Oral History transcript, Interviewer: Robert Penn Warren, February 9, 1964, Jean and Alexander Heard Library, Vanderbilt University, 13.

39. For the definitive history of the Freedom Rides, see Raymond Arsenault, *Freedom Riders: 1961 and the Struggle for Racial Justice* (New York: Oxford University Press, 2006).

40. Clarie Collins Harvey, "Freedom Riders, Please Go Away," *National Funeral Director and Embalmer,* vol. 14, no. 8 (August 1961): 4, 15, 18.

41. Ibid.; Clarie Collins Harvey, Oral History transcript, Interviewers: John Dittmer and John Jones, Mississippi Department of Archives and History (Accession Number: OH 83-04, Acquisition Date: April 23, 1981), 25–30; Clarie Collins Harvey, Oral History transcript, Interviewer: Robert Penn Warren, February 9, 1964, Jean and Alexander Heard Library, Vanderbilt University, 20–23; Medgar Evers, "Memorandum on 'Operation of Other Civil Rights Organizations in the State of Mississippi,'" October 12, 1961, NAACP Papers, reprinted in *The Autobiography of Medgar Evers,* Myrlie Evers-Williams and Manning Marable, eds. (New York: Basic Books, 2005), 235–

239; Arsenault, *Freedom Riders,* 334–335; and Tiyi Morris, "Black Women's Civil Rights Activism in Mississippi: The Story of Womanpower Unlimited" (Ph.D. diss., Purdue University, 2002).

42. Clarie Collins Harvey, Oral History transcript, Interviewer: Robert Penn Warren, February 9, 1964, Jean and Alexander Heard Library, Vanderbilt University, 14–17, 51–52; Clarie Collins Harvey, Oral History transcript, Interviewers: John Dittmer and John Jones, Mississippi Department of Archives and History (Accession Number: OH 83-04, Acquisition Date: April 23, 1981), 28; Dittmer, *Local People,* 98–99.

43. Clarie Collins Harvey, "Women Strike for Peace," *National Funeral Director and Embalmer,* vol. 15, no. 5 (May 1962): 15–17; Clarie Collins Harvey Papers, Amistad Collection, Box 17, FBI Files.

44. Mississippi Sovereignty Commission online, mdah.state.ms.us, SCR # 1-16-1-57-4-1-1; John R. Salter, Jr., *Jackson, Mississippi: An American Chronicle of Struggle and Schism* (Hicksville, N.Y.: Exposition Press, 1979), 138.

45. Myrlie Evers-Williams and Manning Marable, eds., *The Autobiography of Medgar Evers: A Hero's Life and Legacy Revealed through His Writings, Letters, and Speeches* (New York: Basic Books, 2005), 280–283. For detailed histories of the Jackson movement, see Salter, *Jackson, Mississippi;* Myrlie Evers with William Peters, *For Us, the Living* (Jackson: University Press of Mississippi, 1996), 235–311; and Dittmer, *Local People,* 157–169.

46. Evers with Peters, *For Us, the Living,* 267.

47. Mendelsohn, *The Martyrs,* 72–81.

48. Salter, *Jackson, Mississippi,* 208–223.

49. Evers with Peters, *For Us, the Living,* 313–322; Mendelsohn, *The Martyrs,* 72–81; Dittmer, *Local People,* 165–169; Salter, *Jackson, Mississippi,* 208–223.

50. Andrew Manis, *A Fire You Can't Put Out: The Civil Rights Life of Birmingham's Reverend Fred Shuttlesworth* (Tuscaloosa: The University of Alabama Press, 1999), 93–94.

51. Fred L. Shuttlesworth, "An Account of the Alabama Christian Movement for Human Rights," in Jacquelyne Johnson Clarke, "Goals and Techniques in Three Civil Rights Organizations in Alabama" (Ph.D. diss., Ohio State University, 1960), 133–153.

52. Ibid., 149–150.

53. For more detailed discussion of the founding of the ACHMR, see Manis, *A Fire You Can't Put Out,* 93–112; and Glenn T. Eskew, *But for Birmingham: The Local and National Movements in the Civil Rights Struggle* (Chapel Hill: University of North Carolina Press, 1997), 121–151.

54. "Birmingham Undertaker Is Beaten," *Pittsburgh Courier,* August 13, 1932; "Urges Congress to Probe NRA Stand on Race," *Pittsburgh Courier,* July 14, 1934; "Citizens Make Plea for Civil Liberties," *Pittsburgh Courier,* October 3, 1942; "The Birmingham Story," *Pittsburgh Courier,* February 7, 1959; Manis, *A Fire You Can't Put Out,* 117, 190, 284.

55. Manis, *A Fire You Can't Put Out,* 311–312; Diane McWhorter, *Carry Me Home: Birmingham, Alabama: The Climactic Battle of the Civil Rights Movement* (New York: Simon and Schuster, 2001), 267; "Alabama Rights Fighter Escapes Shots of Bigot," *Chicago Defender,* April 17, 1962; "Would Be Assassins Bullets Misses Willie E. Shortridge," *National Funeral Director and Embalmer,* vol. 15, no. 4 (April 1962): 19.

56. For more details on Gaston's life story, see Carol Jenkins and Elizabeth Gardner Hines, *Black Titan: A. G. Gaston and the Making of a Black American Millionaire* (New York: One World/Ballantine Books, 2004); A. G. Gaston, *Green Power: The Successful Way of A. G. Gaston* (Birmingham, Ala.: Southern University Press, 1968); Patricia Thompson Stelts, "Black Midas: Arthur George Gaston" (M.A. thesis, Dept. of History, Georgia Southern College, August 1973).

57. "Disorderly Crowd Breaks Windows of Car Carrying Student to Ala. U.," *Birmingham World,* February 7, 1956; "Student Body at U. of Ala. Blasts Mobs," *Pittsburgh Courier,* February 11, 1956; "Courageous Miss Lucy Denies Being High-Handed," *Pittsburgh Courier,* March 3, 1956; J. A. Rogers, "Miss Lucy's Fans," *Chicago Defender,* March 17, 1956; "History Shows," *Pittsburgh Courier,* March 31, 1956.

58. "Gaston Using a Buck to Aid B'ham Battle," *Chicago Defender,* May 18, 1963; "Millionaire Funeral Director Tells Role in Birmingham Truce," *National Funeral Director and Embalmer,* vol. 16, no. 6 (June 1963): 16; McWhorter, *Carry Me Home,* 264; Gaston, *Green Power,* 112–113; Eskew, *But for Birmingham,* 207.

59. "$300,000 Motel for Birmingham," *Chicago Defender,* July 17, 1954; Gaston, *Green Power,* 110; Manis, *A Fire You Can't Put Out,* 114; "Gaston Opens New Office Building," *Chicago Defender,* March 26, 1960.

60. Manis, *A Fire You Can't Put Out,* 321–324.

61. Howell Raines, *My Soul Is Rested* (New York: G. P. Putnam's Sons, 1977), 156; Manis, *A Fire You Can't Put Out,* 324–326; Eskew, *But for Birmingham,* 202–205; Martin Luther King, Jr., *Why We Can't Wait* (New York: Harper and Row, 1964), 45–47.

62. King, *Why We Can't Wait,* 48–56.

63. Gaston, *Green Power,* 120–121; McWhorter, *Carry Me Home,* 335–337.

64. Eskew, *But for Birmingham,* 230–231; Ben Burns, "Uncle Tom Trouble in Birmingham," *Chicago Defender,* April 16, 1963; McWhorter, *Carry Me Home,* 343. McWhorter claims that Gaston told Hibbler he canceled the concert because "he didn't want to go against the good white folks in Birmingham." Other sources, including Gaston's *Green Power* and Eskew's *But for Birmingham,* note that a bureaucratic mix-up was partly to blame for the concert's cancellation. Gaston, *Green Power,* 124–125; Eskew, *But for Birmingham,* 379, n.28.

65. Eskew, *But for Birmingham,* 231–233; Manis, *A Fire You Can't Put Out,* 352; David J. Garrow, *Bearing the Cross: Martin Luther King Jr. and the Southern Christian Leadership Conference* (New York: William Morrow, 1986), 239–240.

66. Garrow, *Bearing the Cross,* 241–243; Manis, *A Fire You Can't Put Out,* 356.

67. Martin Luther King, Jr., *Why We Can't Wait,* 70–72; Eskew, *But for Birmingham,* 239–240.

68. Gaston, *Green Power,* 115, 125; Eskew, *But for Birmingham,* 259–297; Manis, *A Fire You Can't Put Out,* 371–372.

69. Stelts, "Black Midas: Arthur George Gaston," 116.

70. King, *Why We Can't Wait,* 111–113; Eskew, *But for Birmingham,* 299–340.

71. "Gaston Using a Buck to Aid B'ham Battle," *Pittsburgh Courier,* May 18, 1963; Gaston, *Green Power,* 123–124.

72. McWhorter, *Carry Me Home,* 504; "Bomb Home of Alabama Negro Millionaire, A. G. Gaston," *Chicago Defender,* September 9, 1963; Gaston, *Green Power,* 131.

73. "Bomb Victims Rode Segregated Ambulances to Hospital, Morgue," *Chicago Defender,* September 18, 1963.

74. James L. Hicks, "No One Can View Cynthia," *New York Amsterdam News,* September 21, 1963. The press coverage of Carole Robertson's funeral also made particular note of "the child's *sealed* blue casket" (italics mine). See Leon Daniel, "'Bombing' Victim Buried," *Birmingham World,* September 21, 1963.

5. THE AFRICAN AMERICAN WAY OF DEATH

1. Jessica Mitford, *The American Way of Death* (New York: Simon and Schuster, 1963), xiii–xvi.

2. Gary Laderman, *Rest in Peace: A Cultural History of Death and the Funeral Home in Twentieth-Century America* (New York: Oxford University Press, 2003), xxi–xxxi; Jessica Mitford, *The American Way of Death Revisited* (New York: Alfred A. Knopf, 1998), 237–253.

3. Mitford, *The American Way of Death Revisited*, xvi–xvii.

4. "Rumors Explode into State Investigation," *Casket and Sunnyside* (December 1963): 18; "Savage Attacks on Funeral Service Are Heard and Read by Millions of Citizens," *Casket and Sunnyside* (December 1963): 22.

5. Robert H. Miller, "Morticians Set for Confab," *National Funeral Director and Embalmer*, vol. 16, no. 8 (August 1963): 5; Dr. Benjamin E. Mays, "An Age of Dramatic Dimensions, Part I," *National Funeral Director and Embalmer*, vol. 17, no. 1 (January 1964): 14–16; Dr. Benjamin E. Mays, "An Age of Dramatic Dimensions, Part III," *National Funeral Director and Embalmer*, vol. 17, no. 3 (March 1964): 18–19; "Morticians to Back March," *Chicago Defender*, August 17, 1963.

6. John Nathan MacIntosh, "The Man in the Decent Black Suit," *National Funeral Director and Embalmer*, vol. 16, no. 11 (November 1963): 7, 17; "Miller-Meteor Leads Rebuttal against Funeral Smears," *National Funeral Director and Embalmer*, vol. 16, no. 12 (December 1963): 6; C. W. Lee, "President's Report: Proposes Creating Position of Liaison Officer," *National Funeral Director and Embalmer* (September 1965): 5, 15, 17; Robert H. Miller, "Report of General Secretary Robert H. Miller," *National Funeral Director and Embalmer* (October 1966).

7. "NFDA Opens Membership to Non-White Persons," *Casket and Sunnyside* (November 1963): 26.

8. Ibid., 26–27.

9. William Manchester, *The Death of a President* (New York: Harper and Row, 1967), 432; Mitford, *The American Way of Death Revisited*, 136.

10. Albert R. Kates, Editorial: "Traditional Symbols and Accustomed Ceremonials," *American Funeral Director* (December 1963): 21–23; Ralph W. Loew, "Mrs. Kennedy's Fortitude Fine Example to U.S.," *Buffalo Courier Express* (December 2, 1963): 14; Robert L. Fulton and Howard C. Raether, "The World Stood Still," *The Director* (December 1963): 4–5; Laderman, *Rest in Peace*, xxxi–xlii.

11. Clarie Collins Harvey, "A Tribute to John Fitzgerald Kennedy of the United States of America," *National Funeral Director and Embalmer*, 17, no. 1 (January 1964): 4.

12. Ibid.

13. Thomas E. Turner, "Negro Home Now Handling All of Ft. Hood's Funerals," *Dallas Morning News,* reprinted in the *National Funeral Director and Embalmer,* 17, no. 1 (January 1964): 5.

14. Turner, "Negro Home Now Handling All of Ft. Hood's Funerals," 5.

15. "The Business Side of Bereavement," *Black Enterprise,* vol. 8 (November 1977): 57.

16. Coretta Scott King, *My Life with Martin Luther King Jr.* (New York: Holt, Rinehart and Winston, 1969), 244; Alex Haley, *The Autobiography of Malcolm X* (New York: Ballantine, 1988), 301.

17. Seth Cagin and Philip Dray, *We Are Not Afraid: The Story of Goodman, Schwerner, and Chaney and the Civil Rights Campaign for Mississippi* (New York: Bantam, 1991).

18. David M. Spain, "Mississippi Autopsy," *Ramparts,* special ed. (1964): 42–49.

19. "It's a Shame," *Chicago Defender,* August 22, 1964; Dave Dennis, "Address at the Funeral Service for James Chaney," First Union Baptist Church, Meridian, Mississippi, August 7, 1964, reprinted in *Rhetoric, Religion and the Civil Rights Movement, 1954–1965,* Davis W. Houck and David E. Dixon, eds. (Waco, Tex.: Baylor University Press, 2006), 775–778.

20. Dennis, "Address at the Funeral Service for James Chaney," 775–778.

21. Peter Goldman, *The Death and Life of Malcolm X* (Urbana: University of Illinois Press, 1979), 230–231; John Herbers, "Non-Violence—Powerful Rights Weapon," *New York Times,* February 28, 1965.

22. Haley, *The Autobiography of Malcolm X,* 426–427; Scott King, *My Life with Martin Luther King Jr.,* 255–256.

23. Homer Bigart, "Black Muslim Guard Held in Murder of Malcolm X," *New York Times,* February 27, 1965.

24. Haley, *The Autobiography of Malcolm X,* 451; Paul L. Montgomery, "Malcolm Buried as True Moslem Despite Unorthodox Ritual," *New York Times,* February 28, 1965.

25. Haley, *The Autobiography of Malcolm X,* 442; "Vigil against Violence at Malcolm X's Bier," *Chicago Defender,* February 25, 1965; Peter Kihss, "Mosque Fires Stir Fear of Vendetta in Malcolm Case," *New York Times,* February 24, 1965; Peter Kihss, "Hunt for Killers in Malcolm Case 'On Right Track,'" *New York Times,* February 25, 1965.

26. "Bishop Defies Home, Church Threats over Malcolm's Rites," *Chicago Defender,* March 2, 1965; "Malcolm X's Followers Follow Him to Grave," *Amsterdam News,* March 6, 1965.

27. Martin Arnold, "Harlem Is Quiet as Crowds Watch Malcolm X Rites,"

New York Times, February 28, 1965; "Ossie Davis' Stirring Tribute to Malcolm X," *New York Amsterdam News,* March 6, 1965; Goldman, *The Death and Life of Malcolm X,* 303; "Malcolm X's Followers Follow Him to Grave," *New York Amsterdam News,* March 6, 1965.

28. Jack Mendelsohn, *The Martyrs: Sixteen Who Gave Their Lives for Racial Justice* (New York: Harper and Row, 1966), 133–135; Thaddeus T. Stokes, "Hatred, Violence, Death," *Atlanta Daily World,* February 28, 1965.

29. Mendelsohn, *The Martyrs,* 137–138.

30. Roy Reed, "Wounded Negro Dies in Alabama," *New York Times,* February 27, 1965; Mendelsohn, *The Martyrs,* 146–147.

31. Roy Reed, "Hero's Burial Set for Slain Negro," *New York Times,* February 28, 1965; "Hundreds File Past Bier of Jimmie Lee Jackson," *Chicago Defender,* March 4, 1965; "Unknown Jimmie Jackson Gets Two-Hero Funerals," *Chicago Defender,* March 6, 1965.

32. Paul Weeks, "Dr. King under Heavy Guard on Arrival Here," *Los Angeles Times,* February 25, 1965; Mendelsohn, *The Martyrs,* 149.

33. Mendelsohn, *The Martyrs,* 149; Adam Fairclough, *To Redeem the Soul of America: The Southern Christian Leadership Conference and Martin Luther King Jr.* (Athens: University of Georgia Press, 1987), 240–241.

34. "Reaction to Murder . . . A National Disgrace," *Southern Patriot* 23 (April 1965): 3; David Riley, "Who Is Jimmie Lee Jackson?" *New Republic* 152 (April 3, 1965): 8–9; Mendelsohn, *The Martyrs,* 150–151.

35. Charles E. Fager, *Selma, 1965* (New York: Scribner's Sons, 1974), 157; Carol Jenkins and Elizabeth Gardner Hines, *Black Titan: A. G. Gaston and the Making of a Black American Millionaire* (New York: Ballantine, 2004), 221–226; Willard Clopton, "Gov. Wallace Agrees to Meet Today with 20 Selma Civil Rights Delegates," *Washington Post,* March 30, 1965.

36. Karla F. C. Holloway, *Passed On: African American Mourning Stories* (Durham: Duke University Press, 2002), 36–37. For more details on Jones's role as eyewitness to the King assassination, see Gerold Frank, *An American Death: The True Story of the Assassination of Dr. Martin Luther King Jr. and the Greatest Manhunt of Our Time* (New York: Doubleday, 1972), 71–76; Scott King, *My Life with Martin Luther King Jr.,* 317; Taylor Branch, *At Canaan's Edge: America in the King Years, 1965–1968* (New York: Simon and Schuster, 2006), 766.

37. For first-person reflections on the larger meanings of these assassinations, see Henry Hampton and Steve Fayer, with Sarah Flynn, *Voices of Freedom: An Oral History of the Civil Rights Movement from the 1950s through the 1980s* (New York: Bantam Books, 1990), 449–471, 479–480.

38. Scott King, *My Life with Martin Luther King Jr.*, 330–331, 348–349.

39. Ibid., 332–333, 352–359; Michael Kilian, "Throngs Fill Atlanta for King Funeral," *Chicago Tribune*, April 8, 1968.

40. Two black funeral homes directed King's funeral rites. In Memphis, R. S. Lewis and Sons Funeral Home embalmed King's body and prepared it for viewing. In Atlanta, Hanley's Funeral Home directed his two funeral services.

41. Proceedings of the Eighty-ninth Annual Convention of the National Funeral Directors Association, New Orleans, Louisiana, Wednesday Morning Session (October 28, 1970): 11–13.

42. Robert H. Miller, "Texas Fights Negro Membership in National Funeral Directors Association," *National Funeral Director and Embalmer* (March–April 1971): 8.

43. Robert H. Miller, "Membership Should Promote Employment of Blacks by Funeral Service Companies," *National Funeral Director and Embalmer* (January–February 1974): 5; Robert H. Miller, "Black-Owned Funeral Supplies Firm Epitomizes 'Black Power' in Business," *National Funeral Director and Embalmer* (May–June 1973).

44. Mitford, *The American Way of Death Revisited*, 176; Laderman, *Rest in Peace*, 131–138.

45. Mitford, *The American Way of Death Revisited*, 176–177; Laderman, *Rest in Peace*, 133.

46. Mitford, *The American Way of Death Revisited*, 178.

47. Robert H. Miller, "Disrespecting the Dead Not for Our Day and Time," *National Funeral Director and Embalmer* (July–August 1973): 3.

48. Robert H. Miller, "Blacks Have Traditional Respect for the Dead," *National Funeral Director and Embalmer* (January–February 1975): 9.

49. "Statement by A. A. Rayner Jr. to the Federal Trade Commission, May 18, 1976," *National Funeral Director and Embalmer* (May–June 1976): 7.

50. "Statement of Leon Harrison, Founder and President of Harrison and Ross Mortuaries," *National Funeral Director and Embalmer* (July–August 1976): 4–5.

51. Robert H. Miller, "Checking It Out," *National Funeral Director and Embalmer* (January–February 1974): 6; Ted Watson, "Ordinance for D.C.: Veto Funeral Charge List," *Chicago Defender*, December 19, 1974; Robert H. Miller, "Funeral Service Awaits FTC Bombshell," *National Funeral Director and Embalmer* (May–June 1975): 2; "Officials Rip FTC for Withholding Payments to Black National Funeral Directors Group," *National Funeral Director and Embalmer* (July–August 1977): 3.

52. Robert H. Miller, "Memorializing Civil Rights Site under NFD&MA

Leadership," *National Funeral Director and Embalmer,* Commemorative Issue: Robert H. Miller (Spring Issue 1979); "Robert H. Miller, 82, Noted Funeral Assn. Exec. Dies," *Jet Magazine,* February 1, 1979.

53. Marcia Kunstel, "60 Cry for 'White Power' as Klan Protest Fizzles," *Atlanta Journal Constitution,* August 10, 1979.

54. For many of the NFDMA members in attendance, the growth in black voting was a personal victory. Some funeral directors, especially from Alabama's Black Belt region, had participated directly in the Selma campaign. Others took pride in their individual efforts to encourage black voter participation. After the passage of the 1965 act, African American funeral directors often volunteered their limousines and hearses to drive black voters to the polls on election day. Jeremy Olshan, "May You Vote in Peace: Funeral Directors Offer Ride to the Polls in Limos," *Press of Atlantic City,* August 6, 2002.

55. William G. Blair, "900 Attend Ecumenical Rites of Wilkins," *New York Times,* September 12, 1981.

56. James H. Cleaver, "Wilkins' Funeral Protested," *Los Angeles Sentinel,* September 17, 1981; J. Zamgba Browne, "Black Undertakers Picket Wilkins Rites," *New York Amsterdam News,* September 19, 1981.

57. Angelo B. Henderson, "Death Watch? Black Funeral Homes Fear a Gloomy Future as Big Chains Move In," *Wall Street Journal,* July 18, 1997.

58. Ibid.; Holloway, *Passed On,* 43–46.

59. For details on the problems that besieged the "big three" funeral corporations, see Laderman, *Rest in Peace,* 184–194. For a recent scandal involving SCI, see Josh White, "'I Never Could Have Imagined': Dignity Was Denied the Dead as Bodies Were Stored and Handled Using 'Disturbing' Methods, Area Funeral Home Workers Say," *Washington Post,* April 5, 2009.

EPILOGUE

1. Rosa Parks with Jim Haskins, *Rosa Parks: My Story* (New York: Dial Books, 1992), 28.

2. The first African American to lie in state in the U.S. Capitol Rotunda was Jacob Chestnut, a U.S. Capitol police officer. Chestnut was killed on the job in 1998 when a lone gunman opened fire at the entrance of the building. Debbie Wilgoren and Theola S. Labbe, "An Overflowing Tribute to an Icon," *Washington Post,* November 1, 2005.

3. Jen Kiernan, "Rosa Parks: Making History in Life and Death," *American Funeral Director,* vol. 129, no. 1 (January 2006): 42–51.

4. David Remnick, "The Joshua Generation: Race and the Campaign of Barack Obama," *The New Yorker,* November 17, 2008.

5. Kiernan, "Rosa Parks," 51.

6. Shaila Dewan and Elisabeth Bumiller, "At Mrs. King's Funeral, a Mix of Elegy and Politics," *New York Times,* February 8, 2006; Peter Wallsten and Richard Fausset, "A Eulogy for King, a Scolding for Bush," *Los Angeles Times,* February 8, 2006.

7. Barack Obama, *The Audacity of Hope* (New York: Three Rivers Press, 2006), 227–231.

8. Carter, who was critical of President Bush's warrantless wiretapping of suspected terrorists, also commented that the lives of Martin Luther King, Jr., and Coretta Scott King were made difficult when "the civil liberties of both husband and wife were violated as they became the target of secret government wiretapping, other surveillance, and as you know, harassment from the FBI." "Remarks by Former U.S. President Jimmy Carter at the Coretta Scott King Funeral," http://www.cartercenter.org/news/documents/doc2295.html.

9. For a complete summary of conservative criticism of the Scott King funeral, see "Media Matters—Media Accused Liberals of Politicizing King Funeral, Ignored Conservatives' Use of Reagan Funeral," http://mediamatters .org/items/200602090007.

10. Dewan and Bumiller, "At Mrs. King's Funeral, a Mix of Elegy and Politics"; "How He Did It," *Newsweek,* November 17, 2008: 41; "Elder Bernice King Remembers Coretta Scott King," http://www.eightcitiesmap.com/ TheSeedsOfCorettaScottKing.htm.

11. "How He Did It," 120.

12. For two recent books on this question, see Tim Wise, *Between Barack and a Hard Place: Racism and White Denial in the Age of Obama* (San Francisco: City Lights Publishers, 2009); William Julius Wilson, *More Than Just Race: Being Black and Poor in the Inner City* (New York: W. W. Norton, 2009).

13. Gary Fields, "Deadly Business: Violence Roils Black Funeral Parlors," *Wall Street Journal,* March 26, 2008.

14. Ibid.

15. Ibid.

16. George C. Wright, *Life behind a Veil: Blacks in Louisville, Kentucky, 1865–1930* (Baton Rouge: Louisiana State University Press, 1985), 246–253; "Form New Party in Ky. to Fight G.O.P. Injustice," *Chicago Defender,* September 10, 1921.

17. Burns's reputation as a leading figure in black Louisville was also evi-

dent at his funeral in 1931, which drew a crowd that "probably exceeded that of any black leader." Wright, *Life behind a Veil*, 210.

18. George C. Wright, "Black Political Insurgency in Louisville, Kentucky: The Lincoln Independent Party of 1921," *Journal of Negro History*, vol. 68, no. 1 (Winter 1983): 17; *Louisville Leader*, November 12, 1921.

19. Wright, *Life behind a Veil*, 251–252; W. E. B. Du Bois, *The Crisis*, 23 (January 1922): 119.

20. Wright, *Life behind a Veil*, 252–261; Lee Brown, "Election Day Vandals Run Amuck; Wreck News Office," *Chicago Defender*, November 19, 1927.

21. Wright, *Life behind a Veil*, 210.

22. John Ed Pearce, "Louisville Negro Breaks Vote Pattern," *Christian Science Monitor*, May 19, 1961; Frank L. Stanley, "Being Frank about People, Places, and Problems," *Chicago Defender*, April 28, 1962.

23. For discussion of the recession's impact on the funeral industry, see Dana Milbank, "Funeral Business Feeling Six Feet Under," *Washington Post*, April 1, 2009.

Acknowledgments

Funeral directors bury the dead. Historians resurrect them. Writing a history of funeral directors is, therefore, a unique challenge and a lively adventure. In many ways, writing this book has been one of the most profound intellectual journeys of my life. The years of researching and writing required me to be present with death in ways that were both exhausting and inspiring. I could not have made such a journey without the generous help of others.

First, I would like to thank the funeral directors and other funeral industry professionals who shared their time and knowledge so openly. The membership of the National Funeral Directors and Morticians Association warmly welcomed me whenever I visited their annual convention. I am especially grateful to Dr. Edith Churchman of the James E. Churchman Funeral Home in Newark, New Jersey, who became one of my closest allies during my years of research. Dr. Churchman, herself an educator, never hesitated to answer my questions about African American funeral practices and often sent me valuable sources. Her friendship has been one of the greatest rewards of this project. I offer special thanks to Kathleen Walczak, Information and Education Specialist at the National Funeral Directors Association. When I first visited the NFDA Headquarters and its library, Kathleen was a gracious host who generously shared her own vast knowledge of the history of the funeral industry. Countless times over the years, Kathleen helped me track down sources I could never have found on my own. I am especially indebted to Barbara Miller Holmes, daughter of Robert H. Miller, who went out of her way to send me personal scrapbooks and cherished family photographs, which were critical to my understanding of her father's contributions to African American funeral service. Over the years, many other funeral directors and industry leaders shared their stories and archives, answered questions, and offered encouragement, including John C. Carmon; James E. Churchman, Jr.; Bernard R. Fielding; Doris Furbush; Thurman Higginbotham; Billie Watson Hughes; Theodore Lee, Jr., and JoAnne Lee; John and Lynne McGuire; Lynn Armstrong Patterson; the late Allene Renfro; Elijah Rollins; Joseph L. Russ; J. C. Scarborough, III, and Queen B. Scarborough; Margaret B. Stewart; John T. Stewart, III; and Calvernetta Williams. Finally, I thank Thomas Lynch, whom I have never met, but whose book *The Undertaking: Life Studies from the Dismal Trade* inspired some of my early ideas about funeral directors' service to the living.

Beyond the funeral industry, a number of individuals were instrumental in helping me complete this project. I would especially like to thank Kevin Boyle, Shane White, and Gary Laderman, who read the manuscript in its entirety and offered incisive critiques that greatly improved the book. Jon Butler was unwavering in his support of the project over the years. Laura Wexler, author of *Fire in a Canebrake*, generously shared her research files on Dan Young and the Moore's Ford lynching. Robert Howard and Representative Tyrone Brooks also offered invaluable insights into Dan Young's career as a civil rights activist. David Beito sent me early drafts of his own book on Dr. T. R. M. Howard, as well as several rare primary sources on Mississippi's early freedom campaign. Roger Wilkins shared his personal memories of his uncle's funeral. Deborah Willis was always willing to help me track down photographs of African American funerals. Finally, I thank Jon Picoult, who sent me an important article on the African American funeral industry that helped shape my conclusions.

The National Endowment for the Humanities funded this project at two very critical points in its development. In 1998, I was selected to participate in an NEH Summer Institute on the History of Death in America, hosted by David and Sheila Rothman at Columbia University. The colleagues I met and lessons I learned from that experience were instrumental in my early conceptualizations of the project. Later, in 2006–2007, I was awarded an NEH Research Fellowship, during which the majority of the book was written. I would also like to thank the Kenneth Spencer Research Library at the University of Kansas for awarding me a travel grant, which allowed me to research the John T. Miles collection. Special thanks goes to Ann Schofield, who hosted me during my week at the University of Kansas. Additionally, I thank Marguerite S. Shaffer and the American Studies Department at Miami University, Ohio, for inviting me to participate in their 2004 Public Culture conference and test out some of my early ideas. Portions of two chapters, now substantially revised, previously appeared in earlier publications: "To Serve the Living: The Public and Civic Identity of African American Funeral Directors," in *Public Culture: Diversity, Democracy, and Community in the United States*, ed. Marguerite S. Shaffer (Philadelphia: University of Pennsylvania Press, 2008); and "'Laid Out in Big Mama's Kitchen': African Americans and the Personalized Theme Funeral," in *American Behavioral History*, ed. Peter N. Stearns (New York: New York University Press, 2005). Finally, I would like to express my appreciation to the staff of the Bishop Payne Library at the Virginia Theological Seminary in Alexandria, Virginia, who graciously let me use their facilities and collections during my leave to write the book.

At Harvard University Press, I thank my editor, Joyce Seltzer, who did an extraordinary job bringing this book to life. What most impressed me about working with Joyce was how deeply she cared about every detail of the project, from its title to its main arguments. Her steadfast commitment to the work kept me motivated to see it to its completion. I also thank her for her wisdom in knowing when to offer advice and when to step back and let me figure things out for myself. I am grateful to Christine Thorsteinsson, who copyedited the manuscript and guided the book through the final stages of production. Christine's attention to detail, belief in the project, and good humor made even mundane tasks enjoyable. Finally, I offer my thanks to Jeannette Estruth, whose good cheer helped me navigate all the logistical details of the publishing process.

Many friends and colleagues offered encouragement over the years. At George Mason University, I would like to thank all my colleagues in the Department of History and Art History for their support. I am especially grateful for the friendship of Joan Bristol, Gretchen Buggeln, Dan Cohen, Phil Deloria, Jen Halpern, the late Robert Hawkes, Lois and Jim Horton, Deborah Kaplan, Jennifer Lansbury, Cornelia Levine, Margaret McCaffrey, Tobie Meyer-Fong, Norman Middleton, Laura Mitchell, Deb Raupp, Jim Rennie, Julie Rocchio, Randolph Scully, Leonard and Beth Stark, Ellen Todd, and Rosemarie Zagarri.

Words are insufficient to express my gratitude to my parents, Gerald and Caralee Smith, whose love has been the foundation of everything good in my life. In the decade that I worked on this book, my paternal grandmother, Elizabeth Smith, and my maternal grandparents, William and Aldina Narden, all passed away. I continue to miss them and the pride they took in my accomplishments. My extended family includes the Smith, Fagen, Johnson-Thomas, Goldman, Chaiet, Eardley, Van Loon, Silk, and Gonzalez families. I thank them all for their love and encouragement. I would also like to remember my great uncle, the late Adam Tanceusz; and my grandparents-in-law, the late Sidney Deutchman and the late Bea and Ben Fagen, who all cared about me and this project and are deeply missed.

I have dedicated the book to my husband, Doug Fagen, and our beautiful sons, Evan and Jeremy, as well as to the memory of my former colleagues Lawrence W. Levine and Roy A. Rosenzweig. When I first came to George Mason University in 1995, I had the distinct honor of joining the faculty with Larry Levine, who had come to the department after his retirement from the University of California, Berkeley. As a junior faculty member specializing in African American cultural history, I couldn't believe my good fortune to have a senior colleague who happened to be one of the most preeminent scholars in my field. The department was also led by the vision of Roy Rosenzweig, who was busy defining the field of digital history as well as being one of the most generous individuals I had ever met. Larry and Roy guided the first twelve years of my professional life through their example as scholars and as human beings committed to creating a more just world. They both improved my first book on Motown music through their thoughtful critiques and cheered me on in numerous ways as I worked on this project. When Larry passed away in October 2006 and Roy in October 2007, the loss was a personal one for me and a much larger one for the field of American history. I will miss their friendship always.

I leave my final and deepest thanks to my husband, Doug, and our boys, Evan and Jeremy, who were born in the middle of this book's own gestation. No one person is more responsible for this book's existence than Doug, who has navigated its presence in our lives since we met. When I was buried in diapers and dirty laundry and doubted if this project would ever see the light of day, Doug believed. His abiding love and his own wisdom about the meaning of death and loss anchor me in a world that can sometimes feel unmoored. Our children, Evan and Jeremy, are simply two of the most enchanting beings I have ever known. Above all, death teaches us that every minute counts. One of the biggest joys of finally putting this project to rest is that it frees me to enjoy more time with Doug, Evan, and Jeremy and the vibrant life we share.

Index

Abernathy, Ralph, 148, 150, 152, 158, 170, 176, 180

A. D. Porter and Sons Funeral Home, 203–208

African American funeral customs: during slavery, 25–31; during modern era, 83–87; jazz funeral, 85. *See also* Homegoing celebration

African American way of death: serving the living and, 13–14; perception of death as freedom, 17–18; origins in the slave funeral, 25–31; hearses and, 60–61, 86–87, 225n12; gospel music and, 83, 85, 95–110, 180, 197; homegoing celebration, 83–87; open caskets and, 124–125, 127, 154–155; African Americans' allegiance to, 184–185; preference for embalming, 185, 191

African burial customs, 18–25; survivals in the New World, 27–31

Alabama Christian Movement for Human Rights (ACMHR), founding of, 141–143, 146–149, 152

American Way of Death, The (Mitford), 156–160, 162, 183

Atlanta College of Mortuary Service, 77, 106

Batesville Casket Company, 182

Bevel, James, 170, 177

Birmingham campaign (SCLC). *See* Southern Christian Leadership Conference

Black benevolent societies, 40–42, 221n21. *See also* Burial leagues

Black capitalism, 39, 42, 44–45, 55, 62, 66, 74, 81, 117–119; race patronage and, 46–48, 51–52, 70, 78, 190–191

Black power movement, 165, 170, 179, 182

Brooks, Tyrone, 1–2, 12

Browder v. Gayle (1956), 130, 142

Brown v. Board of Education (1954), 11, 110, 116, 118–120, 155

Brown Chapel A. M. E. Church (Selma), 170, 175–176, 187–188

Burial insurance, 40–43, 87–88, 97–102, 104–105, 118, 144

Burial leagues, 40–43, 82, 88, 225n14

Burns, Harvey, 205–207, 242n17

Bush, George H. W., 189, 197

Bush, George W., 195, 197–200, 242n8

Carter, Jimmy, 199, 242n8

Caskets: modernization of, 38; covert uses for, 115–116, 153, 230n6

Casket and Sunnyside, 68, 81, 88–89, 157–158, 160
Cemeteries, racial segregation in, 57, 60, 64–66, 168, 181
Chaney, James, 13, 167–169, 176
Civil rights movement: voting rights campaigns, 3–4, 9–11, 112–115, 167–171, 173–199; African American funeral directors' relationship to, 49, 57–66, 110–111, 115–116, 164–166, 190; desegregation campaigns, 57–59, 61–64. *See also* March on Washington; Nashville Streetcar Boycott; Till, Emmett
Civil Rights Act of 1964, 117, 163–166, 187, 189
Civil rights funeral: examples of, 123–124, 127–128, 139–140, 154–155, 167–181, 204; definition of, 166–167
Civil War, U.S., 18, 31–35, 38–39, 43, 57, 59–60
Coffin, Levi, 16–17
Cole, Robert A., 98–102, 105, 106
Collins, Malachi C., 46–47, 133
Colored Embalmer, The, 69–70, 74, 77, 78
Congress of Racial Equality (CORE), 112, 115, 134, 138, 167, 169
Connor, Eugene "Bull," 141, 143, 147–150
Cornelius, W. R., 33–34
Courts, Gus, 129. *See also* Regional Council of Negro Leadership
Cremation, 83, 183–185, 191

Dennis, Dave, 139, 168–169, 176
DePriest, Oscar, 97
Detroit Memorial Park, 64–66, 121
Diggs, Charles C., Jr.: involvement in Mississippi civil rights campaign, 120–123; participation in Emmett Till case, 128–129; support for Montgomery Bus Boycott, 132; relationship to NNFDA, 132–133, 155
Diggs, Charles C., Sr., 64–65, 121–122, 231n15. *See also* House of Diggs Funeral Home
Drew, Robert L., 120, 137
Du Bois, W. E. B., 18, 39, 42, 44, 48–50, 206

Ebenezer Baptist Church (Atlanta), 180, 197, 200
Ebony magazine, 79–80, 87, 101–103, 105, 122–123, 224n2
Eckle's Embalming School, 121
Emanuel Jackson Funeral Home, 96–97
Embalming: history of, 18, 32–35, 50, 68, 73, 83, 86, 214n11; schools of, 36–38, 56, 77, 81, 106–107, 121, 217n35; of civil rights martyrs, 124, 155; arguments against, 156, 183; African Americans' preference for, 185
Epsilon Nu Delta (E.N.D.), 78
Evers, Medgar: civil rights activism of, 123, 137–139; assassination and funeral of, 139–140, 163, 166, 176
Evers, Myrlie, 138, 163

Farmer, James, 112–115, 134
Fayetteville Casket and Coffin Company, 55–57
Federal Bureau of Investigation (FBI): Moore's Ford lynching case, 6–7, 11, 13; George W. Lee murder case, 123; Goodman, Schwerner, Chaney murder case, 167; homicide statistics of, 202
Federal Trade Commission (FTC), 165–166, 182–187

First ladies. *See* Mortician's nurse
Frazier, E. Franklin, 103, 224n2
Frazier and Collins Funeral Home, 120,
    133, 135, 139–140
Freedom Rides, 112, 134–135, 137
Freedom Summer project, 13, 167–169
Funeral directors: professionalization of,
    35–39; public image of, 79–81, 89–90,
    94, 97, 101–103, 111, 133; ethical
    concerns with, 80–83, 87–88, 104–
    105, 111; advertising and, 94–95; in-
    volvement in underworld economies,
    95–98, 101, 111, 205–207; sociologi-
    cal research about, 103–105
Funeral fans, 94–95. *See also* photo gal-
    lery
Funeral homes: emergence of, 67–68,
    89–90; as refuge from Jim Crow, 90–
    91, 99–100, 109, 203; as site of civil
    rights organizing, 114, 204, 207; vio-
    lence at, 172–173, 202–204
Funeral industry: emergence of, 31–39;
    African Americans' early participa-
    tion in, 39–45; racial discrimination
    in, 56–57, 66, 116–117, 186–187;
    growth in modern era, 67; criticism
    of, 81–83, 156–158, 159–161; federal
    investigation of, 182–187; rise of
    multinational funeral conglomerates,
    191–192

Gabriel's Rebellion, 27–28
Gaston, A. G.: as successful entrepre-
    neur, 109, 144, 146, 152; involvement
    in Birmingham civil rights campaign,
    141–142, 145–155, 163, 178, 236n64;
    assistance to Autherine Lucy, 144–
    145; firebombing of his home, 153–
    154. *See also* Gaston Motel; Smith
    and Gaston Funeral Home

Gaston Motel, 144–146, 149–150, 152–
    153
Georgia Association of Black Elected
    Officials (GABEO), 12
Georgia Bureau of Investigation (GBI),
    6, 13
Goodman, Andrew, 13
Gospel music, 83, 85, 95, 108–110, 180,
    197
Grave decoration: African, 23–24; Afri-
    can American, 30–31
Greenwood Cemetery (Nashville), 60,
    64, 92
Greenwood Park (Nashville), 92–93,
    97
Greer, Prince, 34

Harlem's Book of the Dead, 86. *See also*
    photo gallery
Harrison, Loy, 4, 6–7
Harvey, Clarie Collins: involvement in
    civil rights movement, 120, 155;
    founding of Womanpower Unlim-
    ited, 133–137, 140; directing of
    Medgar Evers funeral, 139–140
Hearses: history of, 38, 77; as important
    feature of homegoing celebration,
    60–61, 86–87, 225n12; as security
    protection during civil rights move-
    ment, 115–116, 179; as ambulances,
    129–130, 154; other uses, 108, 134,
    189, 241n54
High Cost of Dying, The, 157, 183
Holmes, Thomas, 33, 34, 37, 216n30
Homegoing celebration, 8, 18, 39, 81,
    83–87, 103, 181, 185, 196–197, 201
House of Diggs Funeral Home, 64, 121,
    132
Howard, Robert "Bobby," 1–2, 12–13
Howard, T. R. M.: as founder of RCNL,

Howard, T. R. M. *(continued)*
119–120, 122–123; death threats
against, 129
Hurricane Katrina, 197–198
Hush harbors, 13, 25, 27, 31, 203

Independent National Funeral Directors
Association (INFDA), 66, 68–77, 88,
105–107

Jackson, Charles, 98–99
Jackson, Daniel "Dan" McKee, 95–98,
101, 227n28
Jackson, Emanuel, 96
Jackson, Jesse, Jr., 189, 194
Jackson, Jimmie Lee, 169, 173–178, 180,
187
Jackson, Mahalia, 95, 108–110, 180
Jazz funeral, 85
Jim Crow segregation: general history
of, 9, 18, 39, 44–45, 47–49, 52, 57–59,
71, 128, 134, 147, 191, 204; businesses
established as a response to, 51, 55–
57, 61–66, 93, 100, 117, 146; at cemeteries, 57, 60, 64–66, 168, 181; as
practiced in the funeral industry, 70,
75–76, 117, 125–126, 136, 164, 191;
funeral home as refuge from, 91, 109,
203
Johnson, A. N., 72, 86, 90–91
Johnson, Lyndon B., 163, 177–178
Johnson, T. V., 120, 123, 129

Kennedy, John F.: engagement with the
civil rights movement, 139, 151, 153,
162–163; assassination and funeral
of, 161–164, 166–167, 196
Kennedy, Robert, 151, 161, 180, 200
King, Bernice, 196, 200–201

King, Coretta Scott, 136, 166, 170–171,
180; death and funeral of, 196–201
King, Martin Luther, Jr., 2, 136, 139,
166, 191, 200; as leader of Montgomery Bus Boycott, 130–132; relationship with African American funeral
directors, 130–131, 158, 165; as leader
of SCLC Birmingham campaign, 140,
143, 145–153, 163; as leader of Selma
voting rights campaign, 169–171,
174–177; assassination and funeral
of, 179–181, 196–197; memorial to,
187–188
Ku Klux Klan, 2, 4, 5, 7, 13, 47, 133, 153,
178, 188

Labat, Alcée, 58–59, 64
Lee, C. W., 130–131, 159
Lee, George W., 122–124, 129
Lee, Hampton D., 175, 178
Lincoln, Abraham, funeral of, 34–35,
176
Lincoln Independent Party (LIP), 204–
206
Liuzzo, Viola, 178, 187
Loewen Group, 191–192
Lowery, Joseph E., 180, 194, 199–201
Lucy, Autherine, 141, 144–145

Malcolm X: comments on Kennedy as-
sassination, 166; involvement in
Selma voting rights campaign, 169–
171; assassination and funeral of,
171–174, 176, 179, 204
March on Washington, 112–113, 159
Mays, Benjamin E., 158–159, 163, 180
Melchor, John C., 119, 137
Metropolitan Funeral System Associa-
tion (MFSA), 97–102

Miller, Chester, 125–126
Miller, Robert H.: early biography of, 106–107, 109–111, 229n43; as leader of NFDMA, 106, 110–111, 116–117, 130–131, 159–160, 178, 182, 184–186; as Mahalia Jackson's manager, 108–109; as "Mayor of Bronzeville," 110; death of, 187; Selma memorial campaign, 187–188
Mitford, Jessica, 156–157, 159–162, 165, 167, 181, 183–184. *See also American Way of Death, The*
Montgomery Bus Boycott, 116, 130–132, 141–142, 159, 189, 194
Montgomery Improvement Association (MIA), 130–132
Moore's Ford lynching (1946): facts of the case, 1–8, 10–11; Moore's Ford Memorial Committee, Inc., 12; recent developments, 13, 212n20
Morehouse College, 158, 180
Mortician, origin of the term, 35
Mortician's nurse, 85–86
Mutual aid societies. *See* Burial leagues
"My Man's an Undertaker," 79, 87
Myrdal, Gunnar, 103–105, 238n30

Nader, Ralph, 183
Nashville Streetcar Boycott, 61–64
Nation of Islam, 166, 171–172
National Association for the Advancement of Colored People (NAACP): involvement in Moore's Ford lynching investigation, 4–7, 10–11; history of, 49, 72–73, 118–119, 189–190, 195, 206, 208; African American funeral directors and, 118–120, 133; in Mississippi, 119–120, 123, 125, 128–129,

133–134, 137–141, 167; in Alabama, 141–142, 175
National Baptist Convention, 109, 192
National Funeral Directors Association (NFDA): founding of, 36–38; discriminatory membership policies of, 47, 49, 53–55, 66, 116–117, 160, 165–166, 181–182; membership statistics, 67; relationship to the INFDA, 68–69, 75–76; response to Jessica Mitford, 160–161
National Funeral Director and Embalmer, 106, 131, 135, 164, 182
National Funeral Directors and Morticians Association (NFDMA), 116, 132, 192, 202–203; engagement with civil rights, 158–160, 163, 178, 181–182; response to FTC investigation, 185–189; sponsorship of Selma memorial, 187–189
National Negro Business League (NNBL), 48–52, 55–56, 62, 66–68, 74–75
National Negro Funeral Directors Association (1907 NNBL group), 51, 55, 67–72
National Negro Funeral Directors Association (NNFDA, established in 1940): reaction to Moore's Ford lynching, 10; history of, 77, 105–106; relationship to the civil rights movement, 110–111, 130–133, 143; name change, 116, 132
National Recovery Administration (NRA), 75–76
New Orleans, Louisiana: *Plessy v. Ferguson* case (1896), 58–59, 66; jazz funerals of, 85; modern civil rights movement, 115, 134; Hurricane Katrina, 198–199

Obama, Barack, 198–202
"Oh, Freedom" slave spiritual, 18, 139
Organization of Afro-American Unity, 171–172

Parks, Rosa: as civil rights leader, 130, 180; death and funeral of, 194–199, 201
Parkway Ballroom (Chicago), 99–100
Plaquemine, Louisiana, 112–115
Plessy v. Ferguson (1896), 44, 49, 57–59, 66
Porter, A. D., 204–207
Porter, Woodford R., 207–208
Powell, Lizzie, 114–116
Price, A. D., 90
Progressive National Funeral Directors Association, 77

Ragsdale, Lincoln, 165
Rayner, Ahmad A., 98, 127–128, 185
Reeb, James, 177–178, 187
Reed, Robert R.: leadership in the INFDA, 68–76, 105–107, 117, 164; criticism against, 76–77; concern about the public image of funeral directing, 81–82, 94; fight against burial leagues, 88, 99
Regional Council of Negro Leadership (RCNL), 119–120, 122–123, 128–129
Renouard, Auguste, 36–38
Roosevelt, Franklin D., 75–76, 121

Schwerner, Mickey, 13, 167–169
Secret societies. *See* Black benevolent societies; Burial leagues
Selma voting rights campaign (SCLC), 169–171, 173–179; memorial to, 187–189

Service Corporation International (SCI), 191–192
Shabazz, Betty, 171
Sharpton, Al, 194
Shortridge, William, 131, 141–144, 149, 155, 158
Shuttlesworth, Fred L., 140–144, 146–148, 152
Sixteenth Street Baptist Church bombing, 154–155, 163
Slave funeral, 25–31. *See also* African American way of death
Slave trade, transatlantic, 13, 17–18, 24, 26
Smith and Gaston Funeral Home, 80, 109, 119, 141, 145
Smyer, Sidney, 147–149, 151–153
Southern Christian Leadership Conference (SCLC), 1, 2, 199; Birmingham "Project C" campaign, 140, 144, 146–154, 163; Selma voting rights campaign, 169–171, 174–176; Poor People's campaign, 179
Student Nonviolent Coordinating Committee (SNCC), 167, 169–170, 175
Swanson, O'Neil D., Jr., 195–196
Swanson, O'Neil D., Sr., 192
Swanson Funeral Home, 195

Talmadge, Eugene, 3–4, 8–11
Taylor, Preston: biography of, 59–61, 96; founder of Greenwood Cemetery, 60, 221n23; as President of the Union Transportation Company, 61–64, 92, 116; founder of Greenwood Park, 92–93
Thomas, James C., 43–45, 50–51
Till, Emmett: historic significance of the case, 6, 116, 124–125, 154, 167, 176,

189; role of funeral directors in the case, 125–128, 185, 232n27; murder trial of, 128–129

Till Bradley, Mamie, 6, 125–127, 154, 232n27

Tri-State Casket Company, 72–74

Truman, Harry, 5, 10–11

Underground railroad, 15–17

Undertakers. *See* Funeral directors, professionalization of

Union Transportation Company, 62–64, 92

Unity Funeral Home, 171–173

Van Der Zee, James, 86

Voting Rights Act of 1965, 177–178, 187, 189

Washington, Booker T., 42–44, 48–50, 52, 61, 66–78, 94, 165

Washington, Dinah, 79, 87

White, Walter, 4–5, 7, 10

White Citizens Council (WCC), 118–120, 123, 129

Wilkins, Roy, 139, 189–191

Wilkerson, Wayman, 69, 72–74

Womanpower Unlimited, 135–136, 140

Worsham College of Embalming, 77, 107

Wright, Mose, 126–127. *See also* Till, Emmett

Young, Andrew, 170, 180

Young, Dan, 1–14, 116, 204

Young's Funeral Home, 1–5, 8